WASHINGTON IRVING: Moderation Displayed

WASHINGTON IRVING:

Moderation Displayed

EDWARD WAGENKNECHT

Rip, where does Rip Van Winkle live? HERMAN MELVILLE

New York

OXFORD UNIVERSITY PRESS   1962

B
Irving

WALTER WAGENKNECHT, his book

PREFACE

In 1862-63 Irving's nephew, Pierre Munro Irving, published a four-volume *Life and Letters of Washington Irving* which, despite its air of family piety, is still an indispensable work. As a definitive biography, however, it has been superseded by Stanley T. Williams's *Life of Washington Irving* (1935). Williams, George Hellman, William P. Trent, and John Francis McDermott, among others, not only through their writings, but even more by the documents they have published, have laid the foundation for modern study of Irving, while *The Spanish Adventures of Washington Irving* by Claude G. Bowers (1940) and Walter A. Reichart's *Washington Irving and Germany* (1957) provide expert guidance in special fields. Further important contributions have been made in five unpublished dissertations: Francis Prescott Smith, "Washington Irving and France" (Ph.D., Harvard, 1937); Marguerite Mallett Raymond, "Washington Irving and the Theater" (M.A., Wellesley, 1940); Pete Kyle McCarter, "The Literary, Political, and Social Theories of Washington Irving" (Ph.D., Wisconsin, 1939); Robert Stevens Osborne, "A Study of Washington Irving's Development as a Man of Letters to 1825" (Ph.D., North Carolina, 1947); and William Leonard Hedges, "The Fiction of History: Washington Irving Against a Romantic Transition" (Ph.D., Harvard, 1953). McCarter, Osborne, and Hedges have kindly given me permission to quote from their work, and the last-named has done me the kind service of reading my manuscript. Francis Prescott Smith is no longer living, but the Harvard College Library has given me permission to quote from his dissertation.

The only objection that can be made to the Williams biography is that, as if reacting to Pierre Irving's laudatory tone as sharply as possible, the author is often so hypercritical toward Irving as to raise some wonder in the reader's mind that a man should have devoted so much of his life to the study of an author he apparently could not greatly admire. In the present—and presumably, for all essential purposes, the permanent—state of Irving knowledge, a fresh biography could not be much more than a paraphrase of Williams. When it comes to a "portrait" the situation is different, and this is what I have tried to provide. Irving himself invites such study when he writes, "If my character and conduct are worth enquiring into they will ultimately be understood and appreciated according to their merits nor can any thing I could say or do in contradiction place them an iota above or below their real standards."

A list of the printed material consulted is given in the Bibliography. Manuscript material has been drawn from the following institutions:

> The New York Public Library, including the Berg Collection and the Seligman and Hellman Collections of Irvingiana
> The Sterling Library, Yale University
> The Houghton Library, Harvard University
> Peabody Institute
> The Henry E. Huntington Library
> The Massachusetts Historical Society
> The Boston Public Library
> The Pierpont Morgan Library

Thanks are due, and are gladly given, to all these, their

librarians and curators, and their co-operative staffs, for much help and many courtesies, and to the Johns Hopkins University Library and the Chenery Library, Boston University, for help in securing microfilms.

Dr. Harold Dean Cater, executive director of the Sleepy Hollow Restorations, gave me a delightful morning at "Sunny-side," and added to my obligation by reading my manuscript.

Irving was probably one of the worst spellers on record, and I have not thought it necessary, in a book addressed to the general reader, to preserve all his idiosyncrasies. This seemed particularly uncalled for since some material had to be quoted from texts which had already been corrected. Occasionally, when I thought it might save the reader an unnecessary stumbling, I have even altered or added a mark of punctuation, but I have not "standardized" quotations, as the reader will very shortly discover.

Quotations set apart from the text have generally been indented whether they begin a paragraph in the original or not. The conventional three and four periods are used to indicate omissions within quoted matter; since I do not pretend to be quoting complete documents, I have avoided the use of this device at the beginning and the end of quotations.

Irving's position in American literature is a rather odd one. So far as his name goes, he is still one of the most famous American authors. There is also a conventional honor paid to him as the Father of American Literature. Yet the living body of his work is small, and in the critical estimate generally placed upon his effort as a whole, he now ranks below any of the others who enjoy a comparable fame. Perhaps some of these paradoxes may be explored in the following pages. The personality in any case, as I hope to convince the reader, is well worth knowing; it was also considerably more complicated than it is generally supposed to have been.

I have given my book the subtitle *Moderation Displayed,* which has not been set down apologetically. Much of what makes life worth living comes from the temperate zone; both in literature and in life there may even be some who are getting a little tired of intensity.

Edward Wagenknecht

Boston University
October 1961

CONTENTS

WASHINGTON IRVING: Moderation Displayed

I

THE LIFE

Born in New York City on April 8, 1783, Washington Irving escaped being a colonial by the narrowest of margins. "The town," as Bryant was later to observe, was then "scarcely built up to Warren Street; Broadway, a little beyond, was lost among grassy pastures and tilled fields," and the Park which was afterwards to hold the City Hall was "an open common." Though the war ended in April, the treaty was not signed until September, and it was almost the end of the year before the last redcoats had left what had now become American shores. At one time during the conflict, hated lobster-bellies had actually been quartered in the house on William Street, and its inhabitants had fled to Jersey. But when King George's men came there too, the Irvings decided to return to Manhattan, and there they stayed until the end.

Washington gave William Irving's eleventh and last child a name as well as a country. Six years later, the child's Scottish nurse exercised more prescience than she can possibly have been aware of when she dragged her charge after the President into a Broadway shop: "Please, your Excellency, here's a bairn that's called after ye!" And Washington, all unknowing, placed his hand upon the head of his future biographer, who, in years to come, used to like to imagine not only that he remembered the incident but that in some way it had cast its spell upon him.

In New York, William Irving traded in hardware, wine, and

3

sugar, but though he built up a prosperous business, he belonged neither to the old Manhattan aristocracy (inevitably Dutch) nor to the new, developing, commercial plutocracy that in time would take over the city. Born in the Orkney Islands, he had followed the sea in his youth; at Plymouth, in 1761, he married a curate's granddaughter, Sarah Sanders. Two years later they came to America. They left one dead child behind them in an English grave; two more children died here. This was a good record for those days; Sarah Sanders must have been a good mother. "I dream of her to this day," Irving was to write only a few years before his own death, "and wake up with tears on my cheeks." One who frequented the William Street house remembered her as "of elegant shape, with large English features, which were permeated by an indescribable life and beauty. Her manners were full of action, and her conversational powers were of a high order."

We have no evidence that Irving dreamed of his father; no man ever clung with warmer affection to the family into which he was born, but so far as he was concerned, the family had no head. It was not William Irving's fault; it simply meant that his temperament and his son's would not go together. Yet the same observer who recalled Mrs. Irving's "elegant shape" and the "indescribable life and beauty" of her features, also remembered her husband at seventy as

of grave and majestic bearing, and a form and expression which, when once fixed in the mind, could not easily be forgotten. . . . His countenance was cast in that strong mould which characterized the land of his birth, but the features were often mellowed by a quiet smile. . . .

His mode of conducting family worship was peculiarly beautiful. . . . On such occasions, it was a most touching spectacle to see the majestic old man, bowed and hoary with extreme age, leaning upon his staff, as he stood among his family and sung a closing hymn . . . while tears of emotion ran down his cheek.

We may well be less impressed than the observer by the "extreme age" of a man of seventy, and there is nothing to indicate that his youngest child was ever impressed by the "tears of emotion" he shed as a family priest. Every Sunday he required the boy to attend three church services, with *The Pilgrim's Progress* for recreational reading, and on Thursday afternoons, when there was no school, he kept him at home to recite his catechism. There is a possibly apocryphal story to the effect that when young Washington wanted to go to the John Street Theater, he had to sneak out and home again for family prayers at nine, and then out the bedroom window, Tom Sawyer-fashion, and back to the theater. But it may not have been as bad as that, not quite "John Knox trying to curb the tricksy Ariel," as George William Curtis imagined it, for Irving himself says he first went to the theater in 1796, when James K. Paulding took him openly, and his father seems to have made no objection. Irving rebelled against the teachings of his home much less seriously than Robert Burns did, but "The Cotter's Saturday Night" showed an imaginative capacity for youthful response to family piety which was apparently lacking in the more tractable American.

Washington Irving went to school until he was sixteen, attending four different establishments (his first teacher took him for a dunce). He afterwards told a friend that he was "a poor scholar—fond of roguery." It is clear that like most human beings of his inclination, he gave himself freely to the studies which stimulated his imagination and ignored the rest, having no objection, for example, to writing other boys' compositions for them if they, in turn, would do his arithmetic for him.

When he was fourteen he planned, as many a boy has planned, to run away to sea, and trained himself for the great adventure, delicate as he was, by chewing and swallowing salt pork, which he detested, and sleeping on the hard, bare floor of his bedroom. We do not know why he did not follow his brothers to Columbia College, but it is clear that he was not deprived of anything he desired. He spent six years reading law in three different lawyers' offices, and even managed to pass a bar examination in 1807, though according to his own account what he knew was not so much "a little law" as "damn little." In Richmond he served in a minor capacity as one of the counsel at Aaron Burr's trial—"I was one of the counsel for Burr, and Burr was acquitted"—but though he got quite sentimental over the fallen hero, it does not appear that either of them ever found out quite what he was expected to do at the trial.

Sailing up the Hudson River, young Irving found his way into the heart of the old Dutch country which his imagination was to make his own:

Of all the scenery of the Hudson, the Kaatskill Mountains had the most witching effect on my boyish imagination. Never shall I forget the effect upon me of the first view of them predominating over a wide extent of country, part wild, woody, and rugged; part softened away into all the graces of cultivation. As we slowly floated along, I lay on the deck and watched them through a long summer's day; undergoing a thousand mutations under the magical effects of atmosphere; sometimes seeming to approach; at other times to recede; now almost melting into hazy distance, now burnished by the setting sun, until, in the evening, they printed themselves against the glowing sky in the deep purple of an Italian landscape.

In those days "all the world had a tinge of fairy land," and a trip up the Hudson was as wonderful as a trip to Europe could have been:

I was a lively boy, somewhat imaginative, of easy faith, and prone to relish everything that partook of the marvellous. Among the passengers on board the sloop was a veteran Indian trader, on his way to the lakes to traffic with the natives. He had discovered my propensity, and amused himself throughout the voyage by telling me Indian legends and grotesque stories about every noted place on the river.

Irving met real hardships, however (some of them he was to recall many years later when he wrote *Astoria*) on the trip he took in 1803 with his employer, Josiah Ogden Hoffman, and others, up into the Canadian wilderness as far as Montreal, and on this occasion he displayed more hardihood than anybody had supposed the delicate youngster to possess. Yet it was health considerations which prompted his brothers to send him on the Grand Tour in the spring of 1804; he had to be helped up the gangplank, and the captain prophesied that he he would go overboard before the voyage ended.

The six weeks' passage to Bordeaux proved a smooth one, however, and Irving confounded prognostications by running all over the ship like a monkey, "climbing to the masthead and going out on the main topsail yard." With Napoleon just about to become emperor, those were exciting times in Europe, and the young American did not escape their fascination. In Nice his passport was taken up; between Genoa and Sicily his ship was captured by pirates; once he came close enough to Nelson's fleet to admire the great admiral's seamanship. Meeting Washington Allston in Rome, he became enough interested in art to ponder the possibility of settling down there to study painting, but this came to nothing, and his brother rebuked him sternly for "galloping" through Italy and the approved cultural sightseeing in his anxiety to reach the pleasures of Paris with young Joseph Carrington Cabell.[1] He was not planning a wholly recreational stay in the French capital; had he not declared his intention of attending "a course of lectures . . . on botany, chemistry, and different other branches of science"? But the theaters, the restaurants, and the ballrooms proved too alluring for him to do much studying.[2] After three months of the same kind of life in London, he sailed for home on January 17, 1806.

As far back as 1802-03 Irving had contributed, as Jonathan

Oldstyle, Gent., to the *Morning Chronicle*, which was owned by his brother Peter, and his work was not without merit, for William Dunlap, Brockden Brown, and Aaron Burr were all impressed by it at the time (as George C. D. Odell was to be impressed in retrospect), and a college student named William Cullen Bryant memorized a portion of one of Irving's papers as a declamation but was so overcome by laughter that he could not deliver it. The real beginnings of Irving's career as an author date from 1807-08, when he joined with James K. Paulding and his own brother William to publish, at irregular intervals, twenty numbers of the *Salmagundi* papers.

"Salmagundi" indicates a salad of minced veal, chicken, or turkey, chopped up with onion and pickled herring, and moistened with oil and lemon juice. The avowed purpose of the publication was "to instruct the young, reform the old, correct the town, and castigate the age," but the moralists were very gay about it all, and more like Sterne than Addison; it was not for nothing that they traveled down to "Cockloft Hall" near Newark, where they played leapfrog on the greensward and drank somewhat freely. They were very saucy and independent too: "So soon as we get tired of reading our own works we shall discontinue them without the least remorse, whatever the public may think of it." Waltzing, tea-drinking, and feminine nakedness all drew the authors' disapproval, and they complained that "many people read our numbers merely for their amusement, without paying any attention to the serious truths conveyed in every page." Some thought was given to politics and a good deal to the theater, and there was enough fiction to give Irving a chance to try his hand at the creation of character.[3]

The year after the *Salmagundi* papers ceased, Irving achieved the first of his two great literary triumphs with *Diedrich Knickerbocker's History of New York from the Beginning of the World to the End of the Dutch Dynasty* (1809). He had begun it with his brother Peter as a take-off on a handbook by Dr. Samuel Latham Mitchill,[4] but when it was left in Washington's hands it developed into one of the giant burlesques of literature. He had already called New Yorkers "Gothamites" in the *Salmagundi* papers; now, in Diedrich Knickerbocker, he created the first of his two enduring contributions to American folklore, who was destined to personify New York City thenceforward and forevermore.

Publication was prepared for by one of the cleverest hoaxes in the history of publishing. On October 26 the New York *Evening Post* carried a notice of the "distressing" disappearance of

a small elderly gentleman, dressed in an old black coat and cocked hat, by the name of KNICKERBOCKER. As there are some reasons for believing he is not entirely in his right mind, and as great anxiety is entertained about him, any information concerning him left either at the Columbian Hotel, Mulberry-street, or at the Office of this paper will be thankfully received.

Eleven days later there was a reply from "A Traveller," who reported that such a person had been seen

by the passengers of the Albany stage early in the morning, about four or five weeks since, resting himself by the side of the road, a little above Kingsbridge—He had in his hand a small bundle tied in a red bandana handkerchief; he appeared to be travelling northward, and was very much fatigued and exhausted.

On November 16, Knickerbocker's landlord, Seth Handaside, announced that *"a very curious kind of written book"* had been found in his room, and that if he did not return to settle his account, this would be disposed of for the landlord's benefit. Publication of *A History of New York* was announced on November 29. "This work was found in the chamber of Mr. Diedrich Knickerbocker, the old gentleman whose sudden and mysterious disappearance has been noticed. It is published to discharge certain debts he has left behind." It appeared on December 7. There had been no advance indication that it was to be a humorous work.

Knickerbocker's History did not convince Irving that he was a successful writer, and he had no idea as yet of making writing a career. During the ten years that followed, he wrote little; once he tried to become Clerk of the Court at Albany, and once he applied for a post in the American embassy at Paris. It may well be that he was in no position to see either himself or his career very clearly; indeed, it is one of the anomalies of literary history that such a book should have been written and published at such a time, for only a few months before it appeared, on April 26, death had robbed Irving of the girl he loved, Matilda Hoffman, seventeen-year-old daughter of his employer. Many years later he wrote, "She died in the flower of her youth and of mine but she has lived for me ever since in all womankind. I see her in their eyes—and it is the remembrance of her that has given a tenderness in my eyes to everything that bears the name of woman."

He had been accepted as her suitor on condition of his establishing himself in the law, and this was the only time in his life when he was seriously interested in legal success. After her death, however, it was not the law but the family hardware business which claimed his practical energies. In 1810 his brothers made him a partner with a one-fifth interest but without onerous duties. In their behalf he traveled to Albany and Philadelphia; since they were importers, he even lobbied in Washington, where he admired Dolly Madison but found her husband—"poor Jemmy"—"a withered little apple-john." In 1811 he took an apartment with his friend Henry Brevoort; this gave him the run of Brevoort's excellent library. Beginning in January 1813, he edited the *Analectic Magazine*, resigning in 1814 after the publisher had suffered financial reverses. In-

censed by the British attack on Washington during the War of
1812, he became aide-de-camp to Governor Daniel D. Tomp-
kins of New York, with the rank of colonel. On May 25, 1815,
he went to Liverpool to assist Peter to look after the English
branch of the business. It was not until after P. and E. Irving
and Co. went bankrupt in 1818, however, that he really began
to look to his pen for support, resolutely refusing govern-
mental and editorial positions which some of his friends
thought him foolish not to accept.

Napoleon had been bound up with Irving's first visit to
Europe, and he reappeared in another capacity in connection
with the second, for the news of his defeat at Waterloo had
reached Liverpool just before Irving arrived there. Though the
American had plenty of indolence in his nature, he could always work hard when he had to, and he did not slight the
family business. But he would not have been himself if he had
neglected his social contacts or the association with authors,
artists, and actors in which he really lived. Of all his friends, nobody else was quite so important to him as Walter Scott, not
yet the acknowledged author of the "Waverley Novels," who
received him as graciously as any great writer has ever welcomed a junior, and lent his offices toward the publication of
The Sketch Book, "by Geoffrey Crayon, Gent.," which appeared in parts, on both sides of the Atlantic, in 1819-20, and
with which Rip Van Winkle and Ichabod Crane became part
of the literature of the world. It was the second and the more
impressive of Irving's two great "strikes"; he was not destined
ever quite to equal it again.

George Hellman has commented upon the circumstance that
Irving was fifty before he ever saw his own name on a title
page. It was "Jonathan Oldstyle, Gent." in the *Morning
Chronicle* and "Anthony Evergreen, Gent." in the *Salmagundi*
papers, and *A History of New York* had, of course, been at-

tributed to Diedrich Knickerbocker. The biographical sketch which preceded the 1810 edition of Thomas Campbell's poems was by "A Gentleman of New York," and even his edition of François-Joseph de Pons's *A Voyage to the Western Part of Terra Firma, or the Spanish Main in South America* (1806) was "Translated by an American Gentleman." The emphasis upon "Gentleman" is as interesting as the fondness for anonymity or the use of pseudonyms.

In 1821 Irving was in Paris again, with Peter, and now he became friendly with the Irish poet Thomas Moore and the American playwright John Howard Payne, whom he had already known in New York, the author of some sixty plays as well as a popular actor, but now best remembered for the song "Home, Sweet Home" in his *Clari; or, The Maid of Milan*. Irving made important contributions to at least two of Payne's plays—*Richelieu* and *Charles II*—though he never permitted his name to appear in connection with them; he also made fresh librettos for two of Carl Maria von Weber's operas—*Abu Hassan* and *Der Freischütz*, which latter he called *The Wild Huntsman*. But he left to other hands all attempts to dramatize "Rip Van Winkle," which, as acted by Joseph Jefferson, became one of the great artistic and popular triumphs of the American stage; indeed he himself is said to have expressed amazement that the story could be dramatized.

In 1822 Irving published the second of his miscellanies, *Bracebridge Hall*, in which he treated himself and his readers to a book-length visit with the English family he had already introduced in the Christmas papers included in *The Sketch Book*. The character sketches and the descriptions of family life, interests, and recreations bring us to the threshold of the novel, but Irving warns us that we must not look to him for continuity. With *Bracebridge Hall* out of the way, he set off for Germany in search of new material.

In November 1822 he reached Dresden, where he at once became a member of his first court circle. More important, he formed his intimacy with the English Foster family, and if Washington Irving was ever in love again, after his unhappy affair with Matilda Hoffman, Emily Foster, later the wife of an English clergyman, was the girl involved. From Dresden, after the Fosters returned to England, he went to Paris, then to London, then back to Paris again; in 1826 he became a member of the American legation at Madrid.

Meanwhile, in 1824, he had published what he himself regarded as his best book, *Tales of a Traveller*, which, though popular on the Continent, particularly in Germany, received a savage press both in England and in America. "It is suggested that Mr. Washington Irving's new work would sell more rapidly," said the *New-York Mirror*, "if the Booksellers would alter the Title, and call it 'STORIES FOR CHILDREN' by *a Baby Six Feet High. . . .*" Not satisfied with condemning this book, the reviewers insisted upon raising the whole question of Irving's literary reputation. He had been overrated, never had been worthy of the plaudits he had received, and much besides. It was Irving's first experience with such savage stupidity, and he was greatly hurt. Probably the ordeal was at least partly responsible for his turn away from "creative" writing in the direction of history and biography during his later years.

He welcomed the appointment at Madrid, in any case, because it gave him a chance to work with Spanish documents. The original idea was that he should make an English translation of Martín Fernández de Navarrete's great collection of materials relating to the voyages of Columbus *(Coleccion de los viages y descubrimientos, que hicieron por mar los españoles desde fines del siglo XV)*. It did not take him long to discover that he was not greatly interested in such a work of translation, and he did not believe the booksellers would be greatly interested in it either. He turned instead to writing *The Life and Voyages of Columbus*, based upon de Navarette and other sources but an independent work of Irving's own composition, published in 1828.

Irving made devoted friends at Madrid, as he did everywhere: Obadiah Rich, the American collector, of whose great library he made excellent use; Pierre D'Oubril, the Russian minister (of French extraction), his wife, and her charming niece, Antoinette Bolviller, to whom he wrote some of his best letters; the Russian Prince Dolgorouki; a well-known English painter, Sir David Wilkie; and, very briefly, a young American named Henry Wadsworth Longfellow, who had just turned up in Spain on his first European tour, designed to qualify him for his position as Professor of Modern Languages at Bowdoin College.

But for all the social pleasantries of Madrid, most of Irving's time there went into grueling work. *Columbus* may not have enlisted, or made demands upon, the deeper, resources of his genius, but it certainly taught him what literary drudgery means. Longfellow was astonished to find his study window already open at six in the morning. "Yes," he replied, when his young admirer asked him about it, "Yes, I am always at work as early as six." The strain on his health was considerable even now; when, as an old man, he devoted himself with comparable zest to his life of Washington, it wrecked him, made his last months on earth a torture, and probably shortened his life.

The Life and Voyages of Columbus published, Irving refreshed himself with Spanish travel. Romanticist as he was, he had already broken in upon *Columbus* to write *The Conquest of Granada* (1829). The story, as he says, "had been a favorite from childhood, and I had always read everything relating to the domination of the Moors in Spain with great delight." He was particularly fond of the last of the Moorish kings Boabdil, and when he was at the Alhambra in Granada, he reveled in his contacts with the places associated with this romantic figure.

The Alhambra is one of the show places of the earth, and for us both Irving and Longfellow have helped to make it so. "There are moments in our lives," wrote the poet, "to which we feel that romance could add nothing, and which poetry itself could not beautify. Such were those I passed lingering about the Alhambra and dreaming over the warlike deeds of other days." He added that during the five days he spent in Granada he "lived almost a century. No portion of my life has been so much like a dream."

Irving had four months instead of five days, and during all this time he does not seem to have awakened; it was, he said, like living in *The Arabian Nights*. By grace of the Governor, he occupied apartments in the palace itself, and finally a station overlooking the Court of Lindaraxa, with its fountain and flowers and nightingales, from chambers once occupied by royalty. As he wrote Henry Brevoort:

Never shall I meet on earth with an abode so much to my taste, or so suited to my habits and pursuits. The sole fault was that the softness of the climate, the silence and serenity of the palace, the odor of flowers and the murmur of the fountains had a soothing and voluptuous effect that at times almost incapacitated me for work and made me feel like the Knight of Industry, when so pleasingly enthralled in the Castle of Indolence.

Drawing on the charms of another world to enhance this one, even in its most enthralling aspects, he wrote Catherine D'Oubril, from Seville, on April 21, 1829:

How happy I should be if you were all down here at Seville. I could take you to such pretty places, so romantic and full of strange stories. Such as Alcala de la Guadaira, just a pleasant drive from here, where there is an old Moorish castle on a hill, in one of the ruined towers of which a most beautiful princess was confined in old times, and there she is to be seen on moonlight nights, with a turban all sparkling with diamonds and rubies, waving a white veil from the top of the tower, for her lover, a Christian knight, who was drowned in the Guadaira as he was coming to rescue her. At the bottom of the hill on which stands the castle is the little river Guadaira, winding along among groves and orchards, and its banks covered with rhododendrons and wild flowers of every kind: and not far from the river is a fountain as clear as crystal, that rises among reeds and lilies and roses; and this fountain they say is enchanted, because the Moors buried money there, and a little old Moor with a green turban and a long white beard sits by the side of it on a white stone, and is often heard sighing heavily, by the women of the village when they go, to draw water; but he can only be seen on the eve of St. Iden's day at midsummer, when you know all enchanted beings, fairies and people of that kind become visible. For my part I do not believe above one half of all these stories, yet one half is enough to make a reasonable person stare.

It is impossible not to envy Irving, and impossible not to sympathize with him, when, on July 18, 1829, he received letters offering him an appointment as secretary of the American legation at London. "As it appeared to be the general wish of my friends that I accept this appointment I have done so; but I assure you when I took my last look at the Alhambra from the mountain road of Granada, I felt like a sailor who had just left a tranquil port to launch upon a stormy and treacherous sea."

Irving was to continue to reap the harvest of his Spanish years in *Voyages of the Companions of Columbus* (1831) and, more importantly, in *The Alhambra* (1832). In 1835 "Legends of the Conquest of Spain" were to make up part of *The Crayon Miscellany*, and *Mahomet and His Successors*, a minor work, was not to come along until 1850. Even in *Wolfert's Roost*, published in 1855, only four years before Irving's death, there was to be some material which had sprouted from Spanish soil. Stanley T. Williams calculated that Irving wrote some 3000 pages or 1,000,000 words about Spain, or about one-third of his total output. Until he began his concentration upon Washington during the last years of his life, "it is difficult to name a year after 1825 when he was not engaged in writing or publishing a history, a story, or a sketch connected with Spain." [5] Judged by any standards, it had been a fruitful sojourn.

Irving reached London in October 1829 and stayed there until 1832. From June 22, 1831 to April 1, 1832, he was, to all intents and purposes, in charge of the legation. "I do not pretend to any great skill as a diplomatist; but in whatever situation I am placed in life, when I doubt my skill I endeavor to make up for it by conscientious assiduity." He took part in important diplomatic negotiations over West Indian trade and was well liked by the new King William IV. He renewed his associations with Wilkie, Moore, Payne, and others, and received a gold medal from the Royal Society of Literature and a Doctor of Civil Laws from Oxford, which he was always too modest to use. At Barlborough Hall in Derbyshire he enjoyed an old English Christmas of the kind he himself had enabled all the world to enjoy in *Bracebridge Hall* and *The Sketch Book;* at Newstead Abbey he slept in Byron's room, waited eagerly and vainly for ghosts, and gathered more material for *The Crayon Miscellany.* On his forty-ninth birthday, April 8, 1832, he went to Paris to say good-by to Peter; on May 21 he arrived at Sandy Hook.

New York welcomed him with a public dinner at the City Hotel, an ordeal he contemplated with horror because it involved speechmaking, but which gave him a chance to vindicate his Americanism against those who thought he had stayed too long abroad. "I am asked how long I mean to remain here? They know but little of my heart or my feelings who can ask me this question. I answer—As long as I live!" As he sat down, the roof "rung with bravos, handkerchiefs were waved on every side, three cheers were given again and again. . . . Mr. Irving put his hand over his eyes a moment and showed signs of deep emotion."

He was not destined to remain in America as long as he

lived, but neither was his knowledge of that country much longer to be confined to New York and its environs. For he made a great tour of the West and South, experiencing and relishing the most primitive conditions and proving himself as good at "roughing it" as any American. He himself told the story with incomparable vividness in a letter written from Washington, on December 18, 1832, to a friend in Europe:[6]

We [7] embarked at Black Rock on Lake Erie. On board of the steamboat was Mr. Ellsworth, one of the commissioners appointed by the government to superintend the settlement of the emigrant Indian tribes on the west of the Mississippi.[8] He was on his way to the place of rendezvous, and on his invitation, we agreed to accompany him in his expedition. The offer was too tempting to be resisted. I should have an opportunity of seeing the remnants of those great Indian tribes which are now about to disappear as independent nations, or to be amalgamated under some new form of government. I should see those fine countries of the "far west," while still in a state of pristine wilderness, and behold herds of buffaloes scouring their native prairies before they are driven beyond the reach of a civilized tourist.

We, accordingly, traversed the centre of Ohio, and embarked in a steamboat at Cincinnati for Louisville, in Kentucky. Thence we descended the Ohio River in another steamboat, and ascended the Mississippi to St. Louis. Our voyage was prolonged by repeated running aground, in consequence of the lowness of the waters, and on the first occasion we were nearly wrecked and sent to the bottom, by encountering another steamboat coming with all the impetus of a high pressure engine, and a rapid current. Fortunately, we had time to sheer a little so as to receive the blow obliquely, which carried away part of a wheel, and all the upper works on one side of the boat.

From St. Louis I went to Fort Jefferson, about nine miles distant to see Black Hawk, the Indian warrior and his fellow prisoners—a forlorn crew, emaciated and dejected—the redoubtable chieftain himself, a meagre old man upwards of seventy. He has, however, a fine head, a Roman style of face, and a prepossessing countenance.

At St. Louis we bought horses for ourselves, and a covered wagon for our baggage tents, provisions, etc., and traveled by land to Independence, a small frontier hamlet of log houses, situated between two and three hundred miles up the Missouri, on the utmost verge of civilization. . . .

From Independence, we struck across the Indian country, along the line of Indian missions; and arrived, on the 8th of October, after ten or eleven days' tramp, at Fort Gibson, a frontier town in Arkansas. Our journey lay almost entirely through vast prairies, or open grassy plains, diversified occasionally by beautiful groves, and deep fertile bottoms along the streams of water. We lived in frontier and almost Indian style, camping out at nights, except when we stopped at the missionaries, scattered here and there in this vast wilderness. The weather was serene, and we encountered but one rainy night and one thunderstorm, and I found sleeping in a tent a very sweet and healthy repose. It was now upwards of three weeks since I had left St. Louis, and taken to traveling on horseback, and it agreed with me admirably.

On arriving at Fort Gibson, we found that a mounted body of rangers nearly a hundred, had set off two days before to make a wide tour to the west and south toward the wild hunting countries; by way of protecting the friendly Indians, who had gone to the buffalo hunting, and to overawe the Pawnees, who are the wandering Arabs of the west and are continually on the maraud. We determined to proceed on the track of this party, escorted by a dozen or fourteen horsemen (that we might have nothing to apprehend from any straggling party of Pawnees) and with three or four Indians as guides and interpreters, including a captive Pawnee woman. A couple of Creek Indians were despatched by a commander of the fort to overtake the party of rangers, and order them to await our coming up with them. We were now to travel in still simple and rougher style, taking as little baggage as possible, and depending on our hunting supplies; but were to go through a country abounding with game. The finest sport we had hitherto had was an incidental wolf hunt, as we were now traversing a prairie, which was very animated and picturesque. I felt now completely launched in a savage life, and extremely excited and interested by this wild country, and the wild scenes and people by which I was surrounded. Our rangers were expert hunters, being mostly from Illinois, Tennessee, etc.

We overtook the exploring party of mounted rangers in the course of three days, on the banks of the Arkansas, and the whole troop crossed the river on the 16th of October, some on rafts, some fording. Our own immediate party had a couple of half breed Indians as servants, who understood the Indian customs. They constructed a kind of boat or raft, out of buffalo skin, on which Mr. Ellsworth and myself crossed the river and its branches, at several times, on the top of about a hundred weight of baggage—an odd mode of crossing a river a quarter of a mile wide.

We now led a true hunting life, sleeping in the open air and living upon the produce of the chase, for we were three hundred miles beyond human habitation, and part of the time in a country hitherto unexplored.

We got to the region of the buffaloes and wild horses; killed some of the former, and caught some of the latter. We were, moreover, on the hunting grounds of the Pawnees, the terror of that frontier; a race who scour the prairies on fleet horses, and are like the Tartars, or roving Arabs.

We had to set guards round our camp, and tie up our horses for fear of surprise; but though we had an occasional alarm, we passed through the country without seeing a single Pawnee. I brought off, however, the tongue of a buffalo, of my own shooting, as a trophy of hunting, and am determined to rest my renown as a hunter upon that exploit, and never to descend to smaller game.

We returned to Fort Gibson after a campaign of about thirty days, well seasoned by hunter's fare and hunter's life.

From Ft. Gibson I was about five days descending the Arkansas to the Mississippi, in a steamboat a distance of several hundred miles. I then continued down the latter river to New Orleans, where I passed some days very pleasantly. . . .

From New Orleans I set off, on the mail stage, through Mobile, and proceeded on, through Alabama, Georgia, South and North Carolina, and Virginia, to Washington, a long and rather dreary journey, traveling frequently day and night, and much of the road through pine forests, in the winter season.

Irving made literary capital of this journal in "A Tour of the Prairies," which is yet another part of *The Crayon Miscellany*. He was back in New York in the late spring of 1833.

He was now officially a great man. He declined to be nominated for Congress; later he was to refuse to stand as the Tammany Hall candidate for Mayor of New York; still later he was to turn down President Van Buren's offer of the Navy portfolio in his Cabinet. At John Jacob Astor's request, he wrote *Astoria* (1836), a vivid book about the fur trade in the Pacific Northwest; this was followed by *Adventures of Captain Bonneville, U.S.A.* (1837), which was based on the explorer's own papers. With these works the man who created American literature in the consciousness of European readers reached out to possess himself of what was afterwards to be called the "farthest reach" of American civilization upon this continent. From the Hudson River Valley to Granada and back again, and then out to Washington Territory—it cannot be called a narrow range.

By this time, too, Irving had established himself at the place which has ever since been most closely associated with his memory, "Sunnyside" (originally "Wolfert's Roost"), at Tarrytown on the Hudson, where, after one more interlude of public service, he was to spend his last years in the care of his devoted nieces. He called it "a little old fashioned stone mansion, all made up of gable ends, and as full of angles and corners as an old cocked hat." Originally a simple Dutch farm house, it needed a good deal of "restoring" and "improving" before it became the lovely thing we know today,[9] "like one of those little fairy changelings called Killcrops, which eat and eat and are never the fatter." But he could hardly have got along without Sunnyside. "My heart dwells in that blessed little spot, and I really believe that when I die, I shall haunt it; but it will be as a good spirit, that no one need be afraid of."

There was to have been another big Spanish book, a history of the conquest of Mexico, but this Irving generously set aside in 1838 in favor of young William Hickling Prescott, and addressed himself instead to the *Life of Washington* which had haunted him most of his writing life. "In at once yielding up the thing to you," he wrote Prescott, "I feel I am but doing my duty in leaving one of the most magnificent themes in American history to be treated by one who will build from it an enduring monument in the literature of our country." Yet he felt rather at loose ends after he had given it up, "dismounted from my cheval de bataille," nor did he move at once toward the Washington. In 1839 he agreed to write for the *Knickerbocker* the papers later reprinted in *Wolfert's Roost*, and Longfellow shook his head over him, "writing away *like fury. . . ; he had better not;* old remnants—odds and ends,— about Sleepy Hollow, and Granada. What a pity." But Longfellow was wrong, for the *Knickerbocker* papers represented the most creative work Irving had done in a long time. He turned away from Washington too for his *Life of Oliver Goldsmith*, published in its original form in 1840 and revised in 1849, and again for the book which posterity has chosen most completely to ignore, the *Biography and Poetical Remains of Margaret Miller Davidson* (1841), a tubercular young poetess. But the really serious interference, and the thing which postponed the completion of the Washington until Irving was much too old and tired for the labor it entailed, was his appointment, through Daniel Webster's intermediary, as Envoy Extraordinary and Minister Plenipotentiary to the Court of Spain.

Irving was in Spain from 1842 to 1845. On the way thither he revisited England and France, where he was presented to Queen Victoria and to Louis Philippe. The land to which he had been accredited was torn by civil strife. Isabella II was a child, with General Joaquin Baldomero Fernández Espartero as regent, and her mother, Maria Christina, in exile at the Court of France.

Much happened during Irving's stay in the peninsula. Espartero fell, and Narvaez came to power, later to be banished in his turn. Madrid was besieged. The Cortes declared Isabella of age at thirteen. Maria Christina returned from exile, ostensibly to care for her daughters, actually to mend her fences and guard her own interests. Through the tortuous ways that opened before the feet of a foreign diplomat in such a land, Irving steered a cautious path, warmly sympathizing with the "little queen," frankly communicating to his government his own views on every conceivable controversial question, but always conducting himself with such circumspection and propriety that no question concerning either his motives or his methods was ever raised. When Madrid was besieged, he tried to rally the foreign diplomats to provide effective protection for Isabella and her sister; when Narvaez took over, he promptly dealt with him as head of the de facto government without waiting for specific instructions from Washington. He took part in delicate negotiations over Cuba, this early an American problem. He rushed to England, to play an important part in bringing Lord Aberdeen and the American minister Louis McLane together in a friendly atmosphere to discuss the Oregon Boundary dispute. In a long and carefully prepared document sent to the Spanish premier, he defended his nation's conduct in the Mexican War. Washington Irving was an amateur diplomat, but his sympathy, common sense, and conciliatory spirit earned a distinguished record for him. Isabella said farewell to him with genuine regret and affection, and his name is loved and honored in Spain to this day.[10]

In 1846 he was back at Sunnyside, never to leave it again. He was now much concerned with preparing a revised edition of his books, many of which had been out of print. In 1848 he found a new and enterprising publisher in G. P. Putnam, his association with whom was to bring profit and comfort to author and publisher alike. Mention has already been made of the *Mahomet* book of 1850 and of *Wolfert's Roost* in 1855, which comprised flotsam and jetsam of most of the important interests of his life. There were some more Alhambra legends in this book, and there was one story which ranks with his best, "Guests from Gibbet-Island," based on Grimms' "The Gallows Guests," as Pochmann points out, but ten times the length of its original. But most of the material contained in *Wolfert's Roost* had been written long before.

There was now nothing to stand in the way of the *Life of George Washington* which he had dodged for so long. Volume I came out the same year as *Wolfert's Roost* (1855), the fifth and last volume not until the year Irving died. He had feared that he might not live to finish it, and this was not an unreasonable fear. "I think I can make it a most interesting book—can give interest and strength to many points, without any prostration of historic dignity. If I had only ten years more of life!"

The first book in which the Father of his Country was portrayed as a human being, the *Life of Washington* left its author nearly a helpless invalid. Preparing for bed on the evening of November 28, 1859, he murmured, "When will this ever end?" sobbed slightly, pressed his hand to his side, and sank to the floor. His labors and his sufferings had ended together; of his fame there was no end yet in sight.

II

THE MAN

1   HOW THE TREE WAS INCLINED

Emily Foster described Irving in her journal as "neither tall nor slight [he was five foot seven], but most interesting, dark, hair of a man of genius, waving, silky, and black, grey eyes full of varying feeling, and an amiable smile." Even though one may not be quite sure what kind of hair a man of genius ought to have, this is not a bad description. The eyes have been described as both blue and brown; "their actual color," says his nephew and biographer, Pierre Munro Irving, "was sometimes a moot point among his friends." Elsewhere we are told that the hair was chestnut-colored, the nose rather long, the mouth of medium size, and the face in general oval-shaped. He was concerned about the hair, and ordered a special kind of oil for it as early as 1809, when it had "come out a little" after a "nervous fever," and in his old age he wore a wig. His tendency to corpulence troubled him too, but he does not seem to have done much about it. In 1853, when illness virtually deprived him of food for nine days, he wrote his close friend, the novelist and publicist, John Pendleton Kennedy that he was "reduced almost to poetical dimensions." The portraits by Newton and Leslie, and especially the one by John Wesley Jarvis, make him look somewhat dandified and man-about-townish; there is more idealism and a benignant look of elegant affability in the beautiful drawing by Sir David Wilkie; Mathew Brady's late photograph is that of a kindly, rather stocky man, with

a definitely well-established, perhaps slightly smug, look. Mrs.
Jameson thought he had "a most benevolent countenance."
His voice, however, was apparently never one of his charms;
Longfellow was not the only one who found it "husky, weak,
peculiar," with "some halting and hesitating" in it. The portraits alone would establish his interest in clothes during his
early life, and we are not surprised when S. G. Goodrich
speaks of his "claret coat, rather more pigeon-tailed than
the fashion at New York; light waistcoat; tights; ribbed,
flesh-colored stockings; shoes, polished very bright." On the
Western tour, Henry Ellsworth was impressed by his cleanli-
ness and especially by his determination to shave every day
even when no glass was available, and his gaining skill and
experience in this art "through *blood*."

In his person Mr. Irving is very neat—he carries a great change of
dresses, and says he never feels well unless he is clean—Before he sits
down to write his sketches or other works, he always washes himself up
nice, and with everything clean on him and around him, he says his
ideas flow properly—but when he is dirty, the power of association dries
up every literary pore.

In his later years, another observer thought he dressed "re-
spectably, but never elegantly; and he often had a peculiar
shambling gait, that would attract the attention even of those
who did not know him." George William Curtis says he wore
low shoes at a time when boots were the general wear.

In his youth, Irving, as we have seen, had delicate health. "I
have had a little better appetite," he writes his parents from
Albany in 1802, "though I have been troubled with the pain in
my breast almost constantly, and still have a cough at night."
One suspects that there was what we would now call a psycho-
somatic element about it and that his moods affected it importantly; he loved the sea, for example, and was always well when
sailing on it. After Matilda Hoffman's death he suffered a fore-

taste of the "dismal horror" and fear of being alone, especially at night, that was to cause him such torture at the end of his life. When family troubles piled thick and fast, "the sight of a letter would agitate me, and a footman's rap was enough to put my nerves in a flutter." Yet at other times, as is the way with such a temperament, he would amaze himself by feeling surpassingly well, as when, on his sixty-second birthday, in Madrid, he caught himself "bounding up stairs three steps at a time, to the astonishment of the porter, and checked myself, recollecting that it was not the pace befitting a Minister and a man of my years." Nerves were clearly at the root of the herpetic complaint which was the plague of his middle years, for which he took "draughts and pills enough to kill a horse" without obtaining any real improvement, and which caused great discomfort and at times even incapacitated his walking.[1]

He died of an enlargement of the heart, after a long period of semi-invalidism during which he suffered agonies from insomnia, difficulty of breathing, and sheer nervous horror, of all of which his pious biographer made a really harrowing record.[2] Yet he sat at the head of his table and carved to the end of his life, and in spite of his sufferings he had many intervals of cheerfulness and gaiety. According to his physician, Dr. J. C. Peters, he had developed catarrh through falling asleep on the ground at Sunnyside and on the settee in the piazza, and had cured the catarrh with a patent medicine which caused him to develop asthma. The physical symptoms themselves were trying enough, but the effect upon his morale was disastrous. Even the noise of the railroad trains passing along the shore could cause a crisis. He tried homeopathic and allopathic remedies with fine impartiality; once he even wrote Mary Kennedy suggesting that her sister "try galvinism," in which a friend had found relief.

He had no health fads so far as I know; neither did he follow any regime of physical training. As a boy he shot squirrels and even robins, and this barbarism meant enough to him so that at the very end of his life he remembered the tree where he had killed his first squirrel and pointed it out to N. P. Willis. There is also a letter to an old friend in which he fondly recalls a fishing expedition of his youth, though this time the emphasis is not on sport but on youthful pranks and high spirits. "Ah well aday, friend Merwin; these were the days of our youth and folly. I trust we have grown wiser and better since then; we certainly have grown older."

On an early trip to Canada he showed courage and blood lust together. (The speaker is Pierre M. Irving.)

About twenty-five miles below the Falls they went ashore, and found lodgings for the night at a log-house, on beds spread on the floor. The next morning it cleared off beautifully, and they set out again in their boat. On turning a point in the river, they were surprised by loud shouts which proceeded from two or three canoes in full pursuit of a deer which was swimming in the water. A gun was soon after fired, and they rowed with all their might to get in at the death. "The deer made for our shore," says the journal. "We pushed ashore immediately, and as it passed, Mr. Ogden fired and wounded it. It had been wounded before. I threw off my coat, and prepared to swim after it. As it came near, a man rushed through the bushes, sprang into the water, and made a grasp at the animal. He missed his aim, and I jumping after, fell on his back, and sunk him under water. At the same time I caught the deer by one ear, and Mr. Ogden seized it by a leg. The submerged gentleman, who had risen above the water, got hold of another. We drew it ashore, when the man immediately despatched it with a knife. We claimed a haunch for our share, permitting him to keep the rest."

Later I get the impresison that he hunted, when he did it at all, as a social recreation. In Bavaria he greatly enjoyed the royal boar hunts, but I think it was the picturesqueness of the accoutrements which appealed to him and the association with royalty:

It was a very cold winter day with much snow on the ground, but as the hunting was in a thick pine forest, and the day was sunny, we did not feel the cold. The King and all his hunting retinue were clad in an old fashioned hunting uniform with green caps—the sight of the old monarch and his retinue galloping through all the alleys of the forest— the jagers dashing snugly about in all directions chasing the hounds— the shouts—the blasts of horns, the cry of hounds singing through the forest altogether made one of the most animating scenes I ever beheld.

On one occasion, in Europe, when twenty hares were killed by the party he was with, he himself had accounted for only one. On his Western tour he killed a buffalo however, and Ellsworth records that when a trail of blood was found, indicating that an elk had been wounded, "Mr. Irving was delighted with the news and begged to accompany the Capt today, not only to look for the stricken Elk but to kill more." Once, near Bordeaux, he even joined a party which went out to look for a "master serpent that haunts the meadow in front of the chateau, which is the talk and terror of the neighborhood . . . which for size and length equals the Boa constrictor or the Sea serpent," but there is no record of their having found it. It was Irving's own opinion, evidently based upon experience, that "man is naturally an animal of prey; and, however changed by civilization, will readily relapse into his instinct for destruction."

Where he really excelled, however, was as a walker. William C. Preston, eleven years his junior, was much impressed by him when they tramped together in Britain. "Our progress from Wrexham to Langollen taught me that though mountain-bred and accustomed all my life to hunting on foot I was inferior as a walker to the city-bred Irvings." In the Scott country they took the first canto of *The Lady of the Lake* as the program of their tramp. In Seville he once climbed the 350-foot ascent to the Giralda Tower three times in two days.

But he also knew his way around with horses, and continued to ride them long past the age when such exercise is prudent, if it can ever be called that. At sixty-seven he would "mount my horse and gallop about the country almost as briskly as when I was a youngster." But he had eight or nine accidents, on horseback or in his carriage, and one of these, at seventy-two, might well have been the end of him. It was on the Western plains that he learned to know horses best and made the most impressive progress in horsemanship, making "excursions at will from the line," and galloping over a dangerously rough terrain, "in pursuit of any object of interest or curiosity." Here he learned what love can exist between a man and his mount. "In a few days he became almost as much attached to me as a dog; would follow me when I dismounted, would come to me in the morning to be noticed and caressed; and would put his muzzle between me and my book, as I sat reading at the foot of a tree." More generously, he rejoiced in the freedom of the horse and felt the pity of its being broken. "I gazed after her as long as she was in sight," he writes of one noble specimen, "and breathed a wish that so glorious an animal might never come under the degrading thraldom of whip and curb, but remain a free rover of the prairies."

Irving's physical resources for confronting life were, generally speaking, adequate, then, if not outstanding, and it seems to me that the same may be said of his temperament. When he said, "I have always had an opinion that much good might be done by keeping mankind in good humor with one another," he may have been consciously echoing Sterne, but the tone and the sentiment are characteristic. "He diffused sweetness and light in an era marked by bitterness and obscuration," writes Bliss Perry. "It was a triumph of character as well as of literary skill."

His temperament is not always judged so admiringly, however. Williams speaks of him as "in some ways . . . unfit for the ways of men," and Hedges stresses his incapacity for development:

None of his commitments were enduring, because none was necessitated by anything except circumstances. He was by nature or temperament a drifter, a man incapable of deep conviction, who never saw the good in anything without being soon distracted either by the bad in the same thing or the good of something else. At times he desired to be united with a people, a place, an idea, some semblance of permanent order, but in alternate moods he wanted to be away, looking for something new—thus the half-hearted exile the other half of whose heart was always at home.

If this seems harsh in its application to so loyal a man as Irving, we must grant that many of those who knew him personally would not have regarded it as completely unwarranted. As a child he seemed to himself to have "an impossible flow of spirits that often went beyond my strength. Every thing was fairy land to me." Yet his teachers and some of his schoolmates thought him sluggish, and one observer commented on his ability for prompt comprehension of whatever did not present too much difficulty. Tom Moore described him as "not strong as a lion, but delightful as a domestic animal," and Henry Ellsworth declared that he had "rather floated along on the surface of life, in a light bark, than stemmed the current with deeper craft." But Emily Foster, young as she was, cut deeper:

Mr. I——— is in want of constant excitement and support [she confided to her journal], interest and admiration of his friends seem the very food he lives on he is easily discouraged and excited I like as I———g says to see a man gather himself up on his pride—pride is the pedestal on which man stands.

Irving says the substance of much of this himself. It was he who told Ellsworth that he had "staggered through the world like a drunken man." The War of 1812, he said, "roused and stimulated" him, but the stimulation did not last long; when he got to England in 1815 he felt "like another being." In 1824 he even warned one of the mothers of the Irving clan against a certain vivacity and quickness of intellect which often shows itself in boyhood. . . . A kind of poetical blossoming of the mind, which cannot be too greatly distrusted . . . when a boy shows early signs of this mental vivacity . . . care should instantly be taken to cultivate and strengthen the more solid and useful properties of the mind.

Of course a modest man must not be read at face value when he bears witness against himself, and from one point of view even the severest charges that have been made against Irving may be read as left-handed compliments. If, as has been said, every man of genius shares the hospitality of his heart with a woman and a child, it is also true that every saint has been a stranger and pilgrim among men. Irving was certainly not a saint; neither was he, except in a very qualified sense, a genius, but his temperamental affinities were with these types rather than with the men of affairs who are perhaps alone in feeling quite at home upon this earth.

We must remember, too, that Irving lived in a time when romantic melancholy was fashionable. In *The Sketch Book* we read both that "the rich vein of melancholy which runs through the English character . . . gives it some of its most touching and ennobling graces," and that "the natural effect of sorrow over the dead is to refine and elevate the mind," and if the sadness of mutability and the pity of man's mortality are anywhere better expressed in literature than in "Rip Van Winkle" and "Westminister Abbey," I am not familiar with the works in question. Irving's own temperament was not free of this, but perhaps he had less of it than readers of *The Sketch Book* might expect. He himself recognized his tendency to melancholy; in one passage he attributes it to his reading! He could be mawkish; it seems not to have been unusual for him to wake up in the morning "with a strange horror on my mind"; in the early days he was not incapable of deliberately indulging himself. "We had met together with the express determination to be miserable, and to indulge in all the luxury of spleen." Generally, however, when his spirits were low, there was good reason for it in the circumstances of his life, and he never seems in any danger of traveling the Road of Romantic Melancholy past the Point of No Return. "Let me not indulge this mawkish feeling and sentiment . . . which has produced a morbid sensibility and fostered all the melancholy tendencies." It is interesting that some of his notes in this vein ascribe recovery to the religious help which some have thought Irving incapable of invoking or receiving. He comes closest to an over-all summary when he writes, "I have had considerable pleasure in my life and have two or three times come very near being happy,—which I believe is as much as most men can say." And this is sensible enough, and certainly not in the least nineteenth-century Romantic.

The truth is that Irving's temperament was much less simple than has often been supposed. The same man who was so dependent upon his family that his brothers regarded him as a kind of baby who must be looked after, lived to become the mainstay of the clan; the man who worried himself sick over trifles carried heavy burdens without complaining; the enthusiast who, at forty-nine, found such "delightful excitement" in his return to America that he was unfitted "for any calm application" was so notorious for catnapping in company, and even at the dinner table, that when he failed to do so, it became occasion for comment; the romantic who dwelt on the sadness of mutability with such skill and charm in his writings was noted for gaiety and affability in the family circle even when he was oppressed by the weaknesses of age.

Irving's letters give the impression of the kind of consistent kindliness and thoughtfulness that comes from thinking about the interests of other people, instead of concentrating upon the wonderful impression you yourself must be making, but their tone is sincere, earnest, and restrained, rarely sentimental and never fulsome. There was a vein of iron in him, nevertheless, and even those who were closest to him recognized it. "I had always too much earnest *respect* for Mr. Irving ever to claim familiar intimacy with him," wrote his last, great publisher, G. P. Putnam. "He was a man who would unconsciously and quietly command deferential regard and consideration; for in all his ways and words there was the atmosphere of refinement." He did not try to get his portraits into books or shop windows, but if they did get there, he wanted them to be good ones. He did not hanker after interviews either, but when it was done, it had to be done right. "I wish you had had a worthier subject for your biographic pen, or that I had known our conversation was likely to be recorded—I should then have tasked myself to say some wise or witty things to be given as specimens of my offhand table talk. One should always know when they are sitting for a portrait." When he is attacked, he will not vindicate himself, but this was not humility but pride: "My writings, my character and life must all speak for themselves, and I must abide by the average opinion which will ultimately be awarded." He was not interested in protocol for its own sake either, yet when he was not properly presented at Dresden, he simply walked off and would not return.

He was only a youngster when in 1803 he was asked to give up his room in a French hotel

to the Chief Engineer of the Department and his lady who had just arrived. They told me he was a grand man and ought to be well accommodated, and that he wished to have my room as he had slept in it before and liked it the best in the house.

But he replied that he would not

give my room for all the engineers in the kingdom, that I was an American gentleman of character and not inferior to any engineer in France— that I was, however, not unwilling to share part of my room and some of my bed with the lady—but as to her husband, I begged to be excused.

It may be that he thought the impudent part of that reply very "French," but none of it was cowardly, whatever else may be said about it. When Ellsworth traveled with Irving, he noticed a clear-cut distinction between his attitude toward discomforts which could be avoided and those which could not.

Mr. Irving is courteous and even kind—cheerful in submitting to those circumstances which are incident to time and place, while he generally censures defects of every kind, which can with proper exertion be remedied—Hence he is sometimes impatient at privations in this western country which its present prosperous condition does not justify.

Irving certainly relished all the comforts and refinements of civilization, and he had an almost feminine sensitiveness to his surroundings,[3] but it is possible that we may sometimes attribute to his "gentleness" that which should be attributed to other things. Thus it may have been kindheartedness which, as a small child, impelled him to ask to be excused from school with the girls when the session was over, instead of remaining while the bad boys were punished, but it may be simply that he priggishly or fastidiously objected to seeing their bare behinds when they were untrussed. He witnessed more than one execution in his time, and his gentleness certainly left him when it came to the bullfight, though at least one must do him the justice to admit that he had the grace to be ashamed of his ability to relish such a filthy and terrible spectacle.

It was Irving's own feeling that his early Canadian journey "seasoned" him to "disagreeables." If so, it was because he met them with deliberate fortitude, determined to be "seasoned" and to stand up to whatever hardships life might bring him, much as young Theodore Roosevelt did. The hardships were great, and so were the trials of the tour on the prairies which he undertook when he was much older:

The night was biting cold; the brilliant moonlight sparkled on the frosty crystals which covered every object around us. The water froze beside the skins on which we bivouacked, and in the morning I found the blanket in which I was wrapped covered with a hoar frost; yet I had never slept more comfortably.

Ellsworth often found himself obliged to get up at night "to brush off small reptiles," finally arranging his blankets "that they might pass over me, and not hurt me, unless they should either creep into the top or bottom in search of a warmer berth." Early in the expedition, Irving himself was much incensed when a skunk was brought into the tent for food, and threw it into the river, but later, "when provisions were scarce, our pork gone, and nothing could be got to fry fritters in, but the grease of a skunk, he liked the meal much, and even ate the roasted meat, and pronounced it very good."

When Irving wrote the letter to his brother about the Canadian apprenticeship having seasoned him for later hardships, he was thinking about the inconveniences he encountered in Europe rather than what he met with later on the Western plains. In Europe, too, he faced real dangers, but he also faced what is even more trying to a fastidious person—stopping in caverns and cabins, "amid filth and vermin," sleeping on chairs and waking up covered with fleas, and making "a hearty meal of cucumbers and onions off a dirty table in a *filthy* log hut on a *black river*."

Once, in a miserable, flea-infested inn, he laid his hand on his pistol to face a threatened intruder, and it turned out to be only "a poor dog who had probably been attracted by the smoke of our supper." But not all his adventures were of this variety. Not many nineteenth-century Americans had the adventure of being captured by pirates. Irving often traveled through bandit-infested regions, refusing the armed guard which many warned him to hire, and the crosses marking the places where previous travelers had been murdered, and the skulls of executed robbers left hanging in iron cages, cannot have added to the charm of the scenery or helped him to forget his peril. At one French provincial inn, "the wild and solitary situation of the house, the rough looks and manners of the people and their apparent indigence were sufficient to awaken disagreeable sensations," yet "in spite . . . of these uneasy sensations—and of a hard bed and a host of hungry fleas I soon fell asleep and woke up the next morning neither robbed nor murdered." At the Alhambra he terrified and astonished his faithful servants by insisting upon exploring the deserted building and taking up his quarters in a remote portion of it, fraught with heaven only knew what dangers, and this too in the face of all the classical shrieks and sound of clanking chains recorded in ghost stories since the dawn of time, which, once they had been identified as of purely human origin, seem to have troubled him so little that he does not even spare a word of sympathy for the "poor maniac . . . subject to violent paroxysms" confined beneath the Hall of the Ambassadors.

Irving always proved equal to handling anybody he needed to handle and facing all the situations he had to face. He never caviled at reasonable charges from those who served him, and he never yielded to extortion. A coward does not tell a brutal postilion to his face, when refusing him a gratuity, that "such a cruel scoundrel as himself deserved to be put in the horse's place and made to feel a little of his own discipline." Once, in France, "three or four stupid fellows" brought a single portmanteau upstairs to his rooms and all demanded a recompense. He paid the one who "seemed to have sustained most of the weight" and cleared out the rest by threatening to call a gendarme. In 1805 he refused to pay the hold-up price which his guide tried to collect for a carriage, and walked the twelve miles to his next stop in three hours, compelling his guide to tramp it with him. When Madrid was under siege, he went fearlessly about the streets for no better reason than that he wanted to see what was going on. On another occasion in Spain he interposed to save a girl from a rowdy who had attacked her during a street fiight, and it might have gone hard with him had a soldier not rushed to his defense.

Even where no duty was at stake, Irving often put himself in the way of perils which there was no earthly reason he should rush to meet. It was chance, not his own will, that kept him from seeing action in the War of 1812. In 1815 he narrowly missed going with Stephen Decatur on an expedition against the Algerine pirates. In Sicily, in 1805, he had himself lowered over a precipice by a rope, so that he might explore the Ear of Dionysius. Later, in Rome, he climbed to the cross on St. Peter's. "The height is fearful and tremendous and I clung to the cross as firmly as the strictest Catholic as a slip would precipitate me to an immense distance, from hence the view was superb." When he got back to the street in one piece, he was astonished how minute both the bell and the cross appeared.

Irving's courage shows up attractively in less physical aspects also. He stood up to the loss of his sweetheart, of his beloved mother, and of other members of his family, and if Emily Foster rejected him in Dresden, he stood up to that too. When business failure menaced his family, he buckled down to uncongenial work to try to prevent it, and when he was not successful in this, he accepted what fate had brought. "It has pleased heaven," he wrote in an 1817 notebook, "that I should be driven in upon my inner strength."

Irving seems to have had little or no fear of disease. When the cholera menaced London in 1832, he was as little alarmed as he was frightened by war in Madrid. He nursed his friend John Cockburn through scarlet fever and his nephew Irving Van

Wart through smallpox. Early in his life, when a Dutch lady threatened to horsewhip him for *Knickerbocker's History*, he made a point of meeting her, and they became good friends. When John Howard Payne whined about play negotiations, he got no sympathy from his collaborator. "Don't cry out before you're hurt, nor send *conjectural* bad news, for want of real." And again: "Write to me whenever you please, or rather when ever you are in good humor, but no croaking letters. . . . Don't get into pets with managers nor cut your fingers in cutting your bread and butter." When necessary, he could even take on the government, which shamefully neglected and robbed him during his services in Spain, and one could not ask him to speak his mind more frankly and boldly on the subject that he did to James Buchanan: "If this silence is meant to intimate that the explanation has not been satisfactory, I can only say that I had rather the rebuke had been fully and frankly expressed than left to mere surmise." Of all the terrors he met in his life, the terror of public speaking seems to have been the only one he could not stand up to. Professor Felton said that his terror at the Dickens dinner was like Mr. Pickwick's with the horse.

2   HOW THE TREE WAS NOURISHED

Temperaments do not thrive of themselves; they need training and fostering, and souls demand a far more rich and varied diet than bodies. Living where he did, and in the nineteenth century, it would have been strange if Irving had not early learned to relish the beauties of nature. "I thank God I was born on the banks of the Hudson!" he wrote late in life. "I think it an invaluable advantage to be born and brought up in the neighborhood of some grand and noble object in Nature,—a river, a lake, or a mountain. We make a friendship with it,—we in a manner ally ourselves to it for life." [1]

He did not confine himself to Hudson River scenery however. "I have been greatly delighted with the magnificent
woodland scenery of Ohio, and with the exuberant fertility of
the soil, which will eventually render this State a perfect garden
spot." The "gigantic trees, rising like stupendous columns,"
overwhelmed him. "Many parts of these prairies of the Missouri
are extremely beautiful, resembling cultivated countries, embellished with parks and groves, rather than the savage rudeness
of the wilderness."

It was the same abroad. In England even the landscape was
moral. "It is associated in the mind with ideas of order, of
quiet, of sober and well-established principles, of hoary usage
and reverend custom." In Germany, the "continual variety of
romantic scenery . . . delights the eye and excites the imagination," while "its happy abundance . . . fills the heart." The
Mediterranean coast, on the other hand, held grandeur and
sublimity. There was sublimity, too, in Spain, but it was de-
pressing in its austerity, so that passing on to France afterwards
was "vivifying." "You cannot imagine how beautiful France
looks to me, with her orchards and vineyards and groves and
green meadows, after naked, sterile Spain."

Irving was not blind to romantic sublimity in nature. "We
were at one time on the dizzy verge of vast precipices, with a
chaos of marble mountains spread before us; at other times we
travelled through deep barrancos and rambias, with red rocks
of immense height absolutely impending over us." He was past
seventy when he wrote a friend, envying her her "voyage up
the Tennessee. I begin to long for a wild, unhackneyed river,
unimproved by cultivation and unburthened by commerce."
And who could ask for a more romantic attitude than he ex-
presses in this entry in an 1824 journal?

The beautiful parts [of the world] are but few and limited and these
in fact have been made by convulsions, which have broken the even

surface of the original world—thrown up mountains—made crags—preci-pices, valleys, etc. etc. So also with the moral world—It is the convul-sions and revolutions that have made all that is romantic and picturesque in morals and manners—what a dull world this would be for poets and painters had there been no deluges or earthquakes and no war—a millen-nium would be death to poetry—a dead sea.

Yet one feels that, on the whole, nature was most valued by Irving in her less spectacular aspects. As he writes his young friend, Mary Kennedy:

You say I cannot imagine how lovely the country is now. Indeed I *can*—though I have not your young eyes and young feelings with which to regard it. I don't know when I have been more conscious of the sweetness of spring than this season. It has opened with uncommon fresh-ness and is surrounding me with its delights. The grass is growing up to my very door,—the roses and honeysuckles are clambering about my windows, the acacias and laburnums are in full flower, singing birds have built in the ivy against the wall and I have concerts at daybreak almost equal to the serenades you used to have at Washington.

Even in austere Spain he could strike the gentle note:

It has been quite a luxury for me to take a long idle stroll, outside of the walls and seat myself by some deserted fountain with the yellow leaves of autumn rustling down from the surrounding trees, and there pass an hour or two enjoying a kind of phantasmagoria of the mind, summoning up past scenes and the images of those that are far away. I am sometimes of the advice of the poor hardworking negro, who, being asked what he would do to kill time if he were free, replied, "Me sit in de Sun, Massa, and let time kill he self!"

Much as Irving loved nature, however, he never made a re-ligion of it. I do not say that he never shows the influence of this tendency; it was too widespread in his time for that. In *Bracebridge Hall* "Forest Trees" become teachers of virtue, and in "Lovers' Troubles" he turns away from the "hollow perfidious courtliness" of Chesterfield to the true and sincere "sentiment and romance" found among people of "an humbler sphere." In *Astoria* there is the wilderness mother with her new-born infant, looking "as unconcerned as if nothing had happened to her; so easy is nature in her operations in the wilderness, when free from the enfeebling refinements of luxury, and the tamperings and appliances of art." But Irving never became a really advanced Romantic along this line. "Some how or another," he writes Brevoort in 1811, "my mind was so bewildered and poisoned by worldly thoughts and cares that the sweet face of nature had not its usual effect upon my feelings." In England, lovely as the scenery was, it was too damp to sit down out of doors, and at Sunnyside he managed to raise his fruits and vegetables "at very little more than twice the market price."

Birds were an important part of the charm nature held for Irving, though he hated parrots, "birds of abomination," which chatter and squall "like a very imp of Satan." At Sunnyside he became a great birdwatcher, with bird houses under the eaves of his tower. Friends sent him wren boxes for his trees; he also kept pigeons.

We have occasional gleams of sunshine and intervals of warmth [he writes Sarah Storrow in 1841], and I think we feel them more sensibly this season on account of their rarity. Within these three days the little bobolinks have begun their tinkling songs among the apple trees and the cat birds are whisking and pecking and carolling about the cottage, and as these are warm weather birds, we hail them as harbingers of sunshine. The nest of the little Phoebe bird under the porch, however, remains unoccupied. This is the second season it has been deserted, but I won't allow it to be disturbed—it shall always remain ready for her— *The Phoebe bird will come back again!*

In one of his journals there are some notes on the song of the Baltimore oriole, and of course the rooks play their part in *Bracebridge Hall.* He praised the skylark before Shelley made it fashionable to do so, and there is one paper in *Wolfert's Roost* ("The Birds of Spring") in which he may be said to have anticipated John Burroughs.

In his European travels, Irving was always sensitive to what he regarded as cruelty to horses, and he certainly was charitable to his own horse after it had thrown him.

At Sunnyside there were dogs, a cat "Imp," cows, ducks who angered Irving by snapping at each other's young, and "Fanny," a pig "of peerless beauty" and a "darling." Pampered dogs are unfavorably viewed in *Bracebridge Hall*, but at Naples in 1805 Irving and his party refused to permit a dog to be overcome by mephitic vapors for their entertainment at the Grotto del Cane. Ik Marvel records his "boyish, eager intentness," watching the preliminary stages of a "dog encounter" on the street, but I am unable tell whether this was a benevolent interest.

Cats gets rather more attention. Ailurophobia is referred to in *Salmagundi*, and there is a reference to Talleyrand's patriotism, "like that of a cat which sticks by the house, let who will inhabit it." On the other hand, Dame Heyliger's cat— "sadly singed, and utterly despoiled of those whiskers which were the glory of her physiognomy"—is faithful to her family after the fire. "But, in truth," writes Irving, "cats are a slandered people; they have more affection in them than the world commonly gives them credit for." He made a detailed and loving record of the behavior of Scott's cat and of Scott's comments concerning him, and at Sunnyside Imp would spend whole days with him, "sometimes clambering on my lap as I sit writing, at other times fondling about my feet, or stretching herself before the fire, clawing the carpet, and purring with perfect enjoyment." In 1852 Irving read some papers of Thomas Wentworth Storrow's "upon the history and character of the cat." He found them "written in a delightful vein of quiet humor and serio comic philosophy," and judged them successfully to "vindicate the cause of a downtrodden people for whom I have always entertained great kindness. If the cats have a proper feeling of gratitude they ought to give you a nightly serenade. You are fully as deserving of one as Jenny Lind or the great Kossuth himself."

Unlike that of the beauties of nature, the appreciation of art requires training. Irving's fondness for making drawings of buildings showed his interest in architecture. His first Gothic building was the Cathedral Church of St. André in Bordeaux, which he saw in 1804, and he was overwhelmed. In Seville in 1828 he compared a saunter about the cathedral to

a walk in one of our great American forests. I cannot compare the scenes, but their sublime and solitary features produce the same dilation of the heart and swelling of the spirit, the same aspiring and longing after something exalted and indefinite; something—I know not what, but something which I feel this world cannot give me.

He looked for revelations of the character of a people in their architecture, perhaps not always quite without prejudices or prepossessions. "In the Chateau of the Tuileries, for instance, I perceive the same jumble of contrarieties that marks the French character; the same whimsical mixture of the great and the little; the splendid and the paltry, the sublime and the grotesque." At the Alhambra he was

led into a consideration of the light, elegant, and voluptuous character prevalent throughout its internal architecture, and to contrast it with the grand but gloomy solemnity of the Gothic edifices reared by the Spanish conquerors. The very architecture thus bespeaks the opposite and irreconcilable natures of the two warlike people who so long battled for the mastery of the Peninsula.

His appreciation of architecture was not, therefore, confined to the Gothic. Sunnyside, which he planned in detail, even to furnishing the architect George Harvey with sketches, is not a Gothic building, though it resembles the Gothic in its highly romantic character, and on its reduced scale it permits a somewhat comparable individuality and ornamentation.

I have found little to indicate that Irving was interested in sculpture. As early as 1805 he began "to be satiated with antique statues, and no longer feel interested in them unless they have something more than antiquity to recommend them." He did visit Canova on one occasion and pronounced him "the first sculptor among the moderns." "I saw at his rooms a group of Cupid and Psyche lately finished which I think surpasses any group I have ever seen for sweetness of workmanship and expression."

With painting he did much better. He was familiar with devotees of paint and pencil from his boyhood; one, John Anderson, aspired to marry his sister Catherine. Later he was intimately associated with Charles Leslie, David Wilkie, and Stuart Newton, in whose work he was greatly interested and to whom he sometimes suggested subjects, generally of a literary character. "You have no doubt heard of Leslie's rapidly increasing reputation. He has done himself vast credit lately by a beautiful picture of Sir Roger de Coverley going to church. He bids fair to take the lead in that most captivating line of painting which consists in the delineation of familiar life."

Perhaps it was this literary bent which, in turn, gave these artists an influence over Irving's writing. The very title of *The Sketch Book* suggests a pictorial conception, and "Geoffrey Crayon" suggests an artist rather than a writer.[2]

A much greater artist, Washington Allston, had an even greater influence upon him, for it was Allston who, in Rome, taught him how to look at paintings and, for a time, even gave him the idea that he wanted to be a painter himself. For Allston's own work, Irving had a proper appreciation:

His Jacob's Dream was a particular favorite of mine. I have gazed on it again and again and the more I gazed the more I was delighted with it. I believe if I was a painter I could at this moment take a pencil and delineate the whole with the attitude and expression of every figure.

Williams compares Irving's own sketches with Thackeray's. The author filled his notebooks with them, and his interest in sketching did not end with his hopes of becoming a professional:

Drawing is a delightful as well as a Gentlemanly accomplishment. The command it gives a person over his time is inconceivable. It has the power of amusing in sickness—rendering home agreeable—and beguiling many a heavy hour of its heaviness.

He lamented that it should be so much neglected "in this age of puppyism," and he wished that he were "a man of opulence," so that he might "take young artists by the hand, and cherish their budding genius!"

His interest was not confined to the work of artists with whom he was acquainted. Like Hawthorne, he was often oppressed by the wilderness of galleries. "How sad that so many fine paintings should be doomed to be only glanced at by the world!" He also had a tendency to care more for out-of-the-way paintings which he had discovered for himself than he did for those which the world held out to him and expected him to admire:

Indeed I carry this so far that I have two or three delicious little Murillos which I have found out in obscure and almost remote chapels or convents, and which I in a manner keep to myself. I carry on a kind of intrigue with them, visiting them quietly and alone; and I cannot tell you what delightful moments I pass in their company; enhanced by the idea of their being so private and retired.

Still he managed to see and to admire a reasonable number of standard painters and paintings, though he was quite unsystematic about it all. Admiring Murillo, he admired Velasquez also, but he overlooked El Greco completely, which was not unusual in his day.

Among the Italians he mentions Veronese, Titian, Tintoretto, and Guido Reni; Veronese's picture of "the Magdalene bathing the feet of our Saviour" seemed "exquisite" to him. The names Rubens, Rembrandt, and Van Dyck appear also; in Rome, in 1805, he enjoyed Gaspard, Nicholas Poussin, and Claude Lorraine. The year he died, Pierre M. Irving records, he made a special trip into New York from Sunnyside to see Church's *The Heart of the Andes*. He was "delighted with it. Pronounced it glorious—magnificent!—such grandeur of general effect with such minuteness of detail—minute without hardness; a painting to stamp the reputation of an artist at once."

His music Irving took generally in connection with his theater-going, and as everybody knows he was one of the most inveterate playgoers of the nineteenth century. In New York he saw all the leading American actors of the time and all the English actors who came to play there. In England he reveled in Mrs. Siddons and her contemporaries; wherever he went—in France, in Spain, in Italy, in Germany [3]—he attended the theater night after night, even when, as, at the outset, in France, he did not care for the style of acting which prevailed.

Though Irving marveled at his brother Peter's ability to enjoy very poor performances, he himself was not incapable of relishing the popular theater. In England, in 1815, he records having witnessed a "slack and tight rope and melodrama, 'Tyger Horde,'" and there is a loving reference to Mr. Punch and the itinerant fair grounds theater in "Buckthorne." There is a widespread impression that Irving was an uncritical playgoer, and he himself lends some support to this view, though he was hurt when he found himself referred to as "the easily-pleased Washington Irving." Certainly he set up no pretensions as a dramatic critic, and he had no more "system" here than he had anywhere else. But it is a mistake to suppose that he was not thoughtful and intelligent in his attitude toward what went on on the stage. In the early days he compared

Cooke with Cooper and Cooper with Cooke. (When Cooper took over the management of the Park Theater, he wrote a versified address for him.) "The more I see of Cooke the more I admire his style of acting—he is very unequal, from his irregular habits and nervous affections—for when he is in proper mood, there is a truth and of course a simplicity in his performances that throws all rant, stage trick and stage effect completely in the background." He compared and contrasted the Shakespearean performances he saw in Germany with those he had witnessed in the United States, and he speculated intelligently concerning the effect which Talma's production of *Hamlet*—"sadly mutilated" and "stripped of its most natural and characteristic beauties—might be expected to exercise on the French drama. Macready he thought "a manufactured kind of actor; wrought after various patterns; with more headwork than heartwork." Edmund Kean was

a strange combination of merits and defects. His excellence consists in sudden and brilliant touches—in vivid exhibitions of passion and emotion. I do not think him a *discriminating* actor, or critical either at understanding or discriminating *character;* but he produces effects which no other actor does. . . . I have seen him guilty of the grossest and coarsest pieces of false acting, and most "tyrannically clapped" withal; while some of his most exquisite touches passed unnoticed.

In one of his letters he achieves a long and discriminating consideration of John Philip Kemble's acting, which, like Macready's, he found extremely studied, but for Kemble's sister Mrs. Siddons, though he saw her only when she was old and had lost "all elegance of figure," he had only praise:

Her looks, her voice, her gestures, delighted me. She penetrated in a moment to my heart. She froze and melted it in turns; a glance of her eye, a start, an exclamation, thrilled through my whole frame. The more I see her, the more I admire her. I hardly breathe while she is on the stage.

Irving sought out his actors in the drawing room as well as on the stage. "I envy you the long quiet conversation with

Alboni about her art," he wrote a friend in 1825. "I delight in conversations of the kind with eminent artists, whom I have always found very communicative and interesting when properly drawn out. So I have found Talma, Pasta, Mrs. Siddons, and Cooke who were the greatest in their respective lines that I was ever acquainted with." He published a record of his conversations with Talma, and when he heard Mrs. Siddons, nearly seventy, read Constance in *King John,* at her own house one evening, he thought it "the greatest dramatic treat I have had for a long time past." But he declined to meet Eliza O'Neil, not because he did not admire her but rather because he admired her so much that he feared being disenchanted. "She is, to my eyes, the most soul-subduing actress I ever saw. I do not mean from her personal charms, which are great, but from the truth, force, and pathos of her acting. I never have been so completely melted, moved, and overcome at a theatre as by her performances." "Well," said Scott, when Irving told him of his determination, "that was very complimentary to her as an actress, but I am not so sure it was as a woman."

As a child, Irving played Juba in a school production of Addison's *Cato* and apparently "hammed" a good deal for his own amusement. (One of his teachers had a considerable interest in the drama.) As a man, he acted with Emily Foster, her family and friends, in Dresden, playing King Arthur in *Tom Thumb,* Sir Charles Rackett in Arthur Murphy's *Three Weeks After Marriage,* and Don Felix in *The Wonder; or Woman Keeps a Secret,* by Susan Centlivre. "I had no idea of this fund of dramatic talent lurking within me," he wrote C. R. Leslie; "and I now console myself that if the worst comes to the worst I can turn stroller, and pick up a decent maintenance among the barns in England."

Music in Irving's life was not quite all theater. Burns's songs were sung to him as a boy by his nurse and his sister Ann, and we are told that he would weep over "The Moon Had Climbed the Highest Hill" and ask to hear it again. He sang a little, and he learned to play the flute—there were even times when this seemed to him "one mode of battling the foul fiend melancholy"—and in "Westminster Abbey" there is at least one passage which shows considerable senitiveness to the grandeur of organ music.

But in general it was opera. He went night after night, hearing the same opera again and again, wherever he might be, and if the performances were not as good in Madrid as they had been in Paris, he could always comfort himself that they were much cheaper. One student has counted 105 performances in less than seven years.[4]

The idea that the opera is necessarily the favorite musical fare of those who do not know much about music is for the most held by those who do not know either music or opera very well, but there can be no doubt that it is possible to enjoy opera for its non-musical aspects, and an interest in musical personalities is often rewarding at the opera house even to those lacking in musical knowledge.

One meets all one's acquaintances at the opera, and there is much visiting from box to box, and pleasant conversation, between the acts. The opera house is in fact the great feature in polite society in New York, and I believe is the great attraction that keeps me in town. Music is to me the great sweetener of existence, and I never enjoyed it more abundantly than at present.

That was in 1848. And four years before in Madrid he had been writing to an otherwise unidentified "dear friend and Colleague":

I often recall with "melancholy pleasure" the astronomical evenings I passed with you in your observatory at the opera where assisted by that far-seeing star gazer, Mr. Martin, we swept the higher regions with our telescopes and scanned all the heavenly bodies. Does the Bird of paradise still figure with full plumage in her nest: I have heard some vague re-

port of her having lost her mate. If so I trust Mr. Martin will have the
gallantry to bear her consolation. Is the momentous qestion decided,
which threatened to shake your legation to its centre—viz. whether Mrs.
W——— was or was not a beauty? For my part I had as little doubt on
the subject as if it regarded her husband.

But such frivolity must not be taken to indicate that Irving
was one of those opera-goers who are more interested in what
was happening in the audience than onstage.

He heard all the great singers of his time and became acquainted with many of them. Pasta was "sublime" and "glorious," Sontag "a beautiful actress" with "blue eyes, auburn hair,
fine teeth, small mouth." Alboni seemed to him "of a frank
happy joyous nature, and I think it is her rich mellow genial
temperament which pours itself forth in her voice like liquid
amber." But Grisi was apparently the only one who was worth
comparing with Mrs. Siddons. "I had scarcely expected ever
again to have seen such a glorious combination of talent and
personal endowment on the stage." Even as late as 1854 he
writes Kennedy about her:

There is a freshness and beauty about her in voice and person that
seem to bid defiance to time. I wish Mr. Gray could see her in Semi-
ramide, and in Rosina (Barber of Seville) which exhibit her powers in
the grand and the comic. I had always seen her in the former and considered her a magnificent being: it was only lately on my last visit to her
that I saw her in comedy; when she played Rosina twice, and surprised
me by the watchfulness with which she could assume the girl; and the
unforced whim and humor with which she could illustrate all her ca-
prices. But to perceive her thorough excellence in this part one must be
able to discern every play of her countenance and especially of her eye.
Her acting, like all great achievements of art, is worthy of especial examination. It is a perfect study. Like all great achievements of art, it is
delightful from its simplicity.[5]

The opportunity to hear Jenny Lind came in America, after
she had retired from the stage, and at first the prospect did not
thrill him. "I am not over-fond of concerts, and would prefer
somewhat inferior talent, when aided by action and scenic

effect of the theatre. I anticipate more pleasure, therefore, from Parodi as *prima donna* of the opera, than from the passionless performances of Jenny Lind as a singer at a concert." He quickly capitulated, however:

> I have seen and heard her but once, but have at once enrolled myself among her admirers. I cannot say, however, how much of my admiration goes to her singing, how much to herself. As a singer, she appears to me of the very first order; as a specimen of womankind a little more. She is enough of herself to counterbalance all the evil that the world is threatened with by the great convention of women. So God save Jenny Lind!

What, now, of the operas themselves? Of course he heard much that modern opera-goers are not familiar with, and which they cannot judge. But there is no denying that there are shocks in the record. Gluck's *Alceste* was "vile French music and singing." The first act of *The Magic Flute* was "delicious," the second "very heavy and tedious." Worst of all was his reaction to *Fidelio*, which he heard in 1822: "some parts very good, some rather in the melodramatic taste; strong contrasts and great noise. Beethoven's style is rather out of fashion—Rossini has introduced a different taste."

But his taste was not really as bad as such a statement would suggest, for he was to live to find *Don Giovanni* the opera of operas. In 1844 he heard *Ernani*, by Verdi, "a new composer who promises great things, and whose music is full of spirit, beauty and grandeur." In general, however, it was the Rossini-Donizetti school to which he adhered. There are thirteen Rossini operas in Earle Johnson's list of the works Irving heard between 1822 and 1829; only one other composer, Mozart, appears as often as three times. He seems to have heard *The Barber of Seville* more frequently than any other opera. Yet he did not hesitate to condemn *Cyrus in Babylon*, "one of Rossini's worst." Of *Lucia di Lammermoor* he wrote from Madrid in 1842, "This opera is my delight. A few steps take me from my lounging chair at home to a comfortable seat at the Theatre: I sit and enjoy the music without any thing to interrupt my attention and return home with my thoughts and feelings all in tune, and am sure to have quiet sleep and pleasant dreams." In Dresden days he became acquainted with Carl Maria von Weber and had the good taste to be attracted by both *Der Freischütz* and *Abu Hassan*. He also met Auber and acquired considerable familiarity with the French *opéra comique*. In Paris, Dominick Lynch once discussed with him his hope of bringing Italian opera to New York. He also admired Méhul's *Joseph*, an opera which is known to this generation almost exclusively through John McCormack's magnificent recording of the "Champs paternels."

But of course literature was even more important to Irving than music, more important indeed than all the other arts put together. He was not, like Longfellow, an accomplished scholar, but he seems to have read quite as vastly. As Miss Simison puts it:

We find him enjoying the works of Chaucer, Shakespeare, Milton, Gay, Goldsmith, Scott, and Campbell, while he is apt to consult such weighty tomes as Bacon, Eachard, Hawkins, Burke, Travis, Pirson, and Ensor. He refers to philosophers like Newton, Playfair, and Stewart, and he quotes from Hume. He knew his Bible thoroughly, too, for he mentions the Decalogue and the Apocalypse, and he cites a favorite passage in the Song of Solomon. From the classics he names Herodotus, Euripides, Aristotle, Theocritus, Lucretius, and Longinus. He alludes glibly to Machaut, specifies Le Sage's *Gil Blas*, and seems particularly intrigued by the Rosicrucians as well as the ancient lore of the Egyptians.

Along the same line, Williams points out that, while traditionally Irving has been thought of as following in the wake of Goldsmith and other eighteenth-century writers, he was actually far more wide-ranging and recondite,

a discursive, miscellaneous reader, an easy victim of old lore, of new languages, of romantic literary associations. It is not generally understood how the process, for example, of his immersion in Spanish history, is duplicated in his intellectual life in minor ways: in his passions for old Dutch stories, for English antiquarians, for Indian wars.

In Scotland, Williams finds Irving "still steeping himself in the traditions of America."

Second, he is browsing in all sorts of books, some on China, some on Scottish history. Third, besides knowing Scott himself, he responds to his stirring legends of the border, and to Burns and Moore; and to the obscure ballads in such collections as Cromek's *Scottish Songs*. He is curious, romantic, this young American idler, a browser, and an antiquarian, volatile perhaps, but with persistence and depth in his literary enthusiasms.[6]

There has been much head-shaking over the curious passage in which Irving warns his nephew Pierre Paris Irving against a too belles-lettristic diet in reading, and there is no denying that this passage has its repellent utilitarian side. Much as Irving himself loved to feed his imagination, however, he had never confined himself as reader to imaginative literature, and certainly he had never confined himself to the currently fashionable books of his time. He did a great deal of antiquarian reading always, showing a deep curiosity about human nature, and, in his comments, an ability to draw inferences and make generalizations on the basis of what he had read. For such a bookish man, he does not have many literary allusions and quotations, except in the Walter Scott-like epigraphs in *The Sketch Book*, which show an impressive range. In *Bracebridge Hall* one may come across such passages as this, about the parson's reading:

He has lately been immersed in the *Demonolatria* of Nicholas Remigius, concerning supernatural occurrences in Lorraine, and the writings of Joachimus Camerarius, called by Vossius the Phoenix of Germany; and he entertains the ladies with stories from them, that make them almost afraid to go to bed at night. I have been charmed myself with some of the wild little superstitions which he has adduced from Blefkenius, Scheffer, and others, such as those of the Laplanders about the domestic spirits which wake them at night, and summon them to go and fish.

From his father's library and other sources Irving made contact with a reasonable number of standard and important works in his youth; later he had the benefit of rummaging in Henry Brevoort's fine collection. That he knew and loved the old nursery tales we know from his loving tribute to their "ingenuity, humor, good sense, and sly satire," though one may question his notion that they were "the sportive productions of able writers," whose "ponderous works on which they relied for immortality have perhaps sunk into oblivion, and carried their names down with them." Elsewhere, Irving gets closer to the folk as a source of literary production and values than this suggestion would indicate, as when he writes his friend, T. W. Storrow, "I mean to get into the confidence of every old woman I meet with in Germany and get from her, her budget of wonderful stories."

Among the older English writers, Shakespeare was necessarily the one Irving knew best; the theater alone would have taken care of that. I suspect he read Chaucer in translation, and no translation could be worse than the one from which he quotes at the beginning of "The Widow" in *Bracebridge Hall*, which also contains an account of his visit to the Tabard (then the Talbot) Inn. The passage on Chaucer in his 1810 journal is as wonderful as any American undergraduate ever achieved in an examination:

In the 16 Century literature dawned in England with considerable brilliancy under the reign of Edward III, but was owing to the genius of a single man. Geoffrey Chaucer, cotemporary of Boccaccio having made himself acquainted with the writings of that illustrious Italian wrote, in his manner, a variety of lively and ingenious tales. This style however is so extremely ancient and loaded with obsolete words, that his works would be almost lost even to the English reader if Pope and Dryden had not taken pains to reduce them into modern English.

Chaucer was learned for the century in which he lived; he was ignorant of nothing that it was possible at that time to know; fortune occasionally smiled upon him, but he experienced the dangerous honor of a brilliant alliance; the fall of his protector drew him along with it, and the merit or the misfortune of having collected the opinions of Wycliff made him desire the crown of Martyrdom.

During his last days Irving told his biographer that "Shakespeare has a phrase for everything." Considering Shakespeare and "one or two others," it seemed "idle for any one else to pride himself upon authorship." Yet when a dispute arose as to whether it was "all our life" or "our little life" in Prospero's famous speech, none of the company could remember what play it was from (Irving misquoted it and put it in *A Midsummer Night's Dream*). He probably quotes from Shakespeare more than from any other author, and his quotations are often correct and apropos.[7] "I have for a few months past led such a pleasant life that I almost shrink from awakening from it into the commonplace round of regular existence—'but this eternal blazon must not be' (Shakespeare) so in two or three days I'll gird up my loins, take staff in hand and return to the land of my fathers." And again: "I was ready to exclaim, 'Stands Scotland where it did?' for it really seemed as if one of the pillars of the earth had quit its base to take a ramble." He read Shakespeare aloud to the ladies on the northern jaunt of 1803, where he was himself impressed by Ann Hoffman's reading of *Romeo and Juliet;* later he read him to the Storrows. The references to the Bard in *The Sketch Book* show affection and familiarity but not much erudition, for Irving is inclined to accept conventional notions concerning the character of poets and too much given to retailing legends and gossip without considering the foundations upon which they rest.

In 1823 he read *The Sad Shepherd* to the Fosters, and Flora Foster seems inclined to credit him with considerable interest in Jonson generally. Both Milton and Bunyan would seem a little austere for Irving, but he refers to both; in 1845 he pictures Sarah Storrow setting forth like Christiana on a Pilgrim's

Progress, and he adds, "I trust you have read the evangelical romance of John Bunyan."

The eighteenth-century writers have generally been considered as influences upon Irving, and in the old days it was taken for granted that he had begun his work under the aegis of Addison and Goldsmith. Recently both Williams and Robert Stevens Osborne have argued that Irving was less indebted to the Augustans at firsthand than has been supposed and more to their imitators in American periodicals. Osborne documents these American influences with considerable convincing detail, though of course this does not rule out all direct contact. Echoing Dante's tribute to Vergil, Irving called Goldsmith his master in the Preface to his biography of that writer, but when his own biographer questioned him about it, he said that "it would never do for an author to acknowledge anything. Was never conscious of an attempt to write after any model. No man of genius ever did." The language is Pierre's; one would give much to know whether Irving spoke of himself as a man of genius; it seems very unlikely.[8]

There are scornful snap judgments of Boswell, Smollett, and Horace Walpole in the life of Goldsmith, but neither Smollett nor Swift can be completely ruled out as influences. Barring his prurience, Sterne lay closer to Irving's spirit. Walter Shandy appears as early as *Salmagundi*, and it is hard to believe that "my uncle Toby" in "The Bold Dragoon" does not echo another and greater Uncle Toby. There are several references to Mrs. Radcliffe, and Irving's "Travelling Notes" of 1804 in the New York Public Library show that he carried *The Italian* on a journey between Bordeaux and Marseilles.

It must be remembered that for Irving nineteenth-century literature was contemporary literature; what to us are far-off battles long ago, to be contemplated with equanimity and evaluated with calm and detached judgment, came to him with all the heat and irritation of current conflicts. He visited Tintern Abbey in 1815 without even mentioning Wordsworth, though, to be sure, he also went to Ludlow Castle without apparently thinking of Milton. He never accepted the extreme romanticism of Wordsworth and Coleridge; the modified romanticism of Scott and Byron was as far as he cared to go. As he writes in one of his notebooks:

> There is an endeavour among some of the writers of the day (who fortunately have not any great weight) to introduce into poetry all the common colloquial phrases and vulgar idioms—In their rage for simplicity they would be coarse and commonplace. Now the Language of poetry cannot be too pure and choice. Poems are like classical edifices, for which we seek the noblest materials—what should we think of the work of the architect who would build a Grecian temple of brick when he could get marble.

Scott and Byron, on the other hand, in Irving's judgment, sailed about the heaven of narrative like an eagle in the sky. Hellman says that the copy of *The Sketch Book* inscribed to "Lord Byron with the author's high respect and admiration" is his only presentation copy of any of his works to a man he had never met. He didn't like the ninth canto of *Don Juan* (he didn't like Scott's *St. Ronan's Well* either), but, like so many of Byron's contemporaries, including some Puritans, he often shows a tendency to carry his admiration for Byron to the length of assuming that sins are not sinful when he sins them. "Newstead Abbey" testifies eloquently to his admiration; so do his successful efforts to get Tom Moore's biography of Byron published in America, and the highly emotional letter he wrote Moore concerning it:

> I cannot tell you how I have been touched and warmed, how often I have felt my heart swelling in my throat and the tears ready to start to my eyes at the exquisite traits af affection, magnanimity, etc. which abound in the childhood and opening youth of poor Byron. I cannot conceive anything more admirable and generous than the manner in

which you accompany him step by step through every scene of his extraordinary career; painting all and illustrating every act calculated to ennoble and endear his memory, and palliating and excusing any thing calculated to disgust or offend. You will teach all the world to love him, and you will make all the world love his biography.

Scott, Irving did know personally, and here there were no personal faults to stand in the way of his admiration; yet at the beginning he seems to have had more reservations about Scott than about Byron. "The Lay of the Scottish Fiddle," written by Paulding but praised by Irving, parodies *The Lay of the Last Minstrel*, and the three adjectives which Irving applies to Scott's work in 1811—"pantomimic, melo-dramatic, romantic"—have not been admiringly chosen. After his visit to Scott in 1817, Irving wrote C. R. Leslie that he could not think of Scott without a warming of the heart. If this meeting had not occurred, or if Irving had not been so warmly and generously received, would his enthusiasm for Scott's "perfect productions" ever have reached the heights it did? In the absence of evidence on this point, one can only conjecture.

The paper Irving wrote to help introduce Thomas Campbell to American readers was, according to his own testimony, "uphill work" and "written against the wall." He complains of a lack of form in "Gertrude of Wyoming": "It is much easier to be fine than correct in writing." Neither was he drawn to Campbell personally when they met. He read Lamb's *Essays of Elia* with great enjoyment, but he could write with great severity about both Thomas Moore and Leigh Hunt. In 1817 he wrote Brevoort:

Moore's poem is just out. I have not sent it to you, for it is dear and worthless. It is written in the most effeminate taste and fit only to delight boarding school girls and lads of nineteen, just in their first loves. Moore should have kept to songs and epigrammatic conceits. His stream of intellect is too small to bear expansion, it spreads into mere surface.

His opinion of Hunt was confided to a notebook:

Leigh Hunt's Rimini shows a heterogeneous taste—in which a fondness for gorgeous material is mingled up with an occasional proneness to the most grotesque—we fancy him a common stone mason with dirty apron and trowel in hand sometimes building with marble and sometimes with rubbish—
His writings are like those edifices which one occasionally sees in Italy—where the architect has purloined the fragments of ancient tables and mingled them with his own rubbish in building the walls.

Irving had his difficulties, too, with Victorian literature. Dickens is considered elsewhere. There is an admiring reference to at least one novel by Trollope—*Doctor Thorne*. But his fussiness over the *Idylls of the King* must seem as ridiculous to posterity as some of the reviewers' troubles with *Tales of a Traveller*. Tennyson "writes from the head," he complained— "too intent on fabricating his verse to write from the heart."

And bared the knotted column of his throat

was Irving's idea of a "beastly" line, "a perfect animal picture," and "very offensive." He was picayunish about

He snatched his great limbs from the bed,

insisting that it meant he pulled himself out by the leg. "Well, I shan't go mad with this poetry—though I dare say I shall learn to esteem it."

Irving's reading in foreign literatures was handicapped by the fact that he was not one of the world's great linguists, yet he managed to get through a good deal of it, either in the originals or in translation (it is not always possible to tell which). *Knickerbocker's History* contains episodes based on the classical epics; Osborne conjectures that he may have learned enough Latin in school to read a little Cicero, but he had no Greek.

He began to study German after his arrival in England in

1815. His visit to Scott furnished him with fresh incentive, and after the bankruptcy of 1818, he "studied German day and night by way of driving off horrid thoughts." In May of that year he wrote Brevoort that he was now able to "read and *splutter* a little." In 1823 we find such entries as "getting very familiar with the German language" and "fighting my way into the German language." In May he records having paid off two German tutors; at one time he rose at five and began his German lessons at seven. Flora Foster gives him credit for only a little German, saying that he had to have the Fosters copy out a simple inscription for him. He may have understood it better than he could speak, or even read, it, however. His 1833 remark that he sat so far from the stage that *Wallensteins Tod* was tedious to him seems to imply that if he had been able to hear what was said, he could have understood it. When, in 1855, he heard that J. P. Kennedy was studying German, he wrote Mrs. Kennedy:

> I should like to rub up my own recollections of the German in the course of a few rides with him in the woods on the back of Douce Davie. I think I could repay him in bad German for some of the metaphysics he occasionally wastes on me in the course of our woodland colloquies.

Schiller was unquestionably Irving's favorite German poet; he has more references to him than to any other German writer, and he tells us that he would rather have written the Wallenstein play than won Wallenstein's battles. Like Longfellow, he had to learn to like Goethe, and he never got as far with him as Longfellow did. He knew Tieck in Dresden, and he apparently had some interest in Carl F. Van der Velde, "the German Scott," one of whose novels, *Die Lichtensteiner*, was in his library at Sunnyside.[9]

Spanish he did not begin until 1824; the next year he wrote Emily Foster that he had devoted himself to it "for a long time with close application," and "made sufficient proficiency to relish the old Spanish poets; from this I was led naturally into a course of Spanish and Moorish history." Perhaps he did better in Spanish than in German because it is a less difficult language and he loved it more. In 1827 he wrote Mrs. Storrow that the farther he went with it, the more he admired it:

There is an energy, a beauty, a melody and richness in it surpassing in their combined proportions all other languages that I am acquainted with. It has less softness and mellifluousness than the Italian, but it is only inferior to the Italian in those respects, while it surpasses it in fire and boldness. It is characteristic of the nation; for with all its faults, and in spite of the state into which it has fallen, this is a noble people, naturally full of high and generous qualities.

Even so, he speaks as one who has not attained. Fernan Caballero knew no English; when he talked with her, he had to use such Spanish and German as he could command. When, in diplomatic service in Spain, he was presented to young Queen Isabella II, he found it necessary to apologize for his Spanish, though she thought—or said—that he spoke it very well. As late as 1846 he complains that, though he understands the language easily, "I find it rather a toil to converse in it; and I hate conversation when it costs me an effort." But he loved Cervantes from his youth and once considered writing a book about him. He was also devoted to Calderon and Lope de Vega, and it made him furious to see modern Spaniards "bending the neck to the yoke of French dramatic rule," and considering modern playwrights superior to their own great giants. "How little do these degenerate Spaniards know of what they ought to be proud of."

Irving's Italian did not get very far, though in 1824 he studied it "again all day in Mr. S's garden and in the Bois de Boulogne, lying on the grass." He knew the *Orlando Furioso* in translation from the age of ten, and it has been shown that, though his familiarity with Dante was not great, he knew at least the "Inferno" well enough to be reminded of it from time to time by other things which he saw and read.[10] He did better with French, in which he acquired a greater competence than in any other foreign language except finally Spanish. On his first visit to Paris, he plunged boldly into speaking French, leaving the grammar until later, as a native does. "I am busily employed in studying the French language, and I hope before I leave France to have a pretty satisfactory acquaintance with it." He did not do quite that, however. In 1806, in collaboration with Peter Irving and George Cannes, he published, at Boston, a translation of François-Joseph de Pons, *Voyage à la partie orientale de la terre-ferme*, but it was the opinion of at least one reviewer that the translators knew very little French and still less English. Francis Prescott Smith has noted that Matilda Hoffman at fourteen wrote better French in her letters than Irving ever did. Still, he went on talking French or talking at it. "I can ask for any thing I want beside a variety of casual questions. I begin to understand what is said to me, and can read and understand tolerably well any simple French book." He was always glad when he found fellow travelers who could speak French. It did not make conversation easy, but it did make it posible. "Two of my fellow passengers talk French and are very polite. I have found that language truly universal and in whatever relation I am thrown I generally find some one or other who can speak it." But he never ceased to disparage either his spoken or his written French. When, in 1837, he gave Longfellow a letter of introduction to a distinguished German, he added a postcript explaining that he writes in English, "being very ill versed in the French language and knowing that you are surrounded by those to whom the English language is familiar." Yet Rabelais, Racine, Chateaubriand, and Molière are among the French writers to whom he refers.[11]

As for the Americans, in James Grant Wilson's *Bryant and His Friends*,[12] Irving is reported as having said that he ignored contemporary poets, having read none since Byron, Moore, and Scott, and that he and Paulding were fortunate in being born when they were. "We should have no chance now against the battalions of better writers." He added:

There are a great deal too many books written nowadays about countries, and places, and people, that when I was young no one knew, or wanted to have any knowledge of whatever; and it is morally impossible for any mortal to read or digest one half of them.

He thought "William Wilson" better than "The Fall of the House of Usher," which he considered too highly colored. "The Raven" puzzled him—a "capital hit," with "a strange weird interest in it," but "too dismal to go to bed upon." He managed to say the conventionally "right" things about all the brilliant new writers of his old age—*Typee* was "exquisite" and its style "graphic"—but they belonged to a world he never made, and it does not seem that they can have meant much to him. Thus *The Scarlet Letter* is "masterly! masterly!! masterly!!!" (the punctuation is Pierre's, for the opinion was given orally), but how much understanding does a man have of Hawthorne when he can lump *The Scarlet Letter* and *The House of the Seven Gables* together as "two very clever works which have made their appearance within a year or so, quite recently"?

He understood Bryant better, and went to real trouble to get him published in England,[13] and certainly his unfailing praise of Cooper is much to his credit, especially in view of Cooper's consistently contemptuous attitude toward him. "They may say what they will of Cooper, the man who wrote this book [*The Pathfinder*] is not only a great man, but a good man." Towards the end, G. P. Putnam managed to introduce the two writers to each other one day in his office.

They chatted cordially for an hour, "and Mr. Irving afterwards frequently alluded to the incident as being a very great satisfaction to him."

Oliver Wendell Holmes was more within his range, and it is not surprising that Irving relished *The Autocrat of the Breakfast Table*. The creator of Diedrich Knickerbocker ought to have relished Charles Godfrey Leland's Hans Breitmann too, and Irving did just that. Naturally he enjoyed the writings of Paulding and Kennedy as the work of personal friends; there is a letter of Kennedy's to Carey in which he speaks of Irving's delight in *Horse-Shoe Robinson*. He also admired Dana's *Two Years Before the Mast* and other works by the same author.

3   HOW THE TREE BORE ITS FRUIT

But Irving did not stop with reading; he wrote. The most elaborate statement he ever achieved of the *quare* and *modus* of his writing was made in a letter to Henry Brevoort, December 11, 1824. It shows him quite as sophisticated in his thinking on these matters as Poe.

I fancy much of what I value myself upon in writing, escapes the observation of the great mass of my readers, who are intent more upon the story than the way in which it is told. For my part, I consider a story merely as a frame on which to stretch my materials. It is the play of thought, and sentiment, and language; the weaving in of characters lightly, yet expressively, delineated; the familiar and faithful exhibition of scenes in common life; and the half-concealed vein of humor that is often playing through the whole;—these are among what I aim at, and upon which I felicitate myself in proportion as I think I succeed. I have preferred adopting the mode of sketches and short tales rather than long works, because I choose to take a line of writing peculiar to myself, rather than fall into the manner or school of any other writer; and there is a constant activity of thought and a nicety of execution required in writings of the kind, more than the world appears to imagine. It is comparatively easy to swell a story to any size when you have once the scheme and the characters in your mind; the mere interest of the story, too, carries the reader on through pages and pages of careless writing, and the author may often be dull for half a volume at a time, if he has some striking scene at the end of it; but in these shorter writings, every page must have its merit. The author must be continually piquant; woe to him if he makes an awkward sentence or writes a stupid page; the critics are sure to pounce upon it. Yet if he succeed, the very variety and piquancy of his writings—nay, their very brevity, make them frequently recurred to, and when the mere interest of story is exhausted, he begins to get credit for his touches of pathos or humor; his points of wit or turns of language. I give these as some of the reasons that have induced me to keep on thus far in the way I had opened for myself; because I find by recent letters from E. I. that you are joining in the oft-repeated advice that I should write a novel. I believe the works that I have written will be oftener re-read than any novel of the size that I could have written. It is true other writers have crowded into the same branch of literature, and I now begin to find myself elbowed by men who have followed my footsteps; but at any rate I have had the merit of adopting a line for myself, instead of following others.

This is an announcement at once unpretentious and ambitious; Irving evidences both an attractive modesty and a fine arrogance. In 1819, too, he admitted to his British publisher John Murray that his writings "have that deficiency in scope and fullness which results from some degree of self diffidence and a want of practice and experience. I may improve as I proceed and shall feel proud and happy if on some future occasion I may have any thing to offer that may be deemed worthy of your attention."

The preoccupation with manner, amazing at so early a stage in the development of a nation's literature, is great enough to suggest decadence; one remembers Maria Edgeworth's objection to *Bracebridge Hall* that "the workmanship surpasses the work. There is too much care and cost bestowed on petty objects." Irving's strength is that he knows exactly what he is doing, and that, in the face of almost overwhelming pressure in the opposite direction, he has chosen to devote himself to literature alone:

I have attempted no lofty theme, nor sought to look wise and learned, which appears to be very much the fashion among our American writers, at present. I have preferred addressing myself to the feeling and fancy of the reader, more than to his judgment. My writings, therefore, may appear light and trifling in our country of philosophers and politicians; but if they possess merit in the class of literature to which they belong, it is all to which I aspire in the work. I seek only to blow a flute accompaniment in the national concert, and leave others to play the fiddle and the French horn.

Thus he wrote of *The Sketch Book*. He felt the same way about *Bracebridge Hall*:

I shall continue on, therefore, in the course I have hitherto pursued; looking at things poetically, rather than politically; describing them as they are, rather than pretending to point out how they should be; and endeavoring to see the world in as pleasant a light as circumstances will permit.

The last part was a matter of temperament, but the "looking at things poetically, rather than politically"—or sociologically or moralistically or even psychologically, as he might have said if all these terms had been in use in his day—was vital to Irving's conception of literature and to the service he rendered. "I am for curing the world by gentle alternatives," he wrote in the Preface to *Tales of a Traveller*, "not by violent doses; indeed, the patient should never be conscious that he is taking a dose." It is the negative, not the positive, part of the statement that is vital; the rest is a sop to the Cerberus of a moralizing age. Poe was to express the same thing more dogmatically; the purpose of art, he insisted, was neither moral exhortation nor truth, but aesthetic pleasure, with the result that he has been widely misinterpreted as wishing to divorce art from morality that she might promptly be remarried to immorality. Nothing was further from his intention; he was simply insisting that she must live unwed.

Irving is fundamentally in agreement with Poe again in his insistence upon a distinction between the short story and the novel, the latter's virtues being, as both writers felt, of a less intense and concentrated variety. Few can doubt that there is more "passage work" in a novel than in the "Ode to a Nightingale," a larger non-literary element, as it were, more orientation, even information; it comes closer than the poem —the realistic novel at any rate—to occupying two worlds simultaneously, the world of actuality and the world of art. In the same manner, a fugue by Bach is more "musical" in the sense of being more exclusively musical in its interest than an opera, which is half drama. Now Irving did not write poetry (of any merit at any rate), but, as we may see by his own statement of his intentions, he treated his sketches as the poet handles his verses, trying to load, as Keats says, every rift with ore.

To be sure, he knew that the successful creation of a work of art—like life itself—requires balance as careful as that of a tightrope walker, and if he could read what I have written here, he would know that in a sense I have falsified egregiously, for every analogy is in a sense a false analogy. Irving valued fine touches—"it is this handling which, like the touching and toning of a picture gives the richest effects"—but he also cherished spontaneity and the insights that come with intuition. He mistrusted writing according to rule: "I feel how a thing ought to be done and how I can render it effective, and if I go counter to this feeling I am likely to come off lamely; yet I cannot reduce this feeling to any rule or maxim by which I can make my plan comprehended in its essential points by others."

For Irving reading and observation were but two sides of his head; like his own Mountjoy he was capable of rambling about with the *Metamorphoses* in his pocket and working himself "into a kind of self-delusion," identifying "the surrounding scenes with those of which I had just been reading." The

Rangers who take him into Pawnee territory seem to him like Robin Hood's merry men. Or he watches the birds at Sunnyside and is "reminded of the tempest-tossed crew of Columbus, when, after their long dubious voyage, the field birds came singing round the ship." Yet this would-be poet was as diligent a notebook keeper as Hawthorne himself, not always noting the "important" things that any keen observer might have seen, but never missing the detail that he could use in his own highly specialized, definitely "literary" kind of work. In the early days, as Miss Simison has observed, the notebook "becomes a kind of exercise book. . . . In it he fumbles with an unwieldy sentence, now crossing out this word, now that, until he finally achieves what he believes to be the perfect phrase. In it, too, he jots down words which please him to stow away for future use." [1] But when the robe is finally woven, there are no seams.

Despite the resemblances between Irving and Poe, it must be understood, as Pete Kyle McCarter has stressed, that he did not, like Poe, aim to unify his writings around the plot. Old-fashioned as he seems to us, he was as impatient of narrative for narrative's sake as the most "advanced" writers of today. Even those of his short pieces which, like "Rip Van Winkle" and "The Legend of Sleepy Hollow," are, by some definition if not by Poe's, "short stories," still have some characteristics of the sketch about them. This may be seen in their leisurely development, in the delighted exhibition of local color, in the way the reader is kept conscious (as in a personal essay) of the writer's personality, and in much besides. "I wish, in everything I do, to write in such a manner that my productions may have something more than the mere interest of narrative to recommend them, which is very evanescent; something, if I dare use the phrase, of classic merit, i.e. depending upon style, etc., which gives a production some chance for duration beyond the mere whim and fashion of the day." Since the short story as a type hardly existed in his day, and in view of his own contemptuous reference to the tales "littering from the press both in England and Germany," it was perhaps easier for him to justify the care he bestowed upon his productions if he thought of them in terms of the well-established and respectable essay.[2]

He understood clearly that if he would really make his mark as a writer, he must "strike out some way of my own, suited to my own way of thinking and writing." Even "Scott's manner," great as Scott was, "must likewise be widely avoided." There were times when he flirted with it, however. There was the semi-connectedness of *Bracebridge Hall*. There was "Buckthorne." There was "The Story of Rosalie," afterwards used in part in "Mountjoy." There was even the novel he planned about the regicide judges. But when, after *Tales of a Traveller*, he veered away from the sketches in whose behalf he had both reasoned and wrought so well, he turned not to the novel but to biographical monoliths like the *Columbus* and the *Washington*. He did not admit to others—perhaps not even to himself—that he was relinquishing a higher form for a lower form. Instead he seems to argue, as against his previously maintained position, that because the new work is bigger it must be better. When, in 1829, Colonel Aspinwall, who was acting as a kind of literary agent for Irving, asked him for another *Sketch Book*, he rejected the idea decisively:

> I have some things sketched in a rough state, in that vein, but thought it best to hold them back until I had written a work or two of more weight, even though of less immediate popularity. A literary reputation, to hold well with the public, requires some *make weights* of the kind. Some massive materials, which form a foundation; the lighter works then become ornaments and embellishments.

"Make weights"? But what, then, is to happen to the "flute accompaniment in the national concert" now suddenly become all "the fiddle and the French horn"?

How much ambition did Irving have, then, as a man of letters, and how much did he believe in his work? He has been scolded often enough for the letters in which he warned Pierre Paris Irving against a literary career:

I hope none of those whose interests and happiness are dear to me will be induced to follow my footsteps, and wander into the seductive but treacherous paths of literature. There is no life more precarious in its profits and fallacious in its enjoyments than that of an author.

And later:

Upon the whole, I am glad that you have entered into your father's counting house. You will there have a certain and prosperous path in life marked out for you, instead of having to adopt and clear away a doubtful one for yourself. You will, in all probability, have the means of living independently, and indulging your tastes and talents at an age when, in another line of life, you might have the whole struggle of existence before you.

Worse still is the letter to his niece Helen about her husband, the other Pierre, Irving's biographer:

Tell him I promise not to bore him about literary matters when he comes up. I have as great a contempt for these things as anybody, though I have to stoop to them occasionally for the sake of a livelihood—but I want to have a little talk with him about stocks, and railroads and some mode of screwing and jewing the world out of more interest than my money is entitled to.

Such utterances are not endearing. But the biographer who takes them as covering the subject of Irving's attitude toward literature, or expressing his settled convictions on the subject —with, in the case of the second instance, the implication that this is what association with that ogre John Jacob Astor has done to him—is twin brother to that other innocent who supposes Mark Twain to be serious when, in ironic letters to W. D. Howells, he describes his gentle wife as a raging virago. The tone of Helen's letter is obviously that of playful exaggeration—it is difficult for a man of letters to resist the opportunity to show himself, now and then, as good a practical fellow as the best (or the worst) of them; as for the letters to Pierre Paris, perhaps it may be enough to say that a father who seeks to save his daughter from being martyred may still be perfectly sincere in his admiration for St. Joan of Arc.

Irving was painfully aware of the difficulties of the literary life, and who shall say he had no right to be?

> I am isolated in English literature, without any of the usual aids and influences by which an author's popularity is maintained and promoted. I have no literary coterie to cry me up; no partial reviewer to pat me on the back. . . . I have nothing to depend on but the justice and courtesy of the public, and how long the public may continue to favor the writings of a stranger, or how soon it may be prejudiced by the scribblers of the press, is with me a matter of extreme uncertainty.

So he wrote Leslie from Paris in 1824. I know of no other writer of his eminence who came so close to being compelled to give up literature in mid-career.

But Irving also knew the advantages of authorship: "Other men are known to posterity only through the medium of history, which is continually growing faint and obscure; but the intercourse between the author and his fellowmen is ever new, active, and immediate."

So long, that is, as his works survive. Irving did not overestimate his writings. He was not such a fool as to suppose that he could stand beside a man like Scott, who "could tenant half a hundred scribblers like myself on the mere skirts of his literary reputation." He was above the kind of exploitation with which minor writers cry up their wares.[3]

> It is a delicate matter [he wrote Charles Oliffe in 1843] for me to meddle with a book which proposes to give favorable selections of my writings. Still, I will venture to suggest that the title should be perfectly simple and unpretending; "Extracts from" or "Specimens of" the writing etc., without prefixing "Beautiful" or "Elegant," or any other laudatory adjective.

"Fragrant Flowers" or any other such sweet scented title would not, I am afraid, have a pleasant odor in the nose of the public.

Late in life, Irving told N. P. Willis that "he was always afraid to open the first copy that reached him of a new book of his own. He sat and trembled, and remembered all the weak points where he had been embarrassed and perplexed, and where he felt he might have done better—hating to think of the book, indeed, until the reviewers had praised it." In the year of his death, when he was asked which book he valued most highly, he replied, "I scarcely look with full satisfaction upon any; for they do not seem what they might have been. I often wish that I could have twenty years more, to take them down from the shelf one by one, and write them over."

The only one that ever really got itself revised was *Knickerbocker's History of New York*, which, indeed, he revised twice. As early as 1820, in a letter, conjecturally to Lockhart, in the New York Public Library collection, he judged it "a raw juvenile production," to be "read with great indulgence. Indeed I feel extremely and I may say painfully diffident in handing my writings to one who is in daily intercourse with the *great Spirits* of the earth." Yet I do not think he was ashamed of this book. In "The Author's Apology" prefixed to the revised edition of 1849, he took credit to himself that even though he had "taken an unwarrantable liberty with our early provincial history," yet he "had at least turned attention to that history and provoked research." Before him "the peculiar and racy customs derived from our Dutch progenitors were unnoticed, or regarded with indifference, or adverted to with a sneer." And he goes on to rejoice and take pride in the popularity of "Knickerbocker" insurance companies, steamboats, omnibuses, etc. He refers to the *History* in other works—in the introductory note to "Rip Van Winkle," where he tells us whimsically that its "literary character" is no better than it should be, but lauds "its scrupulous accuracy, which indeed was a little questioned on its first appearance, but has since been completely established; and it is now admitted into all historical collections as a book of unquestionable authority," and again in *Bracebridge Hall*. There are two references to "The Legend of Sleepy Hollow" in "Wolfert's Roost," and in his paper about Margaret Davidson he does not hesitate to quote her praise of it.

"*Mon verre est petite*," says de Musset, "*mais je bois dans mon verre*." Irving was no Scott and no Dickens, and he knew it, but he was an Irving, and he knew that too. "Whatever my literary reputation may be worth, it is very dear to me, and I cannot bring myself to risk it by making up books for mere profit." He could even stand up to the great and formidable John Murray when the latter made an unauthorized alteration. "I do not conceive that the purchase of the work gave you any right to make such an alteration."

Viewing his life as a whole, we can say that Irving was a more than ordinarily productive writer. There were even times when his application partook of the heroic. Yet compared to a writer like Dickens—who, day after day, year in and year out, spent the morning hours at his desk, regardless of whether he felt like it or not, or of what else he might have to do—Irving was not a systematic or disciplined writer. "My whole course of life has been desultory, and I am unfitted for any period-ically recurring task, or any stipulated labor of body and mind. I have no command of my talents such as they are, and have to watch the varyings of my mind as I would a weathercock." *Knickerbocker's* triumph was followed by years of virtual literary idleness, and even the triumph of *The Sketch Book* brought him no assured literary confidence:

Now you suppose I am all on the alert [he wrote C. R. Leslie]—and full of spirit and excitement—no such thing. I am just as good for nothing as ever I was and indeed have been flurried and put out of my way by these puffings. I feel something as I suppose you did when your Picture met with success—anxious to do something better—and at a loss what to do.

He simply accepted the fact that his "literary impulses" were "uncertain." Conditions for composition had to be right. "I require much leisure and a mind entirely abstracted from other cares and occupations, if I would write much or write well." He couldn't just "hammer" it out; if he tried, it was good for nothing and had to be thrown away. Worry and low spirits were distractions; competing interests were distractions; even "the delights of intimate and social intercourse" were a distraction:

Literary excitement is excessively precarious, and there is nothing an author is made more nearly distrustful of than the picturings of his fancy. We are mere chameleons, fed with air, and changing color with any thing with which we come in contact. We are to be stirred up to almost anything by encouragement and cheering, but the least whisper of doubt casts a chill upon the feelings of the invention.

Obviously there was some self-indulgence here. It is always dangerous to wait for "inspiration." But Irving experienced the advantages of his temperament as well as the disadvantages. When he felt a "literary fit coming on," he was capable of making the most of it. "An author's right time to work is when his mind is aglow—when his imagination is kindled. These are his precious moments. Let him wait until they come; but, when they have come, let him make the most of them." Sometimes he got up in the night to write, or, if he could find no candle, jotted down his ideas on a scrap of paper in the dark. Once he wrote twenty-eight pages in a day—"clear and neat writing." About a third of *Bracebridge Hall* was written in ten days, and many of the Traveller's tales were produced very rapidly also. He devoted himself to "The Bold Dragoon" one morning while the breakfast dishes were being removed, and he wrote

"Wolfert Webber" in two weeks, keeping at it from break-fast until three o'clock in the afternoon. We have already seen something of the diligence with which he devoted himself to the Columbus. He worked into the night; he worked from four o'clock in the morning. In 1827 in Madrid he even worked all Christmas morning. It is true that even now he was capricious, so that we find such entries as "incapable of work," "try to work but incapable," and "could not write without great difficulty." Yet he did stay at it, and he did get the job done.[4] The *Washington* was an even greater achievement, both be-cause it came at the end of his life, when he had supposed his working days were over, and because it involved not only long hours of labor at his desk but also an historian's field re-search—visits to the scenes of Washington's life, examination of newspapers, government records, military despatches, and much besides.

The interesting thing is that, except for the *Washington*, at the end, when his health was no longer good enough to sup-port the burden, he generally felt better for hard work. "I have never found, in anything outside of the four walls of my study, any enjoyment equal to sitting at my writing desk, with a clean page, a new theme, and a mind wide awake." Even when he was not at his physical best, it seemed to help. "For some time past, indeed ever since I have resumed my pen, my mind has been tranquil. I sleep better and feel pleasanter." And he lived to learn that "an abundance of leisure ... if not em-ployed, is the most insupportable of all earthly blessings."

As he grew older, he seemed to need work more, not less, perhaps because some of the distractions that had absorbed him earlier had begun to pall:

I live only in the Revolution. I have no other existence now; can think of nothing else. My desire is to give everything vividly, but to avoid all melodramatic effect. I wish the incidents to be brought off strongly, and speak for themselves; but no hubbub of language, no trickery of phrase, nothing wrought up.

He needed "to mount the pen occasionally as an old huntsman requires to be occasionally on horseback, even though he hunts to no purpose." In 1856 he wrote Emily Foster:

My health is excellent though at times I have tried it hard by literary occupation and excitement. There are some propensities that grow upon a man with age and I am a little more addicted to the pen than I was in my younger days, and much more, I am told, that is prudent for a man of my years. It is a labor however, in which I delight; and I am never so happy of an evening as when I have passed the whole morning in my study, hard at work, and have earned the evening's recreation.

Irving was very sensitive to criticism. In his theoretical views on the subject he differed from time to time. In "The Mutability of Literature" he somewhat cynically pronounced critics useful because they kept down the number of printed books. In his most considered essay on the subject, "Desultory Thoughts on Criticism" (1839), he urged that writers should be left free to go their own gait. His own only critical papers of consequence are his introduction to Thomas Campbell's poems, the *Analectic* essays on Robert Treat Paine and Edward C. Holland, and his account of his conversations with the French actor Talma.[5] This is not enough material to make it possible to dogmatize as to what he might or might not have achieved in this field had he cultivated it more assiduously, though it goes without saying that he did not possess a deeply analytical mind and could never, under any circumstances, have been a great critic. He might very well have been an acceptable one, however, and my own guess would be that his basic kindliness of spirit and unwillingness to sit in judgment, coupled with a certain fear and dislike of elaborate formulations, were more fundamentally at the root of his difficulty than natural inability. The man who wrote as follows of Paine's devotion to Dryden ought not to have experienced much difficulty in understanding what is meant by historical criticism:

> Like all those writers who take up some particular author as a model, a degree of bigotry has entered into his devotion, which made him blind to the faults of his original; or rather, these faults become beauties in his eyes. Such, for instance, is that propensity to far-sought allusions and forced conceits. Had he studied Dryden in connection with the literature of his day, contrasting him with the poets who preceded him, and those who were his contemporaries, Mr. Paine would have discovered that these were faults with which Dryden reprobated himself. They were the lingering traces of a taste which he was himself endeavoring to abolish.

Furthermore, though Irving was no dogmatist, he was not indifferent to ideas, nor did he always eschew generalization. His comparison between Shakespeare and Racine may not do justice to Shakespeare's style, but he perceives and states a distinction clearly, and this distinction has at least a measure of validity:

> Authors whose popularity arises from beauty of diction and harmony of numbers are ruined by translation; a beautiful turn of expression, a happy combination of words and phrases, and all the graces of perfect euphony, are limited to the language in which they are written. Style cannot be translated. . . . Who can form an idea of the exquisite beauties of Racine, when translated into a foreign tongue? But Shakespeare triumphs over translation. His scenes are so exuberant in original and striking thoughts and masterly strokes of nature, that he can afford to be stripped of all the magic of his style. His volumes are like the magician's cave in "Aladdin," so full of jewels and precious things, that he who does but penetrate for a moment may bring away enough to enrich himself.

So far as his own works were concerned, Irving would have been glad to get along without critics altogether. "I should like," he writes Brevoort, "to write occasionally for my own amusement, and to have the power of throwing my writings either into my portfolio, or into the fire. I enjoy the first conception and first sketchings from my ideas; but the correcting and preparing them for the press is unknown labor, and publishing is detestable." Unfavorable reviews hurt him even when he felt a well-founded contempt for their source. A friend said of him that "one condemning whisper sounded louder in his ear than the plaudits of thousands," and while this may be an exaggeration, there are reports of his abandoning enterprises because friends or relatives did not seem sufficiently to believe in them. An American "friend" who sent him unfriendly reviews from the homeland caused him much pain. *"It is hard to be stabb'd in the back by one's own kin,"* he writes on one occasion. And he adds, somewhat petulantly, "No matter—my countrymen must regret some day or other that they turned from me with such caprice, the moment foes abroad assailed me." Less petulantly, upon another occasion, he finds a weight resting upon his mind, "a soreness of heart as if I had committed some hideous crime and all mankind were justly irritated at me. I went about with a guilty look and sought to hide myself. It was not without some effort that I occasionally threw off this weight and recollected that my only crime had been an unsuccessful attempt to please the world."

This being true, he was also helped and encouraged by praise, though even here he could be embarrassed, as when he was compared with his friend Paulding to the latter's disadvantage. "Receive a most kind and gratifying letter from Moore about my work. Has a good effect in reassuring me." He actually wept over the enthusiastic reviews of *The Sketch Book*, though he so little expected them that he would have preferred not to send out any press copies. He was so flattered by Prescott's statement that he had been little "seduced from historic accuracy by the poetical aspect of his subject" in *The Conquest of Granada* that he quoted it verbatim in the introduction to the revised edition.

Irving does not seem to have been so thin-skinned that he

could not acknowledge limitations when they were pointed out to him; thus he acknowledged the truth of Alexander H. Everett's criticisms of his *Columbus* in 1829; a mere laudatory review would not, he says, have been of any value to him. He was reasonable, too, in the early days, when Gulian C. Verplanck took rather heated exception to his treatment of the Dutch in *Knickerbocker's History*:

> I hope he will not put our old Dutch burghers into the notion that they must feel affronted with poor Diedrich Knickerbocker just as he is creeping out in the new edition. I could not help laughing at this burst of filial feeling in Verplanck, on the jokes put upon his ancestors, though I honor the feeling and admire the manner in which it is expressed. It met my eyes just as I had finished the little story of Rip Van Winkle and I could not help noticing it in the introduction to the Bagatelle. I hope Verplanck will not think the article was written in defiance of his Vituperation. Remember me heartily to him, and tell him I mean to grow wiser and better and older every day, and to lay the castigation he has given me seriously to heart.

In 1859 he wrote almost abjectly to both C. C. Felton and Henry T. Tuckerman, to thank them for their praise of *Washington*:

> I have been very much out of health of late [he told Felton], with my nerves in a sad state, and with occasional depression of spirits; and in this forlorn plight had come to feel very dubious about the volume I had committed to the press. Your letter had a most salutary and cheering effect and your assurance that the last volume had been to you *of more absorbing interest than either of the others* carried a ray of joy to my heart, for I was sadly afraid that the interest might be considered as falling off.

To Tuckerman he added, concerning his particular fears for this volume, "Having nothing of the *Drum and Trumpet* which gave bustle and animation to the earlier volumes I feared it might be considered a falling off."

Irving always knew that writing is an art, not a trade, and that its highest rewards cannot be calculated in financial terms.

When Scott fell upon evil days, Irving apparently considered him somewhat quixotic in assuming the crushing financial burden which he assumed.

It grieves me [he wrote David Wilkie] to find that Scott is bestowing so much glorious labor to satisfy the claims of creditors, who, if I understand the affair rightly, are his creditors only by some technical construction of the law. However, I fancy it matters very little to his happiness who gets the profit of his labors: he feels a delight in the labor itself. He has a restless creative principle within him that incites to continual activity, and perhaps there is no livelier and purer source of pleasure than that of successful invention. God bless him! I feel it a happiness to have lived in the same time with him, when one is continually surprized and delighted with the outpourings of his exhaustless genius, and his generous soul.

He could not afford to neglect the financial aspect, however, for he was dependent upon what he could earn for his support, and in his later years he supported others also. "With the exception of a few editors of magazines and reviews," wrote Richard Henry Dana in 1819, "Mr. Irving is almost the only American who has attempted to support himself by literary labors."

In business as such Irving had little interest. "I am not a man of business," he wrote Aspinwall in 1828, "and am easily perplexed in money matters." It was he who coined the phrase "the almighty dollar," for which he was idiotically accused of irreverence, so that he had to explain that "no irreverence was intended even to the dollar itself; which . . . is daily becoming more and more an object of worship."

The bankruptcy of P. & E. Irving & Co. was a great blow to Irving, but not primarily because he craved money. It was rather because "to owe money is with me to feel like a culprit." In some ways the bankruptcy was even harder to take than Matilda Hoffman's death had been: "That was solemn and sanctifying, it seemed while it prostrated my spirits, to purify and elevate my soul. But this was vile and sordid and humiliated me to the dust."

Irving's financial problems did not end when the Irving firm emerged from its financial difficulties. He was very short of funds while working on *Columbus*. In 1838 he was so cramped that he lacked funds for travel.[6] He was hard hit by the Panic of 1841, for whose pangs he could comfort himself only by reflecting that it had come in obedience to the laws of God. "The world at large is suffering the penalty of its own avarice: for avarice for a time was as extensive and deleterious in its sway as the cholera. Every one was seized with the mania of becoming suddenly rich and in yielding to the frantic impulse has impoverished himself." And he wrote Sarah Storrow:

> How I shall be able to keep all afloat with my cramped and diminished means, and with debts incurred on behalf of others hanging over and threatening me is an...harassing question. These things break my rest and disturb my waking thoughts; they haunted me sadly during my illness. However, as poor Scott said, "I have a good deal of work in me yet." If I can but fairly get my pen under way I may make affairs wear a different aspect: but these cares and troubles bear hard upon the capability of a literary man "who has but his good spirits to feed and clothe him." The Doctor who attended upon me in my illness and who was curious in studying my constitution, said "I had a large heart that acted powerfully on my system." God knows I have need of a stout heart at times, but I certainly have always found it rally up to the charge in time of danger or difficulty. On that I will still rely.

Irving's business letters in general give an impression of considerable competence. There is no bluster, but it is always clear that he knows what he wants and means what he says. "I have asked *1000* guineas for the translation," he writes Storrow when the Navarrete proposition is under consideration; "if they do not come to my price I will not undertake the work." In 1824 he wrote Payne that he could not continue to write for the theater in view of the sums Payne had got for *Richelieu* and *Charles II*. "I speak not with any reference to

my talents; but to the market price my productions will command in other departments of literature." In the complicated
negotiations with the aloof, mysterious, and difficult John
Murray he was not without his triumphs—1500 guineas for
Bracebridge Hall and 3000 for *Columbus*—and when in 1832
Murray tried to get an agreement altered he stood firm and
achieved a really masterly statement of his case.[7]

To his publishers Irving was loyal from the beginning; this
was true even of the humble Moses Thomas:

> Whatever may have been his embarrassments and consequent want of
> punctuality, he is one who showed a disposition to serve me, and who
> did serve me in the time of my necessity, and I should despise myself
> could I for a moment forget it. Let him have the work on better terms
> than other publishers, and do not be deterred by the risk of loss.

He was cautious and reasonable even in his dealings with
Murray: "I should exceedingly regret having to change my
publisher, for I think it is to both our interests to keep on together, but I will never sacrifice my feelings or my self respect
to considerations of mere interest." Between Irving and G. P.
Putnam, who made him comfortable in his old age, there was
always perfect trust and understanding on both sides. "John,"
remarked Irving in 1848, when Putnam's first letter reached him
in the law office to which he had fancied himself condemned
to earn his bread, "John, here is a fool of a publisher willing
to give me $2,000 a year to go on scribbling." Putnams paid
Irving $88,143.08 during his lifetime.[8] When they were in finan-
cial difficulties after the Panic of 1857, he had a chance of
making more money by taking his books elsewhere, but he
refused to leave the firm while any member of the Putnam
family remained connected with it, and this determination was
rated an important element in the publishers' survival.

Like other literary men, Irving attempted to improve his
financial position through investments, and like other literary

men he did not always invest wisely. In 1820 it was steam navigation on the Seine. The initial investment was apparently $5000, "which I apprehend is all that I am worth in the world." The ultimate loss, however, was higher. In 1825 he sank more money into mining. "I think," he wrote his sister in 1841, "there ought to be a new clause inserted in the Litany, 'From all inventors, projectors and other devisers of sudden wealth, Good Lord deliver us!'" There are a number of references to investments in his letters to Kennedy. In June 1825 his operations in Wall Street prevented his joining his friend on a hunting trip. Ten years later he asked Kennedy to look into the possible purchase of certain wharfs and buildings in Baltimore; he was not trying to get rich, he protested; he was merely trying to get his money into an investment safer than stocks and one less subject to "sudden depreciation." In December 1835 he lost $3000 in Guardian Fire Insurance stock. "I could not have shown my face in this suffering community," he says, "with a less loss," and all his sympathy seems to be for people of moderate means—widows and "single females"— whose loss was so much more serious than his.

Irving was very sensitive about his relations with John Jacob Astor and rarely missed an opportunity to point out that he had not benefited financially by their association. "He was too proverbially rich a man for me to permit the shadow of a pecuniary favor to rest on our intercourse." Even when Astor wanted to pay for an elegant binding on *Astoria*, he would not hear of it. "I replied that it must be produced in the style of my other works, and at my expense and risk; and that whatever profit I was to derive from it must be from its sale and my bargain with the publishers." As for investments:

The only moneyed transaction between us was my purchase of a share in a town he was founding at Green Bay; for that I paid cash, though he wished the amount to stand on mortgage. The land fell in value; and some years afterwards, when I was in Spain, Mr. Astor, of his own free-will, took back the share from my agent, and repaid the original pur-chase-money.

Which, to be sure, was more than he would have done for a stranger.

4 HOW THE TREE GREW IN THE FOREST

So far we have thought about Irving mainly in connection with his own temperament, his mind, and his art, but it must not be supposed that he lived his life in solitude. "Mr. Irving," wrote Henry Ellsworth, "is very social in his disposition, and no man would bear an exile of solitary confinement, with less comfort than himself."

To show you the mode of life I lead [he writes Brevoort from Wash-ington in 1811], I give you my engagements for this week. On Monday I dined with the mess of officers at the barracks; in the evening a ball at Van Ness's. On Tuesday with my cousin Knickerbocker and several merry Federalists. On Wednesday I dined with General Turreau, who had a very pleasant party of Frenchmen and democrats; in the evening at Mrs. Madison's levee, which was brilliant and crowded with interest-ing men and fine women. On Thursday a dinner at Latrobe's. On Friday a dinner at the Secretary of the Navy's, and in the evening a ball at the Mayor's. Saturday is as yet unengaged.

Ten years later there is a note to a hostess, written in the third person, in which he enumerates the three engagements (dinner, concert, ball) which he gladly breaks to accept her invitation. And as late as 1840 he writes his nieces from New York that he is leading such a busy and dissipated life that he must write them from his bed at four o'clock in the morning, "having no leisure in the day time."

Wherever Irving went, he found sanctuary. Its keeper was not always a pretty girl like Emily Foster whom he could fall in love with, but there was always somebody to look after him.

Naturally this "somebody" was generally a woman, but it does not appear that he had any difficulty with the men either. In a month at Dresden he had seven dinners and three teas with the Fosters and spent eight evenings with them besides. But even in Genoa in 1804, long before he was a celebrity, it was "Lady Shaftesbury's, Madame Gabriac's, and Mrs. Bird's." "From Lady Shaftesbury I have experienced the most unreserved and cordial friendship. I visited her house every night, dined there frequently, and supped whenever I chose." At Madrid he came and went at will in the homes of Alexander Everett, Obadiah Rich, and Pierre D'Oubril. "Anacreon Moore is living here," he writes Murray from Paris, "and has made me a gayer fellow than I could have wished; but I have found it impossible to resist the charm of his society." He was like the debutante who is exhausted and tired to death of the gay whirl yet cannot bring herself to break away from it.

Yet his expressions of weariness and disillusionment are more numerous than his expressions of enjoyment:

> I am sick of fashionable life, and fashionable parties. I have never let myself into the current for a time but I have been ultimately cast exhausted and spiritless on the shore. What a sacrifice of the nobler and better feelings there is in this kind of intercourse.

He warns Pierre Paris Irving against wasting his evenings "in parties of pleasure" instead of devoting them to "valuable reading," and complains to Aspinwall that Newton is "squandering himself . . . upon mere fashionable society." He is even capable of complaining crabbedly of "so many painted faces, and bedizened and bediamonded heads about me, harassing themselves with midnight dissipation."

Some of these expressions of dissatisfaction come, it is true, from his later years, when, as he expressed it, he was "very borable," when "playing the lion" had "killed" him, and "the curse of notoriety" had made "existence in cities a perpetual task and toil." "The dances that are the fashion put me out of countenance, and are not such as a gentleman of my years ought to witness." Having "run the rounds of society for the greater part of half a century," he was now disposed "to consult his own humors and pursuits." As early as 1842 he complains that he now finds it much harder to be amused in Paris than it was on his last visit:

It is possible I may have gathered wisdom under the philosophic shades of Sleepy Hollow or may have been rendered fastidious by the gay life of the cottage; it is certain that amidst all the splendors of London and Paris, I find my imagination refuses to take fire, and my heart still yearns after dear little Sunnyside.

Yet, from the beginning Irving would have society only upon his own terms. He was nobody in 1805, yet he wrote William from Paris:

I will never move in any circle where my society is merely tolerated. I have had a complete surfeit of nobility in Italy and Sicily. It makes my blood boil to see a star on the jacket or a ribbon in the button hole, entitle a blockhead, a puppy, a scoundrel to rank above a man of worth and merit. . . . Thank heaven, we *order these matters better in America*.[1] Every day makes me more and more sensible of the peculiar blessings of my country—every government through which I pass enables me to draw an advantageous comparison. My eyes are opened in respect to many things that were hid from me while in America.

Two years later he writes from Richmond, where he was assisting at Aaron Burr's trial:

For myself I find I am declining very much in popularity from having resolutely and manfully resisted sundry temptations and invitations to tea parties . . . balls and other infernal orgies which have from time to time been celebrated by the little enchantresses of the place. I tried my hand two or three times at an apology for non attendance, but it would not do, my usual ill luck followed me; for once when I alleged the writing of letters, it was plainly proved that I was seen smoking a cigar and lolling in the porch of the Eagle, and another time when I plead a severe indisposition, I was pronounced guilty of having sat at a young lady's elbow the whole evening and listened to her piano—All which brought me into manifest disgrace and reduced me to great extremity.

All his life Irving could turn from sociability to concentrated solitude and enjoy it. There was such a period at Madrid when he was working on *Columbus*. When he visited Prague, he was thankful that he knew nobody there, "and, during the short stay I have to make, I am not obliged to go to evening parties, or to pay formal visits." In 1842 he writes Sarah Storrow from Madrid that he does not

feel the solitariness of my situation so irksome as you appear to imagine [and that] there are times when it suits my humor to be alone. . . . At such times, in the interval of occupation, I give free scope to my old habit of day dreaming, and enjoy the spacious solitude of my saloon, the silent walls of which echo to my footsteps.

Again he says,

Indeed it is not in general the mere absence of Society that makes me feel lonely: it is the absence of those who are peculiarly dear to me: those who are linked to me by kindred ties, which with me are all powerful—above all, I feel the absence of my "womankind," who of late years have been the great sweetness of my domestic life. No male society can make up for the lack of them.

Some observers were impressed by Irving's own social gifts. Young George Bancroft thought his conversation "rich and varied" and himself "a most pure and amiable man," and Fanny Kemble declared that, of all the distinguished persons she had known, he was "one of the least affected by the adulation and admiration of society." Longfellow, too, pronounced him "one of those men who put you at ease with them in a moment. He makes no ceremony whatever with one, and, of course, is a very fine man in society, all mirth and good humor." Others viewed him less admiringly, though I have found nobody else to match De Witt Clinton's savagery: "I have spent an evening in his company, and find him barren of conversation, and very limited in information. His physiognomy is intelligent, and I should, upon the whole, think favorably of him, had he not attempted to play the Joe Miller at a great man's table." This last touch seems completely out of character, but the crotchety John Neal is also very severe on Irving in his social aspects. Having first stressed Irving's tendency to fall asleep in company (the justice of which charge all who knew him admit), and of the "little impediment" in his speech, he goes on to describe him as

indolent; nervous; irritable; easily depressed; easily disheartened; very amiable; no appearance of especial refinement; nothing remarkable, nothing uncommon about him;—precisely such a man, to say all in a word, as people would continually overlook, pass by without notice, or forget, after dining with him.

Some of this is corroborated by friendlier observers. Lord Jeffrey thought him "rather low spirited and silent in mixed company, but . . . agreeable . . . tête à tête . . . and very gentle and amiable," while Marian Gouverneur judged him to have "a genial but at the same time a retiring nature. . . . His manner was exceedingly gentle and, strange to say, with such a remarkable vocabulary at his command, in society he was exceedingly quiet." Philip Hone says he talked freely only under excitement. William C. Preston also found him reticent in the English manner. He had "great dread and distaste" of American exuberance, and tried to discourage it in Preston. Irving himself was well aware of many of his social disadvantages— which cannot have caused them to handicap him less: "I am but a spiritless being . . . at these gay assemblages; I do not dance; I have not the art of talking to people who do not interest me, and am so diffident on my knowledge of the French language, that I cannot force myself to converse in it in mingled society."

There can be no doubt that Irving always disliked large

gatherings and was at his best with those he loved. Even at the Fosters he would "button himself up" when a stranger came in, relapse into dullness, and retire to a recess until the family was left alone again. All his life he loathed public dinners. He broke down at the Dickens dinner. Once, in England, at a Literary Fund dinner, he made a speech consisting of a single sentence, "I beg to return to you my very sincere thanks." Once he actually fled from a theater to avoid acknowledging a public greeting.

One would suppose that those who enjoy social intercourse must like people, and there seems no question that this was true in Irving's case. He was sensitive to experience and to human contacts always; wherever he went, even if he was on a mission, he could not resist noting and commenting upon the characteristics of the people around him. To Diedrich Knickerbocker he attributed a kind of diluted Rousseauism:

> For my part, I have not so bad an opinion of mankind as many of my brother philosophers. I do not think poor human nature so sorry a piece of workmanship as they would make it out to be; and as far as I have observed, I am fully satisfied that man, if left to himself, would about as readily go right as wrong.

This may not be a very profound view of human nature, but that is not the point here; it is certainly a kindly one.

In his own person, Irving takes up a comparably kindly attitude toward the Moors in *The Alhambra* and his other Spanish books; he even objects to what he considers the unfair representation of them in *The Civil Wars of Granada,* for while "great latitude is undoubtedly to be allowed to romantic fiction . . . there are limits which it must not pass; and the names of the distinguished dead, which belong to history, are no more to be calumniated than those of the illustrious living."

Of course this does not mean that Irving was a cheerful idiot in his attitude toward human nature. The Moorish king with whom he sympathized most was the unfortunate Boabdil, but he does not therefore gloss over his faults and limitations:

He was personally brave, but wanted moral courage; and, in times of difficulty and perplexity, was wavering and irresolute. This feebleness of spirit hastened his downfall, while it deprived him of that heroic grace which would have given grandeur and dignity to his fate, and rendered him worthy of closing the splendid drama of the Moslem domination in Spain.

He was less generous to Yankees than he was to Moors; he even called the pro-French Catalonians, whom he disliked, "the Yankees of Spain." Clearly, Irving did not love everybody. "Some of my fellow passengers," he writes, "were *disagreeable beasts* enough, but there were three or four quite agreeable." And again, of his passport difficulties in Bordeaux: "I had . . . to dance attendance on *some dogs* in office." (He could even be a snob on occasion, as when he writes upon embarking from London to Berwick in 1817, "I found the cabins crowded with men women and children, evidently of the inferior order.") [2] And he could be disillusioned about individuals, even friends, as in his reference to "the *small* traits and parasitical tendencies" of Tom Moore, whom he had previously described as "one of the worthiest and most delightful fellows I have ever known." But afterwards, when he was gone, he thought only of Moore's best side again. And even when he tells Sarah Storrow that he does not believe intercourse with a certain family likely to lead to her contentment, he adds:

Do not however suffer yourself to think, and above all to speak of them with asperity. Recollect that towards you and yours they have always manifested esteem and exercised kindness; and recollect also that all that can readily be laid to their charge are foibles not vices, and a too great delight to captivate the admiration of a heartless and sneering world. I only regret that they are not aware how worthless is the fashionable notoriety they are striving after and how surrounded by perils.

Irving is most attractive socially in his relations with the friends and relatives whom he really loved, but young William Hickling Prescott was not a friend, and Irving never appears in a more attractive light than in relinquishing the subject of the conquest of Mexico to the younger man:

> I *am* engaged upon that subject, but tell Mr. Prescott that I abandon it to him, and I am happy to have this opportunity of testifying my high esteem for his talents, and my sense of the very courteous manner in which he has spoken of myself and my writings in his Ferdinand and Isabella, though they interfered with a part of the subject of his history.

It may be that Irving afterwards suspected that he had been too generous for his own good. "I doubt whether Mr. Prescott was aware of the extent of the sacrifice I made." It may be that there mingled with his regret a feeling of relief at getting out from under a time- and strength-consuming job. But none of this importantly modifies the fact that his relinquishment was the spontaneous act of a generous man and not a mean one.

Irving loved Washington Allston. He loved Scott so much that he felt it a happiness to have lived in his time. And as for C. R. Leslie:

> My dear Boy [he wrote from Paris], it is a grievous thing to be separated from you; and I feel it more and more. I wish to heaven this world were not so wide; and that we could manage to keep more together in it. This continual separating from those we like is one of the curses of an unsettled life; and with all my vagrant habits I cannot get accustomed to it.

James Selden Spencer, his pastor at Tarrytown, has told how he comforted him in time of sorrow. "They who minister to others must not themselves refuse the consolation." He was faithful to the sickly John Nalder Hall, whom he nursed at Seville, and with whom he tried to keep a spiritualistic tryst after Hall's death. Even at seventy-three he writes Kennedy that "my intercourse with your family connection has been a

great sweetener of the last few years of my existence, and the
only attraction that has been able to draw me repeatedly from
home." At least once he actually shed tears on parting from
the Kennedys.

Irving was untiring in his efforts to help his literary friends.
He worked to have Bryant's and Fitz-Greene Halleck's poems
published in London, and he acted as American agent for God-
win and Tom Moore. He urged Cooper upon Murray and
Kennedy upon Bentley. He labored long and hard with John
Howard Payne. Sometimes, apparently, he even wrote letters
of commendation which he did not deeply mean. He could be
helpful, too, where no literary considerations were involved.
His sponsorship of the highly individualized James Ogilvie in
New York Society in 1808-09 [3] does not suggest a socially hidebound person. He practically adopted a German boy whom he
met on shipboard, and who went on to become a wealthy man
in Quincy, Illinois. Nor did he ever forget that his devoted
servants were human beings:

Tell Robert [he wrote home in 1853], I charge him not to work in
the sun during the hottest hours of the day, should this intense warm
weather continue. He injured himself by it last summer; and I would
not have anything happen to him for all the hay in the country.

Did Irving ever fail in friendship? He was not entirely above
a healthy human interest in gossip, but there does not seem to
have been anything malicious about this. When he dined with
Samuel Rogers, Rogers "served up his friends as he served up
his fish, with a squeeze of lemon over each. It was very piquant,
but it rather set my teeth on edge." [4] Irving was, however,
rather hyper-sensitive to real or fancied neglect on the part of
even very close and intimate friends. He does not write David
Wilkie, he tells Colonel Aspinwall in 1829, "for really he always scrawls replies in the most hurried and unsatisfactory
manner, as if impatient of the moment he devoted to the task,

and eager to be off to some bluestocking party." In the 'twenties there was even a break in his communication with Brevoort, evidently the result of misunderstandings consequent
upon the miscarriage of letters. But, oddly enough, the case
which really calls for investigation concerns Irving's relations
with one of the two most illustrious men of his acquaintance—
Charles Dickens.

In 1841 Irving broke his rule in such matters by writing
Dickens what would now be called a "fan" letter, afterwards
explaining his position clearly:

> Do not suppose me . . . a man prompt at these spontaneous overtures
> of friendship. You are the only man I have ever made such an advance
> to. In general I seek no acquaintance and keep up no correspondence out
> of my family connection, but towards you, there was a strong impulse,
> which for some time I resisted, but which at length overpowered me, and
> I am glad it did so.

Dickens's response could not have been warmer:

> There is no man in the world who could have given me the heartfelt
> pleasure you have by your kind note. . . . There is no living writer, and
> there are very few among the dead, whose approbation I should feel so
> proud to earn. And with everything you have written upon my shelves,
> and in my thoughts, and in my heart of hearts, I may honestly and truly
> say so. If you could know how earnestly I write this, you would be glad
> to read it—as I hope you will be, faintly guessing at the warmth of the
> hand I autographically hold out to you over the broad Atlantic.

Irving was well aware that he had been praised by a far
greater writer than himself:

> You flatter my languid and declining pride in authorship by quoting
> many of my sketchlings of London life, written long since and too slight
> I supposed to make any lasting impression, but what are my slight and
> erratic sketches to your ample and complete pictures which lay all the
> recesses of human life before us and then the practical utility, the op-
> erative benevolence which pervade all your portraitures of the lowest
> life, and give a value which enables you to carry your readers through
> the various dens of vice and villainy without a breath to shock the ear

or a stain to sully the robe of the most shrinking delicacy. . . . Old Pickwick is the Quixote of common public life, and as with the Don, we begin by laughing at him and end by loving him. . . . And then the exquisite and sustained pathos, so deep, but so pure and healthy, as carried throughout the wanderings of little Barbara [5] and her poor grandfather. I declare to you there is a moral sublimity of fancies in the whole of that story, that leaves me at a loss how sufficiently to express my admiration—and then there are passages (like that of the schoolmaster's remarks on neglected graves), which come upon me so suddenly and gleam forth apparently undesignedly, but which are perfect gems of language.

The two writers met at the Carlton House, in New York, on February 13, 1842, when Dickens was making his first American tour. Irving presided at the New York dinner to Dickens, where he fulfilled his own prophecy by breaking down in his speech, but Dickens seized the opportunity to pay him another such heartfelt tribute as only his own inexhaustible and loving warmth could bring forth:

Washington Irving! Why, gentleman, I don't go upstairs to bed two nights out of the seven . . . without taking Washington Irving under my arm; and when I don't take him, I take his own brother, Oliver Goldsmith. . . . Washington Irving—Diedrich Knickerbocker—Geoffrey Crayon—why, where can you go that they have not been there before? Is there an English farm—is there an English stream, an English city, or an English country-seat, where they have not been? Is there no Bracebridge Hall in existence? Has it no ancient shades or quiet streets?

They said good-by in Washington on March 11, just before Dickens left for Richmond, but afterwards met unexpectedly, once more, in Baltimore. This was the occasion when, as Dickens described it many years later, an admirer sent them "a most enormous mint julep, wreathed with flowers."

We sat, one on either side of it, with great solemnity (it filled a respectably-sized round table), but the solemnity was of very short duration. It was quite an enchanted julep, and carried us among innumerable people and places that we both knew. The julep held out far into the night, and my memory never saw him afterwards otherwise than as bending over it, with his straw, with an attempted air of gravity (after some anecdote involving some wonderfully droll and delicate observation of character), and then, as his eye caught mine, melting into that captivating laugh of his, which was the brightest and best I have ever heard.

So far, so good, but Maunsell B. Field will not leave it there. In his *Memories of Many Men and Some Women* (Harpers, 1874), he recorded the shocking story of Irving's disillusionment with Dickens. When the American called on his friend at his hotel, he found him at dinner, served on a board stained with gravy and wine and "covered with a vulgar profusion of food." Jumping up, napkin in hand, and coming forward to greet him, Dickens cried, "Irving, I am delighted to see you! What will you drink, a mint julep or a gin cocktail?" And Irving is supposed to have been so disgusted by this vulgarity that he could not tell the story afterwards without walking the floor in his fury.

Nobody else seems to have been aware of this cruel disillusionment. Dickens merely records that "Washington Irving came in with open arms, and here he stopped until ten o'clock at night." Dickens's American secretary, George William Putnam, says, "Washington Irving came very often, and the meeting of these two kindred spirits was such as might have been expected. They were delighted with each other." C. C. Felton, who passed much time with them both, thought it "delightful to witness the cordial intercourse" between them. Dickens himself wrote his biographer, "Irving was with me in Washington yesterday, and *wept heartily* at parting."

Williams accepted the Field story without reservations, even permitting himself a fling at Dickens's "tavern manners," a phrase which attests little to his knowledge of Dickens. Both food and drink stimulated Dickens's imagination and furnished him with literary material, but his interest in the pleasures of the table was largely social; he was in general more abstemious than Irving. It is true that Irving's social manners were more elegant and less hearty than those of Dickens, but it is difficult to believe that any graduate of Cockloft Hall could have been so shocked as Field says Irving was by anything he could possibly have seen at the Carlton House.

For all that, the case is not quite open and shut. For when Irving was in England, he does not seem to have made any attempt to see Dickens, and except for Dickens's cordial letter of July 5, 1856, we have no record of any further intercourse between them. E. A. Duyckinck records that Irving once refused an invitation to one of Dickens's private theatricals: "He would not visit a man who had proved himself so insensible to American kindness." F. S. Cozzens reports his having said that Thackeray was a better judge of character than Dickens, but this is not supported by other evidence. In 1853 Charles Lanman recorded Irving's having spoken very admiringly of Dickens as "genial and warm" and contrasting him with Thackeray in this regard. Lanman adds that he called *Pendennis* his favorite Thackeray novel. He described *Vanity Fair* as full of talent but declared that many passages hurt his feelings; *Henry Esmond* he thought queer but deeply interesting. At the very end of his life he is quoted as having placed Dickens "immeasurably above his contemporaries," with *David Copperfield* as his "master-production." [6]

We have, then, no unfriendly word toward Dickens, in Irving's own hand, but there is one entry in Pierre M. Irving's unpublished journal in the Berg Collection which can certainly be admitted as evidence. On June 22, 1859, Pierre asked his uncle whether he had found anything of interest in the first numbers of Dickens's new journal, *All the Year Round:*

"Yes [he replied]—but how changed the feeling with which you read any thing by Dickens now—he had shown himself to have such inferior qualities of heart from what you had given him credit for. He is doing now in England what he did in America—after all our extravagant homage to him which he should have been proud of—felt to be a great compliment—pouring abuse upon us because we stood in the way of his own selfish interest (copyright) so he is trifling with his popularity in England &c—"

As an illustration of what Irving was talking about, Pierre pasted into his journal the New York *Times* editorial of June 16—"Dickens upon Dickens"—in which the novelist's jettisoning *Household Words,* and breaking with its publishers, Bradbury and Evans, because they would not print in *Punch* a statement he wished to make concerning the difficulties consequent upon his separation from his wife, was excoriated.[7]

None of this, of course, necessitates our believing in a trauma at the Carlton. It looks much more as though Irving's personal relations with Dickens were untroubled throughout the American tour, but that he was estranged from him, as many Americans were, by *American Notes*. This would be in line with both Pierre's journal entry and the statement quoted from Duyckinck. If this was the case, it is interesting to note that Irving's indignation was not shared by Henry Brevoort, who wrote him, on December 28, 1842:

I suppose Dickens has written to you, and that you have read his book. It is just what might have been expected from him; but the good people here abuse him for not writing what he neither could nor would write, a dull sensible description of these United States. The Negro and spitting chapters were put in for balance I imagine—but some of the others are admirable and display a warm and sensitive heart.—The little woman and her baby—the reflections upon the poor emigrants, are truly admirable and characteristic.

For some reason, then, Irving does not seem to have wished to keep up his friendship with Dickens in later years; nothing more is known of the cause than has here been stated. The estrangement, whatever its cause, was one-sided, for Dickens never ceased to think warmly of Irving.[8]

But a man must deal with other men not only as individuals but also in terms of groups, and the largest and most irresistible group is the state. In defiance of the facts—and of his own diplomatic service—the legend of Irving's political indifferentism has become as firmly established as his interest in society.

Even during his lifetime he was regarded by some as having been seduced away from his American loyalties by the romantic charms of Europe. That these charms made a powerful appeal to a bookish man there is no denying. "My mind," he wrote in 1822, "was early filled with historical and poetical associations, connected with places, and manners, and customs of Europe." As he tells us in *Bracebridge Hall:*

> The first time that I heard the song of the nightingale, I was intoxicated more by the delicious crowd of remembered associations than by the melody of its notes; and I shall never forget the thrill of ecstasy with which I first saw the lark rise, almost from beneath my feet, and wing its musical flight up into the morning sky.

But he preferred Spanish romanticism to English romanticism, perhaps even responded to it with a clearer conscience, because it seemed to him to have exchanged the sentimental for the heroic. Wherever the Arabs "established a seat of power, it became a rallying-place for the learned and ingenious; and they softened and refined the people whom they conquered." Annals of the Moorish-Spanish conflict "teem with illustrious instances of high-wrought courtesy, romantic generosity, lofty disinterestedness, and punctilious honor, that warm the very soul to read them." In spite of all their faults, even modern Spaniards seemed to him "the most high-minded and proud-spirited people of Europe." In this aspect they even took on a moral significance for him:

In the present day when popular literature is running into the low levels of life, and luxuriating on the vices and follies of mankind; and when the universal pursuit of gain is trampling down the early growth of poetic feeling, and wearing out the verdure of the soul, I question whether it would not be of service for the reader occasionally to turn to these records of prouder times and loftier modes of thinking, and to steep himself to the very lips in old Spanish romance.

He could be thrilled by heroic associations even where no present-day beauty appeared, and he paced the beach at Palos with tears in his eyes, seeing the convent of La Rabida with his inner eye and watching Columbus set sail.

Perhaps Spain was easier for him at the outset than England because his prejudices did not get in the way. His literary prejudices of course were all in England's favor, but his political prejudices drew him in the opposite direction; it was not until 1847, when he read Curwen's journal, that he even realized that the Tories had a case during the Revolution, and that "Tory" and "traitor" were not synonymous terms.

All that I had heard or read to the disadvantage of the English character [he wrote in 1805], seemed to rush to mind—haughtiness, illiberal prejudice, reserve, rudeness, insolence, brutality, knavery were the black traits that presented themselves. I looked round me with distrust and suspicion—my heart was completely closed up and every frank generous feeling had retired within it. I thought myself surrounded by rogues and swindlers and felt that I was a foreigner with contempt and enmity.

Though Irving contrasts this with the "confidence and affability" he encountered when he arrived in Paris, it was not all clear sailing in France either, for if political prejudices did not operate to French disadvantage, moral prejudices did. Even when he was "dazzled, astonished, enraptured" by Europe, he could not suffer himself to be "*ensnared*."

I look in vain in Europe for those warm friendships, that honesty and openness of heart and manners that I have left behind me in America and for which French politeness is a miserable substitute. I turn with disgust from the profligacy and immorality of the *Old World* and reflect with delight on the *comparative* purity of American morals.

He doubted that he was enough a citizen of the world to make a good traveler, he told William; his experiences of Europe only made him a better American.

The English mania for field sports seemed ridiculous to Irving. The British Sunday was dull, monotonous, and commonplace, "like the sands of the desert, which are continually stealing over the land of Egypt and gradually effacing every trace of grandeur and beauty and swallowing up every green thing." While as for the English watering places,

I don't know whether you were ever at an English watering place, but if you have not been, you have missed the best opportunity for studying English oddities, both moral and physical. I no longer wonder at the English being such excellent caricaturists, they have such an inexhaustible number and variety of subjects to study from. The only care should be not to follow fact too closely for I'll swear I have met with characters and figures that would be condemned as extravagant; if faithfully delineated by pen and pencil. At a watering place like Buxton where people really resort for health, you see the great tendency of the English to run into excrescences and bloat out into grotesque deformities. As to noses I say nothing of them, though we had every variety. Some snubbed and turned up, with distended nostrils, like a dormer window on the roof of a house—others convex and twisted like a Buck handled knife and others magnificently efflorescent like a full blown cauliflower. But as to the persons that were attached to their noses, fancy every distortion, tuberance and pompous embellishment that can be produced in the human form by high and gross feeding, by the bloating operations of malt liquors, by the rheuming influence of a damp foggy vaporish climate.

Even the works in which Irving is generally thought of as having glorified England are by no means truckling. Both in *The Sketch Book* and in *Bracebridge Hall* faults are dwelt upon as well as virtues, and though the paper on "John Bull" is certainly sympathetic, the subject is not idealized. Even before the War of 1812 he had been convinced that Europe was "wasting its strength in perpetual commotions," while the United States, "blest with profound peace and an excellent government, is gaining daily accesses of wealth and power and rising by tranquil yet rapid degrees to take the most conspicuous seat among the nations." He hits American subservience to British literary opinion as early as *Salmagundi*, and he repeats his resentment of British strictures on American matters in *The Sketch Book* and warns England, as Hawthorne was to warn her, that she is more likely to need America than America is to need her.

Yet, Irving spent a good many years abroad, and also employed a good deal of energy in explaining how much he wanted to return to America for some time before he actually came. No doubt there were good reasons for delay:

My affections would at once prompt me to return, but in doing so, would they insure me any happiness? Would they not on the contrary be productive of misery? I should find those I love and whom I had left prosperous—struggling with adversity without my being able to yield them comfort or assistance. Every scene of past enjoyment would be a cause of regret and discontent. . . . No—no. If I must scuffle with poverty let me do it out of sight—where I am but little known—where I cannot even contrast present penury with former affluence. . . . Besides I am accustomed and reconciled to the features of adversity in this country; but were I to return to America I should find it under a new face and have to go through something of what I have already experienced, to get on similar terms of familiarity.

Some students of Irving find such reasoning entirely convincing; thus Osborne remarks that he "chose to remain in England as a professional writer and contribute to American literature rather than return to America, accept a post in the Navy Department, and follow writing as an avocation." And this may be entirely correct. Yet I cannot but feel that Irving had developed something of a divided mind, and that if he had really wished to return to America before 1832, he might have found a way to do so. "The fact is," he writes in 1827, "that the longer I remain from home the greater charm it has in my eyes, and all the coloring that the imagination once gave to distant Europe now gathers about the scene of my native country." Did distance not, in a measure at least, lend enchantment to the view? After his return he wrote C. R. Leslie, "The improvements in living, and the resources for living agreeably in the United States have multiplied amazingly since I went abroad. I have enjoyed myself delightfully since my return, and am satisfied that I can live as pleasantly here as in any part of the world." Is there no touch of surprise here?

Irving has been blamed for romanticizing the American West; even Lucy Lockwood Hazard dismisses *A Tour of the Prairies*, in *The Frontier in American Literature*, as "opéra bouffe": "Mr. Irving prepares an elaborate stage setting for his near adventures; he goes through all the gestures of deep emotional excitement; but his artificially induced thrills end in anticlimax." On the other hand, she thinks highly of *Astoria* and *Bonneville* and complains of the neglect which they have suffered: "To one who believes with G. M. Trevelyan that literature ought to be read in the light of history, and history written as though it were literature, *Astoria* and *Captain Bonneville* are valuable as examples of a successful synthesis of historical material and literary art." It should not be forgotten, however, that if Irving often described what he saw in the American West in terms of real or fancied European counterparts, he also described what he saw in Europe in terms of American counterparts—and sometimes to Europe's disadvantage. As far back as *Analectic* days, he knew that "there is an inexpressible charm imparted to every place that has been celebrated by the historian or immortalized by the poet; a charm that dignifies it in the eyes of the stranger, and endears it to the heart of the native." He had praised "Gertrude of Wyoming" because Campbell had convinced many "that our native scenes are capable of poetic inspiration and that our country may be as capable of poetic fiction" as anything in Europe. In all his writings about the West he was trying to create (in the narrower sense of the term) an *American* literature, and he was also trying to incorporate Western Americana into the legendry of the world. Only a very bigoted chauvinist could find anything "un-American" in this.

In a sense Irving has only himself to blame for the legend of his political indifferentism. Look at the famous 1807 letter to Mary Fairlie, describing his attempt to share in a political campaign in New York:

What makes me the more outrageous is that I got fairly drawn into the vortex and before the third day expired I was as deep in mud and politics as ever a moderate gentleman would wish to be—and I drank beer with the multitude, and I talked handbill fashion with the demagogues, and I shook hands with the mob—whom my heart abhorreth.—Tis true for the first day I maintained my coolness and indifference—the first day I merely hunted for whim character and absurdity according to my usual custom. Second day being rainy I sat in the bar room at the fourth ward and read a volume of Gallatin which I found on a shelf, but before I got through a hundred pages I had three or four good Feds sprawling around me on the floor and another with his eyes half shut leaning on my shoulder in the most affectionate manner, and spelling a page of the book as if it had been an engineering hand bill. But the third day—ah—then came the tug of war—My patriotism all at once blazed forth and I determined to save my country! Oh my friend I have been in such holes and corners—such filthy nooks and filthy corners, sweet offices and oyster cellars! "I have been sworn brother to a leash of drawers, and can drink with any tinker, in his own language during my life"—faugh! I shall not be able to bear the smell of small beer or tobacco for a month to come, and a negro is an abomination unto me. . . . Truly this serving one's country is a nauseous piece of business—and if patriotism is such a dirty virtue—pray thee no more of it.

In *Salmagundi*, though less personal, he is considerably less whimsical and more earnest: "To be concise: our great men are those who are most expert at crawling on all fours, and have the happiest facility of dragging and winding themselves along in the dirt." To be "either wise or valiant, upright or honorable" is a disadvantage, since these qualities "are prone to render him too inflexibly erect, and directly at variance with that willow suppleness which enables a man to wind and twist through all the nooks and turns and dark winding passages which lead to greatness." He goes on to present "the aspiring politician" under the figure of

that indefatigable insect, called the tumbler, pronounced by a distinguished personage to be the only industrious animal in Virginia, which buries itself in filth, and works ignobly in the dirt, until it forms a little ball, which it rolls laboriously along, like Diogenes in his tub; sometimes head, sometimes tail foremost, pilfering from every rut and mud hole, and increasing its ball of greatness by the contributions of the kennel.

And he sums up: "A candidate for political eminence is like a dried herring: he never becomes luminous until he is corrupt."

These are bitter words. Moreover, as late as 1833 or 1834, when he had already lived half a century, Irving wrote to his brother Peter:

You are right in your conjectures that I keep myself aloof from politics. The more I see of political life here, the more I am disgusted with it. . . . There is such coarseness and vulgarity and dirty trick mingled with the rough-and-tumble contest. I want no part or parcel in such warfare.

In *Bracebridge Hall*, too, Geoffrey Crayon disdains the label politician and avers his determination to view the world "poetically, rather than politically."

The more I have considered the study of politics, the more I have found it full of perplexity; and I have contented myself, as I have in my religion, with the faith in which I was brought up, regulating my own conduct by its precepts, but leaving to abler heads the task of making converts.

Irving said all these things, and I am sure he meant them—with one side of his head, at least—yet in the larger view he did not lack political interest, convictions, or connections. Of course public affairs were not one of the great interests of his life, but the references to them in his letters are frequent enough and clear enough so that anyone ought to be able to understand that he knew what was going on about him and was ahead of the average intelligent citizen, not behind him, in his capacity to play a responsible and intelligent part in the life of the body politic to which he belonged. Even in Europe, for all his romanticizing and focusing upon the past, he was not indifferent to current considerations. The enthusiasm with which he approached the revolutionary year of 1832 may have been juvenile but it certainly was not indifferentist:

What a stirring moment it is to live in. I never took such intense interest in newspapers. It seems to me as if life were breaking out anew in me, or that I were entering upon quite a new and almost unknown career of existence, and I rejoice to find my sensibilities, which were waning as to many objects of past interest, reviving with all their freshness and vivacity at the schemes and prospects opening around me.

Enthusiasm, humanity, and common sense mingled in his attitude toward that "noble fellow," the Hungarian nationalist leader, Kossuth. Irving approved of all the "admiration and sympathy" he awakened, but he knew that American policy must be determined by "cool judgment" rather than "warm impulses of feeling. I trust we are never to be carried away, by the fascinating eloquence of this second Peter the Hermit, into schemes of foreign interference, that would rival the wild enterprises of the Crusades."

On domestic affairs the tone was more intimate. It is true that Irving praised President-elect Franklin Pierce most of all because "he has at heart to take care of Hawthorne" and that he himself "associated with both parties, and . . . found worthy and intelligent men in both, with honest hearts, enlightened minds, generous feelings, and bitter prejudices." But he also had views on general issues:

Ours is a government of compromise. We have several great and distinct interests bound up together, which, if not separately consulted and severally accommodated, may harass and impair each other. A stern, inflexible, and uniform policy may do for a small compact republic, like one of those of ancient Greece, where there is a unity of character, habits, and interests; but a more accommodating, discriminating, and variable policy must be observed in a vast republic like ours, formed of a variety of states widely differing in habits, pursuits, characters, and climes, and banded together by a few general ties.

I always distrust the soundness of political councils that are accompanied by acrimonious and disparaging attacks upon any great class of our fellow citizens. Such are those urged to the disadvantage of the great trading and financial classes of our country. You yourself know, from education and experience, how important these classes are to the prosperous conduct of the complicated affairs of this immense empire. You yourself know, in spite of all the commonplace cant and obloquy that has been cast upon them by political spouters and scribblers, what general good faith and fair dealing prevails throughout these classes.

This sounds like Federalism, and Irving's early political conditioning was Federalist: he admired Hamilton and mistrusted Jefferson as a demagogue. But since both William and Peter inclined toward what was then called Republicanism as early as 1800, he was not completely surrounded by Federalistic impulses. Peter also supported Burr, as many anti-Jefferson Republicans did. Both the Ogdens and the Hoffmans were Burrites, though Hoffman was later appointed to a judgeship by Andrew Jackson. By the time the "old general" reached out for the White House, Irving had concluded that, "with all his *hickory* characteristics," he still had "good stuff in him, and will make a sagacious, independent, and high-spirited president; and I doubt his making so high-handed a one as many imagine." His association with Louis McLane and Martin Van Buren during his time in England drew him closer to Jacksonism, but by 1836 he was about ready to leave the Democrats and turn to the Whigs, who would carry him back in a measure toward the Federalism of his youth. Jackson's money policy and the panic it caused were in part responsible for this, but he also objected to Jackson's Indian policy and to the government's indifference toward the Northwest, in which his own interest had been awakened through John Jacob Astor. In 1840 he worked against Van Buren. There may well be differences of opinion as to the quality and settled tendency of the mind, and the degree of political conviction, revealed in these shifts, but Irving can hardly be regarded as either a party hidebound or a political innocent.

Irving's general social sensitiveness is attested by a number of passages in which he comments upon the poverty he witnessed, particularly in Europe. His interest in copyright reform was not, of course, entirely unselfish. His hopes for an adequate copyright law went beyond all existing proposals; he wanted an author's rights respected "not for his own life, but *throughout all generations;* not partially and conditionally but absolutely and entirely; there is no property under heaven in which a man has a more natural and indispensable right." But he never doubted that half a loaf was better than no bread. In 1839 he refused to sign a copyright petition which he regarded as inadequate and ineffective, thus bringing upon himself the necessity of writing a letter to the *Knickerbocker* to explain his position, but he did sign a petition in 1852. The next year we find him writing T. W. Storrow somewhat pessimistically:

> I cannot say that I am very sanguine about the copyright law or treaty: there are too many active and sordid interests at work to defeat it and too many mean and despicable feelings to be wrought upon for it to be successful. We are not sufficiently enlightened and high-minded as yet to legislate properly on the true interests of literature.

He showed concern from time to time in other matters in which he had no vested interest. In 1825 he wrote at least part of an essay on dueling which is no longer extant. The whole of the last Oldstyle letter is devoted to ridicule of dueling, including ridicule of those who consider duels romantic:

My sister Dorothy, who is of a humane and benevolent disposition, would, no doubt, detest the idea of duels, did she not regard them as the last gleams of those days of chivalry, to which she looks back with a degree of romantic enthusiasm.

The paper ends with a proposition to license duels through the Blood and Thunder Office, to give notice to the newspapers and admit spectators, continuing the fight until one party or the other fell. "This," Jack Stylish observes, "would, in some degree, be reviving the spectacles of antiquity. . . . We have, at present, no games resembling those of the ancients, except, now and then, a bull or bear bait; and this would be a valuable addition to the list of our refined amusements."

In 1831 Irving wrote a letter to one Edward Livingston, professing interest in his campaign against capital punishment; he had intended to treat the subject himself, he says, in his proposed series of essays on American themes and problems. In 1832 he was greatly concerned about pure water for New York City,

which is nearly as important to health as the air we breathe. We yearly are at great cost of time and money in travelling in quest of pure air, but begrudge a trifling expense that would bring pure water to our door. It is a pity that so rich and luxurious a city which lavishes countless thousands upon curious wines, cannot afford itself wholesome water.

In his life of Columbus, Irving condemns both Indian slavery and Negro slavery, which he sees as inviting divine retribution, and in "The Devil and Tom Walker" the one thing Tom will not do to accommodate the Devil is go into the slave trade. Irving was clear on the secession issue as early as 1832, and when Governor James Hamilton of South Carolina, who had entertained him, hoped he would come again, he smiled and replied, "Oh, yes! I'll come with the first troops." In 1856 he voted for Fremont.

Yet he had no love for Negroes. "A negro is an abomination to me," he told Mary Fairlie in 1807, when he was trying to round up the Negro vote, and this in spite of the fact that the "poor devils" had all accommodatingly turned out Federalists:

I almost pitied them—for we had them in an enormous drove in the middle of the day waiting round the poll for a chance to vote—the sun came out intolerably warm—and being packed together like sheep in a pen, they absolutely fermented, and a cloud of vapor arose like frankincense to the skies—had Jupiter (who was a good federalist) still been there, he would have declared it was of a sweet smelling savor.

He was apparently not impressed by *Uncle Tom's Cabin*, and his trip through the South in 1832 seems to have convinced him that slavery was not so bad as it had been represented. He may seem to be paying the Negroes a compliment when he calls them the "merriest people in these parts—if you hear a broad, merry laugh, be sure that it is a negro—politest people—fine gentlemen," but read in its context this passage is less impressive, for he goes on to minimize what he admits is an evil of slavery, the danger of children being sold away from their parents, by dragging an unabashed red herring across the trail: "but are not white people so, by schooling, marriage, business, &c?" In 1851 he wrote Kennedy that he wished to heaven "nature would restore to the poor negroes their tails and settle them in their proper place in the scale of creation. It would be a great relief to both them and the abolitionists, and I see no other way of settling the question effectually." He liked this figure so much that he remembered it for eight years and used it again in a conversation with his biographer, "I shouldn't mind about the Niggers if they only brought them over before they had drilled out their tails."

On the other hand, Irving's fairness and generosity toward

Indians have been recognized by nearly all writers, though Keiser plays it down somewhat by connecting it with the current romantic enthusiasm for primitivism.[9] Lucy Lockwood Hazard calls him decidedly more friendly than Cooper. Osborne finds that as early as 1814, when he published in the *Analectic* the essays on "Philip of Pokanoket" and "Traits of Indian Character" which were afterwards very widely circulated through *The Sketch Book*, he was already aware both "that Indian behavior was not motivated by the same cultural traditions that motivated the behavior of the transplanted European," and "that Indian cultural traditions were adequate to produce a character of heroic proportions." He did not think it absurd to compare the Pequods who were massacred in a swamp near Plymouth with Roman senators massacred by the Gauls. "For his time, Irving was remarkably well informed on the subject of the Indian."

Irving came by his interest in Indians honestly, for it was shared by his brother William and his great friend Henry Brevoort, both of whom had Indian trading interests. He was not greatly impressed by the specimens he encountered upon his Canadian trip, but not even the amorous advances made to him by a drunken squaw, and what might easily have been a serious attack upon him by her jealous husband in consequence, turned him against the race. *Knickerbocker's History* is full of satirical attacks against the rapacity of the white settlers; here is one of the sharpest, which Irving cut in revision:

The Indians improved daily and wonderfully by their intercourse with the whites. They took to drinking rum, and making bargains. They learned to cheat, to lie, to swear, to gamble, to quarrel, to cut each other's throats, in short, to excel in all the accomplishments that had originally marked the superiority of their Christian visitors. And such a surprising aptitude have they shown for these acquirements, that there is very little doubt that in a century more, provided they survive so long, the irresistible effects of civilization, they will equal in knowledge, refinement, knavery, and debauchery, the most enlightened, civilized and orthodox nations of Europe.

This is consistent with the testimony of other works. (Only in the French and Indian War are the Indians "hell hounds.") Columbus's first impression of the Indians was of their sweetness and gentleness. "They love their neighbors as themselves; and their discourse is ever sweet and gentle, and accompanied with a smile; and though it is true that they are naked, yet their manners are decorous and praiseworthy." Irving condemns the profligacy of the Spaniards and, following Las Casas, minutely documents their hideous cruelties. "Humanity turns with horror from such atrocities, and would fain discredit them."

When the chance came to make his Western tour, Irving welcomed it because it gave him a chance to see "the remnants of those great Indian tribes, which are now about to disappear as independent nations, or to be amalgamated under some new form of government." It was the real, not the stock, Indian that he wished to encounter, and he later felt that he had accomplished this. "In fact, the Indians that I have had an opportunity of seeing in real life, are quite different from those described in poetry." To make more such information available, he encouraged Charles Lanman to collect his writings about the West:

They carry us into the fastnesses of our mountains, the depths of our forests, and watery wilderness of our lakes and rivers, giving us pictures of savage life and savage tribes, Indian legends, fishing and hunting anecdotes, the adventures of trappers and backswoodsmen; our whole arcanum in short of indigenous poetry and romance.

For the same reason he welcomed the *Indian Sketches* of his nephew John Treat Irving. We have not yet had much of the true Indian character, he says; "writers have all represented the Indians according to a conventional and artificial model; this unhackneyed youngster presents them as they are." [10]

Irving has often been reproached for the absence of pro-Indian passages in his Northwest books. Charlton Laird writes:

> If Irving sensed the tragic and ironic possibilities of the tales of Bonne-ville and especially of Astoria, his romantic accounts do not betray him. Did he not know the broad foundation of suffering and debauchery upon which the fortune of his friend John Jacob Astor rested? Was he silenced by the sense of what one gentleman does not say about another? Was he swept along by the desire to please a public who believed that Western expansion was the high destiny of America, and that a dead Indian was a good Indian? Or was he merely growing old?

I do not doubt that all these considerations operated. Romantic imagination in the worst sense glorified the *coureurs de bois:* "It is difficult to do justice to the courage, fortitude, and perseverance of the pioneers of the fur trade, who conducted these early expeditions, and first broke their way through a wilderness where every thing was calculated to deter and dismay them." It is even more shocking that he should quite calmly take it for granted that eventually the fur-bearing animals were going to be exterminated. Yet it will not do to make Irving blinder than he was:

> Many of these *coureurs de bois* became so accustomed to the Indian mode of living, and the perfect freedom of the wilderness, that they lost all relish for civilization, and identified themselves with the savages among whom they dwelt, or could only be distinguished from them by superior licentiousness. Their conduct and example gradually corrupted the natives, and impeded the works of the Catholic missionaries, who were at this time prosecuting their pious labors in the wilds of Canada.

He continued to describe white atrocities against Indians, with the white man, not the Indian, as the aggressor. "We kill white men because white men kill us." He recorded Bonne-ville's opinion that the Nez Percés, in spite of the unfavorable reports of others, are "one of the purest-hearted people on the face of the earth." In *Astoria* he describes an Indian woman who "displayed a force of character that won the respect and applause of the white men."

In one of Irving's Spanish sketches, the pious Fernan Gonzalez comes close to violating the sanctity of an altar inadvertently while hunting. "Being as pious as he was brave, the good count now knelt before the altar and asked pardon of God for the sin he had been on the point of committing; and when he had finished his prayer, he added another for victory over the foe." I am not sure whether Irving was fully aware of the irony here, for his utterances on war and peace are not altogether consistent. "What is the amount of all the evil inflicted by lightning, tempest, earthquake, and volcano, to the overwhelming and widespreading miseries of war!" Yet as late as 1833 we find him urging support of a bill for the improvement of the marine corps on the frivolous ground that "in this money making age, we should endeavor to cherish whatever institutions we have among us that partake of the *game* spirit. Our whole naval service in fact, wants rallying up."

The only war in which Irving himself was even peripherally in service was of course the War of 1812, and even this did not rouse him until after the British had burned Washington. Then, as he told a stranger who wondered what "Jimmy" Madison would do now, it was no longer "a question about *Jimmy* Madison, or *Jimmy* Armstrong. The pride and honor of the nation are wounded; the country is insulted and disgraced by this barbarous success, and every loyal citizen would feel the ignominy and be earnest to avenge it." And though it is true that even now Irving urged British and Americans not to slander each other, lest the seeds of a bitterness be planted which post-war reconciliation would find difficulty in eradicating, this was the only period in his life when he either thought or wrote like a jingo. The sketches of naval heroes which he contributed to the *Analectic Magazine* are perfervid in their praise of martial prowess, even when the hero in question was, like the Boy Who Stood on the Burning Deck, an inspired idiot:

"Where men are fighting for honor rather than profit, the utmost delicacy should be observed towards their high-toned
feelings. Those complaints which spring from wounded pride,
and the jealousy of station, should never be regarded lightly."
Irving's attitude toward fame is as childish as that of a Renais-
sance man: "The bravest soldier would not willingly expose
himself to certain danger, if he thought that death were to be
followed by oblivion." Hence it becomes both "duty" and
"policy" for a nation

to pay distinguished honor to the memories of those who have fallen in
its service. It is, after all, but a cheap reward for sufferings and death;
but it is a reward that will prompt others to the sacrifice, when they
see that it is faithfully discharged.

Irving regretted the Mexican War and thought that it might
have been avoided. Yet when he heard how General Zachary
Taylor and his army had conducted themselves, and how they
had treated their enemies, he wept in sympathy and admiration.
He hoped that "this brilliant victory will be followed up by
magnanimous feeling on the part of our government, and that
the war may be brought to a speedy close on fair and honorable
terms." Yet he seems to have thought the American course in
making war justified; at any rate he argued in its behalf in a
long and carefully prepared document for the Spanish premier,
Don Xavier Isturiz.

Meanwhile, however, he had played a role more creditable
to his head if not also to his heart in connection with two minor
crises. Whether or not Irving's services were as important as
George Hellman believed in preventing war between France
and the United States in 1834,[11] it is certain that he took a large
view and both then and later gave Van Buren good advice. He
was more importantly and unquestionably involved in settling
the Oregon Boundary dispute with Great Britain, for he himself acknowledged having "reason to congratulate myself that,

in a quiet way, I was enabled . . . to facilitate the frank and con-
fiding intercourse of Mr. McLane and Lord Aberdeen, which
has proved so beneficial to the settlement of this question."
While it was still a matter of touch and go, he had written Mrs.
O'Shea:

> It is a question of compromise; of more give and take; where the
> honor of neither party ought to be implicated in the quantity, more or
> less, of land, ceded. The press, however, has roused the pride and pas-
> sions of both parties, and may blow up the flame of war whatever
> diplomacy may do to prevent it. Still I have a strong hope that the ques-
> tion may ultimately be adjusted in a peaceable way and without discredit
> to either party.[12]

Knickerbocker's History is not all on the pacifist side, for
Jefferson's peace policy and especially his reduction of appro-
priations for the navy are bitterly ridiculed.[13] When Peter
Stuyvesant comes in, he reverses his predecessor's policy, believing that only a strong nation is respected by its neighbors
or has any reasonable chance of preserving the peace. Taken
as a whole, however, the book contains much more to distress
militarists than to make them happy. D. K. is in the mood as
well as the manner of Fielding when he describes history itself
as "a kind of Newgate calendar, a register of the crimes and
misdeeds that man has inflicted on his fellow men." Great men,
as the world conceives them, are "tyrants, robbers, conquerors,
renowned only for the magnitude of their misdeeds," and progress is the invention of ever more ingenious ways of murdering
other people. Treaties cause wars instead of preventing them,
and the only time one can feel really safe is while negotiations
are in progress; the wise nation, consequently, will prolong this
period indefinitely. "Thus it may paradoxically be said, that
there is never so good an understanding between two nations
as when there is a little misunderstanding—and that so long as
they are on terms at all, they are on the best terms in the

world!" When the war fever rages, the "drum ecclesiastic" can always be counted upon to whip it up, for "a cunning politician often lurks under the clerical robe." And once the alarm has been sounded, "the public, who dearly love to be in a panic, are always ready to keep it up." Which comes considerably closer to Mark Twain's bitter and painfully accurate description of the development of war fever in *The Mysterious Stranger* than might have been expected of Irving. The great battle in *A History of New York* is a completely bloodless one in which nobody is hurt, but Diedrich Knickerbocker apologizes for disappointing his readers as cruelly as "a multitude of good people" are always disappointed when, having turned out to an execution, they are inconsiderately balked by a reprieve.

There is also an elaborate discussion of whether or not it was right to take the land away from the Indians. Diedrich Knickerbocker does not see how anybody could doubt it. The Indians had no wants and were very unreasonable animals altogether. Did not their conquerors bring them "rum, gin, brandy, and the other comforts of life"? Did they not bring them "a thousand medicines, by which the most inveterate diseases are alleviated and healed; and that they might comprehend the benefits and enjoy the comforts of these medicines, they previously introduced among them the diseases which they were calculated to cure." Did they not offer them salvation, the opportunity to trade in "a little pitiful tract of this dirty sublunary planet in exchange for a glorious inheritance in the kingdom of heaven"? Did they not use "every method to induce them to embrace and practice the true religion—except indeed that of setting them the example"? And, finally, by exercising their unquestioned "RIGHT BY EXTERMINATION" and "RIGHT BY GUNPOWDER," did they not hurry the Indians "out of the world" so they might that much sooner enjoy their reward in another?

Irony predominates in the sketch of the Old Soldier in *Bracebridge Hall* also, and there is a touch of it, with considerable praise for the humanity of the Moors, in *The Conquest of Granada* and its associated writings. When Mahomet grows militaristic, Irving's sympathy for him oozes out at the palms of his hands, like Bob Acres's courage. Basically he believed that

until nations are generous they will never be wise; true policy is generous policy; all bitterness, selfishness, etc., may gain small ends, but loses great ones—it may appear chivalrous, but it is true; expedience may answer for the moment—they gain a point, but they do not establish a principle— there is a return of the poisoned chalice.

As he grew older he became more sensitive about these things, and the military part of Washington's life was the part he enjoyed writing least: "I used to read all the details of a painful nature in wars, but now I skip them. My stomach has lost its tone; I cannot digest horrors any longer."

5   HOW THE TREE WAS DEPRIVED

Irving's emotional life, in its most intimate aspects, presents curious paradoxes. He must surely have been the most affectionate family man who never founded a family. "My heart warms toward you all the farther I am off," he wrote his brother William in 1804. "And I often lay in my berth or walk the deck for an hour or two thinking of home and fancying how you are all employing yourselves, till the tears stand in my eyes." When, in visiting Ashby Hall in 1831, he met a girl of eighteen or nineteen who reminded him of what his sister had been at that age, he "had to turn off to a window to conceal my agitation." And in later years when his family had become what some people would have called a "burden" upon him, he insisted that this was not so, that, on the contrary, his responsibilities gave an interest to his existence. "Had I only myself to take care of I should become as inert, querulous and good for nothing as other old bachelors who live only for themselves, and should soon become weary of life." When he arirved home at Sunnyside from a visit to the Kennedys in the spring of 1853, he alighted at the railroad station and walked home along the tracks. "I saw female forms on the porch and I knew the spy glass was in hand. In a moment there was a waving of handkerchiefs and a hurrying hither and thither. Never did old bachelor come to such a loving home, so gladdened and blessed by womankind."

It was members of the younger generation that made this happy home for him, and Irving's affections had never had any difficulty in embracing the younger generation. In the early days they gravitated about him, enthralled by his story-telling gifts and, it is clear, by his kindness as well. There is a charming letter to his mother from Birmingham in 1815, telling of his arrival at his sister Sarah Van Wart's:

> The little folks had all retired to bed with great reluctance, but early in the morning I heard them about my door, consulting whether they should enter and very anxious that I should make my appearance, but very shy about making any approaches. I dressed myself and went among them, to their great delight and in a few minutes we became the most intimate friends imaginable.

Needless to say, his sympathies were not limited to blood relations. He had his share of contacts with the children of the "great." In Spain he was friendly with the nine-year-old daughter of the Duke of Gor. There was also a three-year-old whom he met at Malaga, a daughter of the Count of Teba; he held her on his lap and told her stories; she was later known as the Empress Eugénie. In Vienna he saw Napoleon's son, the Duke of Reichstadt, whom Rostand was to celebrate in *L'Aiglon,* and found him "a fine boy," and "full of life and

spirit—very handsome, and very much liked by every body."
But he did not need a great name to awaken his interest.

He did not believe in overtraining children or keeping them
on too tight a rein. Approving of her own ways in childrearing,
he once wrote a woman friend:

> Let others aim at making their children precocious prodigies; intellec-
> tual wonders: and wear out their organs of thought, and enfeeble their
> constitutions by early overtasking of the mind, and imprisonment of the
> body: I will always bet in the long run, on those who have had a happy
> untasked childhood, with simple wholesome diet, and plenty of frolic in
> the open air.

It must have cost him at least a slight pang when a strange
woman with whose children he had been playing on a train
took him for "the kind father of a big family."

It is quite clear that, like Hawthorne and like Mark Twain,
Irving preferred little girls to little boys. "A thousand thanks,
most charming and discreet princess, for the little purse you
have sent me, and which will ever be precious to me for having
been wrought by your own fair hands." He can be quite savage
about this preference: "You know my idea of the education
of young people—*the girls to be indulged in everything*—the
boys to be *worked hard* and well WHIPPED." But he can
hardly have meant this seriously. He could be cynical when
the mood struck him about children in general: "How few it
is who know how to instruct children!—and indeed how few
children are worth the trouble." Once he offered to buy a little
boy's eyes, and no agreement being reached as to price, gave
him a sixpence anyway. And once he actually helped a boy
steal apples from his own trees while the youngster cautioned,
"Don't let the old man see us."

It is hard to believe today that some contemporary critics
found Irving indecent, especially in *Tales of a Traveller*.
"There are occasionally coarse and vulgar expressions in some

of them, which do not belong to Washington Irving," wrote
John Neal. Another critic rejected "The Adventure of My
Aunt" because of "a want of delicacy in the story." "The Bold
Dragon" was pronounced "offensive to the chastity of the
Georgian home," and "The Italian Banditti" awakened "pure
unmingled digust." One periodical, *The United States Literary
Gazette,* even offered documentation of its charges, or was it
only supplying a guide to prurient readers?

> We refer . . . to the description of the comic shape of the Strolling
> Manager's Clown; to the indecency drowned in the crack! crack! of the
> postillion's whip at Terracina; the innuendoes in the "Bold Dragon"; the
> indelicacy with which that is slyly smothered in the description of Dolph
> Heyliger's mistress, which might have been said openly without any
> breach of propriety; and finally, the shocking story of the "Young
> Robber," where a scene the most revolting to humanity is twice un-
> necessarily forced on the reader's imagination.

Is this Washington Irving? The Irving who believed that
"there are some senses that tend to elevate and spiritualize our
natures—others that debase it and bring it to the earth"? who
praised "the innate purity and goodness of Goldsmith's nature"? and Fernan Caballero for her "warmth and purity of
heart" and "an unworldly spirit, rarely met with in one who
has mingled so much with the world," and G. P. R. James for
"the kindliness of feeling, the purity of taste and the soundness
of principle maintained throughout your various writings: this
too at a time when there is such a meretricious taste and such
a specious profligacy prevalent in literature throughout the
world"?

But even absurd ideas must be accounted for, and whatever
else one may say about the reviewers I have just cited, one
does know what they are talking about. If Cooper's females
are "flat as a prairie," as Lowell charged, nobody could say this
of the daughter of Wolfert Webber:

I have no talent at describing female charms, else fain would I depict the progress of this little Dutch beauty. How her blue eyes grew deeper and deeper, and her cherry lips redder and redder; and how she ripened and ripened, and rounded and rounded in the opening breath of sixteen summers, until, in her seventeenth spring, she seemed ready to burst out of her bodice, like a half-blown rose-bud.

And again:

The chain of yellow virgin gold, that encircled her neck; the little cross, that just rested at the entrance of a soft valley of happiness, as if it would sanctify the place. The—but, pooh!—it is not for an old man like me to be prosing about female beauty; suffice it to say, Amy had attained her seventeenth year.

Of her admirer Dick Waldron we are told that he

could boast of more fathers than any lad in the province; for his mother had had four husbands, and this only child; so that though born in her last wedlock, he might fairly claim to be the tardy fruit of a long course of cultivation. The son of four fathers united the merits and vigors of all his sires. If he had not had a great family before him, he seemed likely to have a great one after him; for you had only to look at the fresh bucksome youth, to see that he was formed to be the founder of a mighty race.

In *Bracebridge Hall* Inez is praised for her lack of prudery, which quality Irving associates with sophistication and corruption, and we are told frankly that it is a woman's job in marriage "to keep passion alive." There is no squeamishness in indicating Mahomet's sexuality; neither is Irving coy in indicating the profligacy of the Spaniards in the New World nor the sexual habits of the inhabitants of that place. After the death of his first wife, the mother of King Fernando is anxious that he should marry again: "True, he was a saint in spirit, but after all in flesh he was a man, and might be led away to those weaknesses very incident to, but highly unbecoming of, the exalted state of princes."

But if Irving is to be attacked for vulgarity, his first work must not be left unexamined: "From time immemorial, it has been the rule of the Cocklofts [of *Salmagundi*] to marry one of their own name; and, as they always breed like rabbits, the family has increased and multiplied like that of Adam and Eve." Especially since "the female members of the family are most incredibly fruitful; and . . . seldom fail 'to throw doublets every time.' " The Cocklofts are also "bewildered with church-yard tales of sheeted ghosts, white horses without heads, and with large goggle eyes in their buttocks."

Of the canonical works, one would think, however, that *A History of New York* might be the one a moralist would be most inclined to attack, especially in the first edition, for Irving removed much of this material in his revision, the reference to "the great Plato" in Book I, Chapter 2, for example, "that temperate sage, who threw the cold water of philosophy on the form of sexual intercourse, and inculcated the doctrine of Platonic affection, or the art of making love without children." The worst obscenity was left unexpurgated, however, prob-ably because, since it is in Dutch, Irving thought most of his readers would not understand it. And since William the Testy was Thomas Jefferson, Irving may well have felt that he could not attack Jefferson's alleged obscenities without in some man-ner illustrating them.[1] But there remained numerous references to bottoms, bundling, illegitimacy, and much besides, to say nothing of the Dutch ship always modeled after the "fair forms" of the Dutchwomen:

> Accordingly, it had one hundred feet in the beam, one hundred feet in the keel, and one hundred feet from the bottom of the stern-post to the tafferel. Like the beauteous model, who was declared to be the greatest belle in Amsterdam, it was full in the bows, with a pair of enormous cat-heads, a copper bottom, and withal a most prodigious poop!

So far as I have observed, there is only one "four-letter word" anywhere in Irving's journals,[2] and it is true that he sometimes omits unpleasant things which have been recorded by others, for example, certain disgusting incidents included in Robert Stuart's manuscript, which was one of his sources for *Astoria*.[3] Yet he will write about the "little roundbellied Spanish marquis," whom he describes as

a battered rake of sixty—as round as a pumpkin yet pale and withered in the face—his plan of amusement for the day—to the bull-fight in the morning—then to dine at a Fonda—to the bull-fight in the evening—then to the theatre—then to have a girl for the night.

And again: "An officer of service in the peninsular war kept a Spanish girl—on his return to England a friend asked if he had brought her with him—He replied—no, that it was only a transient connection—oh observed the other I presume she was hors du combat."

He is equally adept in dealing with unpleasantness of a non-sexual character. In 1804 he complains of a small French town that it was made loathsome

from the quantities of manure piled up against the house which at certain seasons they carry into the fields and spread it about to fertilize the soil. The abominable smells occasioned by these heaps of manure, together with the vileness of the Inns destroy all idea of comfort to a traveller unaccustomed to them.

But he adds:

For my part I try to take things as they come, with cheerfulness, and when I cannot get a dinner to suit my taste I endeavor to get a taste to suit my dinner. I have made a hearty meal of Cucumbers and onions off of a dirty table in a filthy log hut on the banks of Black river and I have made as hearty a one in a vile French auberge of a stale fowl that I verily believe had mounted guard on the table a half score of times. There is nothing I dread more than to be taken for one of the Smell-fungi of this world.

In 1826 he "went with Smith and Peter to place of La Celada to see execution of a man for robbing and murder—hanged—

took place about one." In the evening he heard *The Barber of Seville* from the French ambassador's box.

Does this, then, mean that Irving was indifferent to moral considerations? Of course it does not mean anything of the kind. He could always take a high moral tone when it was called for. He advised a nephew about his reading:

As far as I can judge . . . the literatures the most free from licentiousness in morals are the Spanish and the German. The Spanish, because the greater part was written at a time when romantic notions prevailed in Spain of manly honor and female virtue; and the German, because almost all its *belles-lettres* have been produced within the last fifty years under the restraints of modern decency.

He advised Prince Dolgorouki upon more important matters:

The world is pretty much what we make it; and it will be filled up with nullities and trifles if we suffer them to occupy our attention. . . . Fix your attention on noble objects and noble purposes, and sacrifice all temporary and trivial things to their attainment. Consider everything not as to its present importance and effect, but with relation to what it is to produce some time hence.

He even advised President Van Buren when he thought he needed it:

You have now arrived at the most distinguished post in the world, at the head of the *great republic:* it depends upon yourself to make it the most honorable. There is but one true rule for your conduct: act according to the sound dictates of your head and the kind feelings of your heart, without thinking how your temporary popularity is to be affected by it, and *without caring about a re election.*

He objected decidedly to the rakish ways of Comte de Pourtalès on the Western tour, and, as early as 1829, he saw New York City deteriorating:

I am afraid our good city is in a bad way as to both morals and manners. What the cities of the old world take moderately and cautiously she gets roaring drunk with. I must say all this rioting and dancing at the theatres, with public masquerades every night in the week, has a terribly low-lived, dissolute, vulgar look. We are too apt to take our ideas of English life from such vulgar sources as Tom and Jerry, and we appear to be Tom-and-Jerrying it to perfection in New York.

But Irving was not obsessed with morality, and he was not a prude. He knew when to make a judgment, and he knew when to refrain from making one. Thus, he believed that one important function of history was to furnish examples for the living. He condemned Britain's treatment of her American colonies. He condemned Arnold's treason. He would not even have considered not condemning the Spanish cruelty toward the Indians. But he also knows when not to judge, when to keep silent, when to present his materials objectively, and when to leave judgment to the reader. He does not, for example, tell us what he thought of Columbus's trick of deceiving the Indians about an eclipse—an astonishing anticipation of *A Connecticut Yankee in King Arthur's Court*.

Such is the testimony of his work; what now of his life, specifically where women were concerned? "I am easily affected by female beauty," he writes in *Bracebridge Hall*. It was the understatement not merely of the year but of many a year. Wherever he went, in Europe or in America, it was the women and girls he looked at most closely and lovingly. "Returned by coach—pretty woman in it." "By advice of Mr. Sennet, the lawyer, I go to the Ship in Distress—a small but civil inn—with a comely landlady." The landlady at the village ale house was a "tidy, short little woman. We were waited upon by her daughter, a very pretty girl with fair complexion and fair hair." "It was delightful once more to hear my native language spoken by a pretty girl." "Go to M. Tieck's at six o'clock in company with Baron de Malsburg—conversation, he in German, I in English—his daughters very pleasing girls." "The family is very agreeable. Mrs. Van Ness is a pretty and pleasant little woman, and quite gay; then there are two pretty girls

likewise . . . ; you see I am in clover—happy dog!" So it goes
on, almost monotonously; it is a waste of labor even to try
to arrange the references chronologically, for the note is the
same from youth to age.

Almost any pretty girl was worth looking at, but some were
more worth looking at than others. Who could resist "that
little assemblage of smiles and fascinations, Mary Jackson"?

> She was bounding with youth, health, and innocence, and good humor.
> She had a pretty straw hat tied under her chin with a pink ribbon, and
> looked like some little woodland nymph, just lured out by spring and
> fine weather. God bless her light heart, and grant that it may never
> know care or sorrow! it's enough to cure spleen and melancholy only
> to look at her.

Then there was Mrs. D——, to whom he was introduced by
her husband:

> I won't speak all that I think of her; you would accuse me of hyper-
> bole; but, to say that I admire her would be too cold, too feeble. I think
> she would be a belle in heaven itself.

In Rome he found few women worth looking at among the
nobility, but among the rugged peasantry antique dignity sur-
vived, along with "great sweetness and intelligence of expression." In 1804 he met a French officer and his wife, with
whom he walked about the town and on the public walks in
the evening. "She was very agreeable and the time passed
pleasantly." There was also an Italian lady whose handkerchief
he carried about with him for a time, and once on a Spanish
steamer en route to Marseilles there was a lovely young Spaniard, who, though accompanied by her husband, was obviously
not averse to a mild flirtation. He had been gazing upon her,
describing her perfections, catalogue-fashion, in a letter he was
writing to a friend, when she broke in upon his absorption
with "Really, señor, one would think you were a painter taking my likeness." And she and he and her husband were very

good friends for the rest of the journey. He even tried flirting with nuns, describing one novice as "the most lovely girl that I have seen in Italy." At one convent, the Abbess was careful, he says, "to keep the handsome nuns out of sight," though the sisters themselves were very pleased "to see anything particularly gentlemen and Americans." And there is one simply incredible journal entry in which we may hope his observation was no better than his spelling: "Nuns on the top of the convent talking to Baker, Lieut. Morres & myself & making lacivious gestures."

When bodies are displayed he observes them, though he seems to disapprove of immodesty. "Be not you ashamed to show," says Hamlet, "he'll not shame to tell what it means." At a small French town he notes a "great scarcity of petticoats" among the women washing clothes in the canal. At Bordeaux the dancers in the ballet

were dressed in a flesh colored habit fitted exactly to their Shapes so that it really looked like the Skin, over this was a light robe of white muslin ornamented very tastily but so transparent that their figures were perfectly visible through it and in dancing particularly were completely exposed. As I was unaccustomed to see women expose themselves thus publicly I felt my American blood mounting in my cheeks on their account and would have been happy to have given them another petticoat or a thicker robe to cover their nakedness. . . . These lascivious exhibitions are strong evidence of the depraved morals and licentiousness of the public. The Stage which should be employed by "holding the mirror up to nature" to inform the understanding and improve the heart is degraded by performances devoted to sensuality and libertinism.

But he was not always so austere as that. That same year, describing, how fashion now permits Frenchwomen to display their legs to the garter, he writes:

With such fascinating objects around me, think what a warfare there is between the flesh and the spirit, and what dreadful conflicts I have with the "divinity that stirs within me." You can't imagine how many narrow escapes I have every day from falling in love.

How often in walking the street, do I see a fair nymph before me trip-ping along in airy movements. Her form of the greatest symmetry, while the zephyrs are continually betraying

> The alluring line of grace
> That leads the eye a wanton chase
> And lets the fancy rove

I hurry after her to catch a nearer view, to feast my eyes with the bright vision before it disappears. The sound of my steps call her attention, she turns her face towards me—the charm is broken—and all my admiration and enthusiasm is dissipated. I see a wide mouth, small black eyes, cheeks highly rouged and hair greased with ancient oil and twisted from the forehead to the chin till it resembles the headdress of a Medusa!

It is amusing that both Irving and Hawthorne should have been so much taken with Lely's pictures of the beauties of Charles II's dissipated court. Hawthorne found Nell Gwyn as painted by Lely "one of the few beautiful women whom I have seen on canvas"; Irving, speaking in more general terms of "amorous, half-dishevelled tresses, and the sleepy eye of love," says that he "blessed the pencil of Sir Peter Lely, which had thus enabled me to bask in the reflected rays of beauty."

Not only did Irving notice the women wherever he went, but he was fond of comparing those of every region with those he had seen everywhere else. When he arrived at Genoa in 1804, he pronounced Genoese women "generally well made with handsome features and very fine black eyes. They are infinitely superior in my opinion to the French women." He also thought them amorous, a charge he repeats concerning the women of Catania, whom he pronounced "lecherous in their intrigues" and "fond of strangers." As for Spain,

There are beautiful women in Seville as (God be praised for all his mercies) there are in all other great cities; but do not, my worthy and inquiring friend, do not come to Seville as I did, expecting a perfect beauty to be staring you in the face at every turn, or you will be awfully disappointed.

He considered Dutch women to have been somewhat slighted by nature in the matter of personal charms, but thought they had nobody but themselves to blame for having "recourse to dress to make their figures still more uncouth, and load themselves with stays and petticoats till they have no longer either 'shape or comeliness.' " He found the same fault with English-women, in spite of their beautiful faces: "they load on garment over garment without taste and their clothes hang about them as if hung on pegs. They have a fashion of wearing huge tippets of bear or fox skin, which added to an habitual stoop in the shoulders gives them the appearance of having a hunch there equal to a dromedary's." Their ankles suffered, too, in comparison to those of Frenchwomen, and their ways in love were different (one wonders how he knew):

French woman dips into love like a duck into water,—'tis but a shake of the feathers and a wag of the tail and all is well again, but an English woman is like a heedless hen venturing into a pool, who is drowned.

But there was one thing he was always sure of:

For fine girls, one need not quit New York. I'll assure you the girls of Bordeaux in my opinion are not to be compared to them for beauty. Many a wishful thought I send to the fascinating little creatures I have left behind me, and full often do I wish it was in my power to spend the evening in their company.

He never changed his mind about this. "I do not know when I have seen more delightful parties," he wrote much later from Tarrytown, "or more elegant little groups of females."

Irving's chivalry toward women appears as early as the Old-style letters, where he objects to a farce in which "an ancient maiden" was made a buffoon:

I think these attempts to injure female happiness, at once cruel and unmanly. I have ever been an enthusiast in my attachment to the fair sex—I have ever thought them possessed of the strongest claims to our admiration, our tenderness, and our protection. But when to these are added still stronger claims—when we see them aged and infirm, solitary and neglected, without a partner to support them down the descent of life—cold indeed must be that heart, and unmanly that spirit, that can point the shafts of ridicule at their defenceless bosoms—that can poison the few drops of comfort heaven has poured into their cup.

He even interprets the generosity of women toward the fallen Burr charitably, and will not account for it "in so illiberal a manner" as to suppose it motivated by his having "ever been a favorite with the sex"; instead he prefers to view it as resulting "from that merciful, that heavenly disposition, implanted in the female bosom, which ever inclines in favor of the accused and the unfortunate." The fidelity and fortitude of women are celebrated in "The Wife," "The Broken Heart," and elsewhere in *The Sketch Book;* in "The Pride of the Village" Irving even comes fairly close to Poe's notion about the death of a beautiful woman being the most poetical subject. In *Captain Bonneville,* too, there is "an instance of female devotion, even to the death, which we are well disposed to believe and to record." [4]

Was Irving, then, a hopeless sentimentalist about women? It is generally assumed that the supreme expression of his sentimentalism is his book about Margaret Miller Davidson, the child poetess, whose verses he edited, with an enthusiastic appreciation, after her death. I disagree. I am not prepared to deny that Irving's attitude toward Margaret is sentimental, but has not his sentimentalism been somewhat overplayed? What he writes is not nearly so unreasonable as it is the fashion for people who have not read it to believe. Most of the verses he quotes do not suggest that if Margaret had lived she could have been anything better than another Mrs. Sigourney, but there are some few which may perhaps give us pause. About the girl's ardor, intelligence, and passion there can be no question at all. She was no hypochondriac, no bigot, and no prig. She was ambitious; she loved the joys of this world; and though she was religious, she was not afraid to use her mind in religion; she even suffered the shock of doubt. To conceive of her as merely an anticipation of Huck Finn's Emmeline Grangerford will not quite cover the case.

Moreover if a normal man is going to be sentimental about anybody, this helpless, doomed girl is exactly what he ought to be sentimental about. This is a great deal more manly than being sentimental about drunkards, drug addicts, and "madames" with hearts of gold, as is the fashion among sophisticated modern writers. If you are going to make a case against Irving for his sentimentality, it is much safer to attack him for his attitude toward Napoleon, toward Byron in his stickier aspects, and toward Aaron Burr than for his attitude toward Margaret Davidson. Toward Napoleon he wavered considerably, being much less sympathetic toward him in power than he was when he fell. In 1815, however, he concentrated more upon the Emperor's sufferings than upon the harm he had done, though it is only fair to add that his indignation was motivated at least in part by the not indefensible proposition that, with all his sins, Napoleon was more respectworthy than the jackals howling around the fallen lion.

Irving's attitude toward Byron has been sufficiently considered elsewhere. But his really indefensible sentimentality was toward Burr: "Though opposed to him in political principles, yet I consider him as a man so fallen, so shorn of the power to do national injury, that I feel no sensation remaining but compassion for him." It was not, surely, due to the goodness of Burr's own heart, or accountable unto him for righteousness, that he had been shorn of the power to do national injury.

Obviously these are all highly subjective matters, and it is idle to judge them by our standards. Who weeps over "The

Broken Heart" today? Yet it was Byron himself who wrote of it, "That is one of the finest things ever written on earth. Irving is a genius; and he has something better than genius,— a heart. He never wrote that without weeping; nor can I hear it without tears." For all that, Irving was certainly not on the whole a tearful writer, and there was plenty burlesque and satire in him. Charles Dudley Warner thought that "The Legend of Sleepy Hollow" would have been better if Irving "had displayed a little touch of pity for Ichabod Crane, had endowed him with some little shade of pathos." And—though here we move far beyond sentimentality—we must always remember that it was not Irving but Joseph Jefferson who infused the character of Rip Van Winkle with its most moving pathos.

Moreover Irving was not always so generous toward women as in the instances quoted. Having condemned those who make fun of old maids, he does the same thing himself, and in the story of "Annette Delarbre" he shows his awareness of the fact that even good women may be cruel to their lovers. In view of the admiration he felt for Jean Jeffries Renwick—who had once been admired by Robert Burns—it is difficult to understand the frivolous and cynical tone of his remarks about women in his letters to her son James Renwick.

Irving could speak without blinking of a "scolding bitch trollope of a housemaid," and he could dismiss as "seldom remarkable for beauty" or worthy of being enrolled in the "immaculate train" of "the chaste Diana" the "half naked nymphs" he saw washing their clothes in a European stream. But it was not only peasant women of whom he could speak disrespectfully. His enjoyment of at least one concert was lessened by the "vast number of ugly old women" he saw there. "Bath," he adds, "is quite a perch for these old birds." There are sharp remarks about individuals too. One girl is dismissed

as an *"agreeable rattle,"* and the truth is that Irving did not
find her society in the least agreeable. "God defend me from
such vivacity as hers, in future. Such smart speeches without
point or meaning—such bubble and squeak nonsense. I'd as
leave stand by a frying pan for an hour and listen to the cook-
ing of apple fritters." Again he speaks of one "Cousin Betty
—rigged out in fierce blue silks with diamond necklaces, breast-
pins, brooches, earring bobs and three score rings on each
finger, that I never see her without thinking of some of the
eminent pawnbrokers' ladies I have seen in London." He also
sometimes listened to, and even recorded, gossip about women,
as that concerning Madame Vestris, which he got direct from
her mother—"an old bawd who had been pander to her own
daughters" and "an old pimp," and also about the singer Pasta,
who "does not seem to be happy—her husband gambles—when
Pasta sits by her (Miss G) at music the tears will stream down
her cheeks."

There is no reason to suppose that Irving ever had sexual
relations with any woman whose name is known to us. Were
there any casual amours in his life?

Williams speaks of "probably, the occasional free living in
certain periods of his life." This is general and conjectural. It
refers to the Cockloft Hall days and possibly to the days in
Paris when Tom Moore made him "a gayer fellow than he
could have wished." In Germany he was friendly with Barham
Livius, whose morals were not above reproach, which was well
understood by Emily Foster, and which seems to have affected
her attitude toward Livius. (We do not know what circumstances contributed to the weakening of the tie between Livius
and Irving in later years.) Looking back to the days of their
youth from his mid-sixties, Irving asked Gouverneur Kemble,
"Who would have thought that we should ever have lived to
be two such respectable old gentlemen!" And he tells us that

when he was in Paris with Joseph Carrington Cabell, even the Italians "stared at us often with surprise and called us the wild Americans." But the accent with which "wild" is here to be read is doubtful, and it is not always fair to take elderly gentlemen musing back upon having heard the chimes at midnight as fair witnesses against themselves, especially when they do not particularize.

Irving was teased, upon his first visit to Paris, for having gone first of all to "the most disreputable theater in the city," the Theatre Montansier; as he himself said, he had "caught Paris by the tail." This house was "much frequented by the frail fair ones," and while he strolled in the garden of the Palais Royal after the performance, he was accosted by one of them who begged him to buy her a bouquet. "I saw it was a mere scheme of the poor girl's to get a few sous to buy herself some bread for the next day, she having had no custom that night. It was evident she and the old woman who sold bouquets acted in concert. I pitied her and paid double price for the bouquet. The poor creature kissed me, thanked me a dozen times, and wanted me to go home with her." Evidently he did not go home with her, and indeed it is difficult to see how any young man could have behaved much better than he did upon this occasion, free of libertinism and pharisaism alike. On the same trip he wrote home to William:

Be assured, my dear brother, that the importance of being guarded in my intimacies is sufficiently impresed on my mind. Left to my own discretion I feel the great necessity of keeping a steady eye on my conduct and of endeavoring to convince my friends that the confidence they reposed in me was not misplaced. . . . Travelling has made me better acquainted with myself, it has given me a humiliating conviction of my own insufficiency—and of my own ignorance and how very much I have to learn, how very much to acquire. Still however I flatter myself that I have not let any opportunity of instruction pass by without endeavoring to profit by it, and on reviewing my conduct while in Europe, though I here and there observe little follies that a young man surrounded by allurements cannot always avoid—yet it is with satisfaction that I reflect that there is no action which I would seriously blush to acknowledge.

This is probably essentially—and also generally—true. If Irving ever threw his cap over the windmill, there are no traces of where it fell; neither did the action leave any obvious marks upon him. The girls that really captivated his imagination were as innocent and high-minded as Matilda Hoffman and Emily Foster. He himself admitted that he was always tempted to think a pretty woman an angel until she was proved something else; his final wistful gallantry toward Mary Kennedy shows that this was so to the end of his life. He knew how to look at a woman as a man looks at her, but he also knew how to see a woman as another woman sees her, and he often observed details of clothes and manners that one ordinarily expects only another woman to see. Much of the pleasure he derived from women's society came from his delight in domesticity and had nothing amorous about it: "I wish Mrs. Storrow would write me a letter and tell me all about the little household in Rue Thevenet. I should be sure of getting from her all that domestic chit-chat which is so interesting and delightful, and which only women can write."

It is possible that Irving's sighing over the dissipations of his youth does not refer primarily to sex. He did not, to be sure, do much smoking in his life. At a meeting of the New York Historical Society after his death, George Bancroft declared that Irving "detested tobacco in every form, with all the abhorrence of Doctor Franklin or Daniel Webster." This is certainly an overstatement, for we do have a few references to Irving smoking a cigar, but most of his references to tobacco are uncomplimentary. In *A History of New York* the Dutch are much belabored for their smoking, and Irving's notations on the Germans and Dutchmen he encountered in Europe are much in the same vein. Emily Foster quotes him as saying that "the pipe is the feature of a German face like the proboscis of an elephant," and he himself writes of a garden where he used to like to walk in the morning "before the Germans come to poison the air with themselves and their tobacco pipes; as the pure air is too insipid for a German. Indeed, he knows as little what pure air is, as a drunkard does of pure water; they both must qualify the element to their palates." In *Columbus* tobacco is a "singular and apparently nauseous indulgence," and "a weed, which the ingenious caprice of man has . . . converted into an universal luxury, in defiance of the opposition of the senses." In his trip to the South he found the soil "worn out by vile tobacco weed." In *Astoria* he even complimented the rattlesnakes on their "proper abhorrence" of it. During Irving's last years, his asthma may have increased his dislike of smoking, though at the very end, Oliver Wendell Holmes, distressed by his difficulties in speaking, sent him some medicated cigarettes, in which he professed to find relief.

Many of Irving's references to drinking, though not indicating a comparable dislike, do accent the note of caution. On the 1803 trip into the northern wilderness, he was made to drink "a large quantity" of brandy after he had been "overcome with the fatigue and the cold water I had drank." It cured his "chills and weakness" but "threw me into a fever for the night." In 1811 he writes Mrs. Ogden Hoffman, complaining of his hosts of the night before: "they so confounded—or as Lady Macbeth says *convinced* my brain with apple toddy and whisky punch, that I am mere animal this morning." In 1833, ordering a large quantity of "the VERY BEST brown sherry" from Böhl von Faber, he rejoices in the displacing of madeira by sherry among the wine drinkers of New York, "a change particularly favorable to my stomach." In 1852 he declined an invitation to the Century Club: "I have had one of my customary bilious attacks

and the temptation of oysters and champagne might lay me
up." He praises the Chinook Indians for their "abstinence from
ardent spirits," and sees the Mohammedan abstinence as a
factor in their military success. Ellsworth says no liquor at all
was carried on the Western trip, and G. P. Putnam is sufficient
authority for the statement that Irving was a complete tee-
totaler during the last two years of his life.

In early life, however, it was different, nor does he seem
always to have avoided excess. After twenty-five years he
could still recall getting tipsy with Jack Nicholson in Richmond at the time of Burr's trial. He got tipsy in New York
too. "We all sent an invitation in form to the Commodore and
his lady to dine with us this afternoon," he writes Henry
Brevoort in 1811, "but they declined on account of the heat of
the day and invited us to tea and gin in the evening. We went
over there in full force and passed a very pleasant evening."
In 1828 in Spain he spent a night with some companions drinking gin and water and singing songs till two o'clock in the
morning.

By this time Irving had become something of a connoisseur
in wine. Falernian wine disappointed him in 1805, causing him
to think that "either the ancients were unacquainted with the
superiority of foreign wines—or that they had a mode of manu-
facturing their wines that their degenerate successors have long
since forgotten," and in Germany he paid considerable attention to the different wines and learned how to differentiate
between them.

On the whole, however, one gets the impression that it may
have cost Irving more effort to be temperate in eating than in
drinking. It is amusing to find him, in 1804, discovering ravioli
as "one of the rarest tid bits I had ever tasted." He first heard
of it when a condemned robber demanded it for his last meal.
Ellsworth reports his suffering from skin eruptions on their

Western trip. He would not accept Ellsworth's diagnosis that this was

owing to his diet which is chiefly meat, salted when eaten very highly—a vegetable diet moderate in quantity would cure him; but it is extremely difficult to moderate the appetite when hunger is so great—all of us are ashamed of our voracity, and were we not kept in countenance by others around us, we should feel bound to make apology.

He adds, "Mr. Irving has also a sweet tooth and mine is proverbial." We may infer that his interest in food was not limited to sweets by his appalling account of the "excellent" dinner he enjoyed at a French inn in 1824:

soup—stewed veal with brown sauce and onions—dish of sausage and onions and white sauce—roast pigeon—dessert of cheese—baked pears—nuts, grapes, etc.—bottle of wine—coffee, three glasses of brandy—all for two francs and half each—very civil people.

Since Matilda Hoffman is the only woman we have positive evidence Irving ever desired to marry, she must still be pronounced the most important woman in his life, in spite of all the efforts that have been made of late years to displace her. He was first attracted to her when she was thirteen and he twenty-one. The only picture we have of her—the miniature by Edward G. Malbone—is not, to my eyes, that of a pretty girl, but I am willing to believe that Malbone did not do her justice. Irving himself has a charming description of her after a separation:

She came home from school to see me. She entered full of eagerness, yet shy from her natural timidity, from the time that had elapsed since we parted, and from the idea of my being a *travelled man*, instead of a stripling student—However what a difference the interval had made. She was but between fifteen and sixteen, just growing up, there was a softness and delicacy in her form and look, a countenance of that eloquent expression, yet that mantling modesty—I thought I had never beheld any thing so lovely.

Another observer, who was not in love with her, was more specific but no less complimentary:

Her auburn hair played carelessly in the wind, and her features, though not of classic outline, were radiant with life. Her eye was one of the finest I have ever seen—rich, deep-toned, and eloquent, speaking volumes in each varying expression, and generally suggestive of pensive emotion.[5]

Her letters do not suggest pensiveness, however. She was a gay, light-hearted girl, fond of clothes and of the theater, and as yet quite untouched by life. There is but one reference to Irving. "Washington says he saw a beautiful girl at Coldenham whose name was Ellen. Tell her that." One letter is signed "believe me your Affectionate not in love sister Matalinda dinda dinda."

Irving himself described her death to Mrs. Foster:

I saw her fade rapidly away beautiful and more beautiful and more angelical to the very last. I was often by her bed side and in her wandering state of mind she would talk to me with a sweet natural and affecting eloquence that was overpowering. I saw more of the beauty of her mind in that delirious state than I had ever known before. . . . Her dying struggles were painful and protracted. For three days and nights I did not leave the house and scarcely slept. I was by her when she died—all the family were assembled round her, some praying others weeping, for she was adored by them all. I was the last one she looked upon—I have told you as briefly as I could what if I were to tell all the incidents and feelings that accompanied it would fill volumes.

He was equally specific about the effect upon himself:

I cannot tell you what a horrid state of mind I was in for a long time—I seemed to care for nothing—the world was a blank to me—I abandoned all thoughts of the Law—I went into the country, but could not bear solitude, yet could not enjoy society—There was a dismal horror occasionally in my mind that made me fear to be alone—I had often to get up in the night and seek the bedroom of my brother, as if the having a human being by me would relieve me from the frightful gloom of my own thoughts.

Pierre M. Irving says that his uncle kept Matilda's Bible and Prayer-Book near him all his life. During the very period he is supposed to have been in love with Emily Foster, he wrote in his journal:

> She died in the flower of her youth and of mine but she has lived for me ever since in all woman kind. I see her in their eyes—and it is the remembrance of her that has given a tender interest in my eyes to every thing that bears the name of woman.

It may very well be that in the following more elaborate passage there is, as Williams has observed, an "infusion of literary with real emotion." Some words and phrases have been rewritten, and there are echoes of the passage in *The Sketch Book.* This does not cancel out its fundamental sincerity, however, nor does Williams so interpret it:

> I heard a soft and plaintive voice singing Angels ever bright and fair— my heart melted at the words I drew into a corner of the cathedral and covering my face with my hands drank in the exquisitely mournful sound. My heart felt as if it would melt within me—the recollection of Matilda—ever allied in my mind to all that is pure spiritual and seraphic in woman came stealing over my soul—I recalled all the scenes of our early attachment—of her gentleness—her purity—and her kind affection —as the soft voice of the music seemed to ascend my soul seemed lifted up with it to heaven.
> I recollected Matilda's parting scene—the agony of her death the seraphic years of her blessedness—She was now in heaven—among angels ever bright and fair—while I—lonely—desolate—humiliated—was grovelling—a miserable worm upon earth—Oh Matilda where was the soul felt devotion the buoyancy the consciousness of worth and happiness that once seemed to lift me from the earth when our eyes interchanged silent but eloquent vows of affection and I seemed to imbibe a degree of virtue and purity by associating with all that was virtuous and pure—How innocent how gentle—how lovely was then my life—How it has changed since— what scenes have I gone through since thou hast left me—what jarring collisions with the world—what heartless pleasures—what sordid pursuits —what gross associations—what rude struggles—How has my heart lost all its tune—that heart that then was all tenderness and melody—How has it become so depraved—hardened—deadened—worldly. Misfortunes

have crushed me to the earth—the cares of the world have harried through my heart and made it bare—I feel like one withered up and blighted—broken heart is like a desert wherein can flourish no green thing—The romance of life is past.

Irving told his biographer that the passages on death in "Rural Funerals" and "St. Mark's Eve" were inspired by his memory of Matilda, and according to Ann Hoffman's granddaughter he was driven from the room, many years afterward, by the sight of some embroidery that she had worked. Forty years after her death, he gave G. P. Putnam her miniature to be repaired and placed in a new case. When it was returned to him, "he took it into a quiet corner and looked intently on the face for some minutes, . . . his tears falling freely on the glass as he gazed."

This would seem to be enough to testify to the depth and sincerity of Irving's love for Maltilda Hoffman. Skeptics have reminded us that he was working on the light-hearted *History of New York* within a few days of her death, and that not long afterward he could joke about his affection for other women, but he would not be the first man who should have turned to work as a refuge from grief, nor would his heart necessarily be less tender for not having been worn upon his sleeve. If he jested about Mary Rhinelander and Mrs. Jerome Bonaparte when he wrote to Renwick, it is also true that he confided a tender memory of Matilda to his journal at the very time he was most under Emily Foster's spell.[6] If he did propose to Emily, she was the only one, and this is not a bad record for fidelity as the world goes.

Emily Foster was the daughter of John Foster, of Bedford, England, and of Amelia Morgan, his third wife. Mrs. Foster, Emily, a younger sister Flora, and three young sons, left Brickhill, Bedford, apparently in August 1820, for a three-year residence in Dresden, where John Foster had relatives.[7] Here

Irving met them, and became very intimate and friendly with them, and here he may have proposed marriage to Emily.[8]

Since Emily was less than half Irving's age, his love for her would witness once more to his incurably romantic attitude toward life and love; from another point of view, it must testify to his excellent taste, for Emily's journal can leave no doubt in any reader's mind that she was an exquisite girl. She lived in fashionable society with a host of suitors trooping after her, but she had not been corrupted by it; she had a mind; and she was intensely religious. She was also, obviously, very fond of "that good dear nice Mr. Irving," and there were times when she exhorted herself not to yield "to capricious coldness fits" and lamented her inability to "feel more than gratitude" for his "esteem and regard." She may have been frightened by the discrepancy between Irving's age and her own; she may have been interested in another man;[9] she was certainly as keenly aware of Irving's weaknesses of character as she was of his goodness and charm; and his inability to share her own passionate evangelicalism was not a good omen. (Both she and her sister married clergymen.) Certainly she did not enjoy the gossip which was circulated in Dresden: "that report that I am to marry 'certo signor autore'—begins to annoy me. . . ." But perhaps there was nothing more to it than that she simply did not love him. If she had done so, all these other considerations would still have existed, but they might have lost their importance. She was very young, and if she gave Irving pangs, she did not altogether escape them herself. When he parted from her and her family at Rotterdam, she recorded:

Mr. Irving accompanied us down the river quite into the sea, when he was put down into the boat, as he looked up to us, so pale & melancholy, I thought I never felt a more painful moment, such starts of regret, a little self-reproach & feelings too quick to analyze.

In the account of the same incident which she furnished for Pierre's biography, she was more discreet, and the discrepancy is itself suggestive:

I shall never, however long I may live, forget his last farewell, as he looked up to us, so pale and melancholy. It was a very painful moment to us all. We have not often felt so grieved at parting with a dear friend.

And Irving himself writes: "Dresden, Dresden, with what a mixture of pain, pleasure, and impatience I look back upon it."

Irving last saw the Fosters in England in the spring of 1832. When he was in England again, ten years later, he made no attempt to communicate with them. Three years before his death, however, on July 2, 1856, he replied to a letter which Emily had written him at Sunnyside, giving him news of herself in later years. Irving's letter, which is very affectionate in tone, refers to her painting of "the head of Herodias, which hangs over the piano in the drawing room." But it is obviously the only communication that has passed between them in many years.

Irving was not "serious" about any other woman, but there were a number of others with whom his friendships were important enough so that they must be mentioned in any account of his life. Some of these were Americans. In the early days, in New York, there was Mary Fairlie, "the fascinating Fairlie," who became Sophie Sparkle in *Salmagundi* and married the tragedian Thomas A. Cooper. At the very end of his life there was John P. Kennedy's niece, Mary Kennedy. On April 10, 1853, Irving praised her in a letter from Sunnyside, writing of her in the third person. She was not at her best, he thought, while presiding "over her little circle of admirers," nor at balls and receptions even though arrayed in that marvellous white dress of woven cob-web with rose colored ribbons in which she once broke upon my sight like a wonder. Neither was it when she mingled in every day life, so bright, so cheerful, so considerate of others, so little mindful of herself—there was something beyond all that. It was that unpretending but strict conscientiousness with which she adhered to a sober path of duty marked out for herself amid the bewildering mazes of gaiety and fashion.

It was this sweet rectitude which seemed to keep her unspotted by the world, drawing round her a robe of light and shedding a grace about her steps of which she was unconscious. I declare to you that the sound of her light step on the stairs going forth to her early devotions while I was yet lingering in my bed has sent a rebuke to my conscience at my own short-comings—There are a daily beauty and purity in her life that read homilies to me—I hope I may profit by them.

And now my dear Miss Mary if to the pure regard and perfect esteem thus inspired you add a little of that sentiment of devotion to the sex which may be permitted to linger about the heart of an old bachelor of seventy, you have an idea of that friendship which it is a happiness for me to entertain for you—for it is by such friendships the heart is softened and purified and made better. I think I profitted greatly in this respect by my intercourse with you and your aunt last winter. God bless you both for it.

When she married, he admitted to her uncle that it was a pity "these charming girls should not always remain young and *single*." But he had already written her to express the "sincerest pleasure" with which he had received the news

of the intended change in your condition. I had some vague idea that such might be the result of the intimacy I saw growing up between the Doctor and yourself during my last visit. In fact I could not conceive how a young gentleman of his apparent discernment and susceptibility could have such a daily opportunity of becoming acquainted with your merit without loving you. I trust my dear Miss Kennedy it will be a happy union.

Two years later he wrote to Mary, now Mrs. Cooke, expressing his satisfaction in her domestic happiness and in her motherhood. He declined an invitation to visit the Cookes because of his absorption in *Washington* but indicated that he would be happy to receive another such invitation at a later date.

But if Germany brought Irving the one girl whom, after Matilda Hoffman, he might have married, the advantage of numbers must always remain with Spain. Upon his first visit in the 'twenties, he was a member of the circle which revolved about Madame D'Oubril. As he somewhat coyly wrote her from Seville, April 19, 1828:

> One thing I will say . . . and that boldly too, that of all the fine women I have seen there is a certain circle consisting of four that assemble every evening around a round table in a certain salon of Madrid, which to my notion excel all the fair dames of Andalusia. One of these four is named Marie, a second Nathalie, a third Inez, but who the fourth is shall be nameless, for I am too modest to praise any one to their face.
> Which is all at present, most discreet princess, from your devoted friend and admirer
>
> Washington Irving.

But if the tone of his letters is a safe criterion, the member of this circle who was closest to him was Madame D'Oubril's niece Antoinette Bollviller. More than one scholar has called Irving's letters to Antoinette the best he ever wrote, and though there is no evidence to indicate that he fell in love with her, one is sometimes tempted to wonder why he did not. During his first stay in Spain he also made a friend of Cecilia Böhl von Faber, daughter of the German scholar and wine merchant, Johann Nikolaus Böhl von Faber, whose great library was important to Irving; as Fernan Caballero, Cecilia had before her a career as a Spanish novelist, not altogether uninfluenced by Irving's own writings.

Later during his Spanish ambassadorship, Irving was friendly with the Marquesa de la Casa Yrujo, who, as the daughter of Governor Thomas McKean of Pennsylvania, had married the Spanish minister in the United States (now deceased), and with

Mrs. Henry O'Shea, whose husband was very much alive but with whom Irving carried on a lively mock-flirtation:

I have made several attempts to see you of late, but have not been able to get inside of your front door. Has your husband any hand in this? I trust not. I trust he has seen and read enough of Spanish plays, which of course "hold the mirror up to nature," to know that when once a young fellow [Irving was sixty-one] is determined to see a fine woman, all the husbands in the world cannot prevent him.

To O'Shea himself Irving wrote in 1845 from Paris, when Mrs. O'Shea was ill and her husband away, "I see her every day and shall continue to pay her every attention consistent with propriety—more could not be expected from me." Even their son, whom Irving called "Papa Quique," seems to have been quite familiar with the terms on which Irving stood with the family, as we may see by the undated letter Irving sent him, complaining of the terrible scolding he had just had from his mother for not having written to her:

Such a letter! Such a passion as she is in! . . . Hombre! if I had known she was such a woman I would have written to her every day in the week. I am frightened out of my wits. I have packed up my trunk on the spot, taken passage for Paris and shall follow this letter as fast as possible. But I shall be afraid to show my face until you, my dear Papa Quique, speak a kind word for me and mollify her passion.

If Mrs. O'Shea had a husband, Leocadia Zamora had not; neither was she ever to acquire one.[10] She was a Cuban prima donna whose eyes were as lovely as her voice, and Irving met her at the home of the Countess of Montijo. There is a touch of possibly revealing sensitiveness on his part in a letter to his niece Sarah Storrow, in which he reports, late in 1844, that he has seen Leocadia but once of late: "I have called on her without finding her at home; and, observing that she appeared to be very much launched in the gay world, I have not followed up the acquaintance as I have a horror of being thought to play the old beau to a young belle." Less than a month later, however, he is passionately praising her singing: "Everybody was in raptures with her: while she received their applause in her quiet, unaffected manner; and with that absence of pretension which gives a charm to her talent. I wish that my friend King could see and hear her; he who is so nice a connoisseur in Female charm—I think she could charm away his rheumatism."

Finally in Spain, there was royalty—the child queen and her younger sister and their mother Maria Christina—to be worshipped from afar, which, if not the very best way of taking women, is not necessarily the worst either. Irving has been criticized for having idealized the kind of woman Isabella II afterwards became. But he was not one of the weird sisters, and he could not look into the seeds of time. That he was not invariably enthralled by royalty *qua* royalty, his cool description of the young Queen Victoria amply demonstrates. Quite aside from his humanity, it is difficult to see how a man of imagination could have been expected to feel other than he did about Isabella: "I could not but regard her with deep interest, knowing what important concerns depended upon the life of this fragile little being, and to what a stormy and precarious career she might be destined." When she behaved well he was happy to give her credit for it: "She acquires more and more a womanly deportment, and acquits herself with a dignity and self-possession hardly to be expected at her years." But those who feel that she threw stardust in his eyes might do well to look up the passages in which he describes her "rough and somewhat *mealy*" skin and stresses the fact that she was decidedly inferior to her sister "both in looks and carriage." "The little Queen, who, by the by, will soon cease to deserve the adjective of *little*, looked rather full and puffy on the occasion, being prehaps rather too straitly caparisoned."

Maria Christina was a far more beautiful woman. "The expression of her countenance as she converses is quite winning and her smile is fascinating; yet I would not have you suppose that she is mannered and artificial; nothing can be more easy, simple and natural than her whole deportment." Here Irving is more open to the charge of sentimentalizing, for he knew what Maria Christina's life had been. What he wrote about her charm was probably well deserved, however, and he does not seem to have been taken in by the show of piety she made upon her return to Spain.

I do not know who was the last pretty woman whose sight gave Irving pleasure; I suspect it was the last pretty woman he saw. When he was seventy he dreamed he was in Mahomet's paradise, and it was to accompany a young lady that he took, at seventy-two, the horseback ride which might have cost him his neck. If the chambermaid who served him in 1853 had been pretty, he writes his sister, he would have kissed her; as she was not, he rewarded her "in sordid coin."

There does not seem to be much question, however, as to who was the greatest woman Irving ever knew well; this was the distinguished philanthropist and civic leader, Rebecca Gratz, who was a close friend of the Hoffmans. "Once in a while," says Holmes's Autocrat of the Breakfast Table, "one meets with a single soul greater than all the living pageant which passes before it." The celebrated beauties of the past often disappoint posterity; Rebecca Gratz is a happy exception. Her portraits by Sully are still breathtakingly lovely, rich in sensuous beauty and spiritual charm, and her letters make it clear that she was as good as she was beautiful. There was, naturally, no question of romance, or even of flirtation, here, but Irving had Rebecca Gratz enough on his mind to sing the song of her perfections to Sir Walter Scott, and there seems no reason to doubt the widely held belief that the Wizard of the North preserved her name and her virtues in *Ivanhoe*.[11]

Irving would undoubtedly have married Matilda Hoffman if she had lived and would certainly have made her a good husband. But however sincere his grief for her death may have been, it did not prevent him from being attracted by other women. All in all, it does not seem that any respectable man can ever have been attracted by a larger number. With the attraction he himself obviously had for them, and with the multitudinous contacts he enjoyed, it certainly would not have been difficult for him to marry somebody else. Why, leaving Emily Foster out of it, did he never attempt to do so?

The very year after Matilda's death we find Irving scribbling some pseudo-profundities in his journal about how, though Aristotle "prescribed a middle age for matrimony," the free mingling of the sexes in America from their earliest years would make it difficult to follow his prescription here. By the time he made his notes for *The Sketch Book* he was inclined to favor early marriages, but he was also of the opinion that

Friendships formed with females in early life are transient—they originate in some attraction of beauty—grace sprightliness or romance which time soon steals from them. Women are like flowers which soon lose their beauty and exhale their sweetness and are dull uninteresting weeds afterwards. They are subject to such changes and perishings. Marriage alters them &c—He that devotes himself to them is like one that devotes himself to raising flowers—He continually sees his favorites changing & fading under his eye—

and more to the same effect. And by 1829 he was talking as if he were eighty, warning his nephew Edgar Irving

against heedlessly getting yourself entangled in any matrimonial engagement, before you have the means or certain prospect of maintaining a family. I speak thus to you now, because I trust your heart is free from any particular attachment. I know that when a young man is once in love, he is not expected to act any more with prudence or discretion. He must then marry in defiance of penury and starvation. Novels and romances have established sound doctrine on this head which is not to be controverted. But believe me, a young man who marries early, without certain and easy means of subsistence, is half extinguished. All his talents and industry, which might otherwise have been freely exercised to their full scope and might have led him to fortune or distinction, must be immediately turned into the limited, anxious and inexpert struggle for mere daily bread. The mere romance of love soon vanishes in such a struggle.

The ghost of Matilda Hoffman must have groaned.

The principal single source of Irving's comments on marriage is his letters to Henry Brevoort. They are not, on the whole, pleasant, and certainly they are not idealistic. What, for example, would Matilda have thought of this, in 1812?

The little Taylor has been here and passed some time since your departure. She is a delightful little creature, but alas, my dear Hal, she has not the *pewter*, as the sage Peter says. As to beauty, what is it "but a flower!" Handsome is that handsome has,—is the modern maxim. Therefore, little Taylor, "though thy little finger be armed in a thimble," yet will I set thee at defiance. In a word, she is like an ortolan, too rare and costly a dainty for a poor man to afford, but were I a nabob, 'fore George, ortolans should be my only food.

As I rode into town the other day, I had nearly ran down the fair Maria M——re. I immediately thought of your sudden admiration for her, which seemed to spring up rather late in the season, like strawberries in the fall—when every other swain's passion had died a natural and lingering death. The fair Maria (for almighty truth will out) begins in my eyes to look, as that venerable Frenchman Todd would say—D——d stringy. She has been acting very much the part of the dog in the manger—she cannot enjoy her own chastity but seems unwilling to let anybody else do it.

When the news of Paulding's engagement came, he felt that

It is what we must all come to at last. I see you are hankering after it, and I confess I have done so for a long time past. We are however past that period when a man marries suddenly and inconsiderately—we may be longer making a choice, and consulting the convenience and concurrence of every circumstance, but we shall both come to it sooner or later.

Four years later, when he learned that Brevoort himself was not about to put on the yoke, as he had supposed, he changed his tune, rejoicing that "if I am doomed to live an old bachelor, I am anxious to have good company." The respite was short lived, for in 1817 Brevoort did marry:

> I am almost ashamed to say that at first the news had rather the effect of making me feel melancholy than glad. It seemed in a manner to divorce us forever; for marriage is the grave of bachelors' intimacy. . . . However, I don't mean to indulge in lamentations on the occasion. Though this unknown piece of perfection has completely escaped my plan, I bear her no jealousy or ill will; but hope you may long live happily together and that she may prove as constant and faithful to you as I have been.

There is a rather nauseating combination of sexual knowingness and moral snobbery in his 1823-24 reference to a rich woman's "nice fresh daughter" as "one that a man would feel no compunction in begetting children upon." But by 1829: "I begin to grow hardened and shameless in the matter, and have for some time past given up all gallanting, and declared myself an absolute old Bachelor."

Irving's most careful attempt to analyze the reasons why he had remained single was made in the manuscript he gave Mrs. Foster at the time he may have made a bid for Emily:

> You wonder why I am not married. I have shown you why I was not long since—when I had sufficiently recovered from that loss, I became involved in ruin. It was not for a man broken down in the world to drag down any woman to his paltry circumstances, and I was too proud to tolerate the idea of ever mending my circumstances by matrimony. My time has now gone by; and I have growing claims upon my thoughts, and upon my means slender and precarious as they are.

In a sense all this is reasonable enough; on a profounder level, it is rationalizing. Millions of men have married under circumstances far less favorable than Irving's, and if he had really wished to marry, he would have done so too.

He knew well the disadvantages of bachelorhood. "You know I was never intended for a bachelor." Or, at greater length,

Your picture of domestic enjoyment indeed raises my envy. With all my wandering habits, which are the result of circumstances rather than of disposition, I think I was formed for an honest, domestic, uxorious man, and I cannot hear of my old cronies snugly nestled down with good wives and fine children round them, but I feel for the moment desolate and forlorn. Heavens! what a haphazard, schemeless life mine has been, that here I should be, at this time of life, youth slipping away, and scribbling month after month and year after year, far from home, without any means or prospect of entering into matrimony, which I absolutely believe indispensable to the happiness and even comfort of the after part of existence.

In the same vein is his report to Sarah Storrow:

God knows I have no great ideal of bachelorhood and am not one of the fraternity through choice—but providence has some how or other thwarted the warm wishes of my heart and the tendencies of my nature in those earlier seasons of life when tender and happy unions are made; and has protected me in those more advanced periods when matrimonial unions are apt to be unsuited or ungenial.

But perhaps the key word is "protected." "Were I what is called a marrying man," he writes, and I think he was not. He accepted bachelorhood so that he might, in a comparatively innocent way, continue his gallanting, without accepting the responsibilities of marriage. And Ellsworth records after one conversation during their trip together:

Our flour was gone except a little which we kept to thicken soup with and I now found my crackers brought from home quite delicious—I gave Irving a few—"he said *what a fine thing it is to have a wife*" Like other bachelors he thinks well of women and is no *ascetic*, but is too much a man of the world to fasten his affections and confine his favors—He will live and die a bachelor and yet make more conquests among the females than other dry fellows can ever do—He knows what women are —he seasons his food for their palate and while he baits successfully; he delays to set his trap—

Irving was very conscious, too, of the danger of being "hen-pecked." "There are not many as well off in domestic life as I."

The testimony of Irving's creative work supports these impressions. Katrine Van Tassel is "a country coquette" to the hilt. "I profess not to know how women's hearts are wooed and won," says Irving, quite as if he were echoing the mock coyness of Chaucer. "To me they have always been matters of riddle and admiration." In the *Tales of a Traveller* love inevitably declines with age: "Whatever poets may say to the contrary, a man will grow out of love as he grows old; and a pack of fox-hounds may chase out of his heart even the memory of a boarding-school goddess." But better material still may be found in *Bracebridge Hall.* Irving admits the difficulty of playing the role of the old bachelor well, and the grave danger of "a young man of pleasure" cooling down "into an obscene old gentleman." But the emphasis still seems to fall on the perils rather than the pleasures of marriage, even though Irving tones it down, "having no inclination to promote the increase of bachelors." Nothing could be more characteristic of him than his feeling that it is "a thousand pities that the season should ever change, or that young people should ever grow older, or that blossoms should give way to fruit, or that lovers should ever get married."

All in all, I cannot believe that Irving was much more passionate in love than he was in other things. A passionate man either marries or becomes a rake. He did neither. He preferred the bud to the full-blown rose and the ballroom (even the kitchen) to the bedchamber. He enjoyed and sought out the innocence of youth; when he supplemented his contacts with girls with associations with older women, they were ladies of unquestionable respectability who safely belonged to somebody else.

6   HOW THE TREE PRAISED ITS MAKER

Except in his youthful rebellion against his father, Washington Irving brought the same geniality to his religion as he did
to the other experiences of his life. He was not philosophically
minded, and he was never in any danger of the terrors of
that metaphysical speculation which so overwhelmed Melville. Only during his last years at Sunnyside could he possibly
be considered a devout man, and this represented a sweet,
twilight mood in which he responded to the comforts rather
than the challenge of the Christian faith.

On the other hand, Irving's religious indifferentism must not
be exaggerated. He never doubted the fundamental truth of
the Christian religion, and reverence (Shakespeare's "angel of
the world") never deserted him. I have already quoted Geoffrey Crayon at the beginning of *Bracebridge Hall:*

> The more I have considered the study of politics, the more I have
> found it full of perplexity; and I have contented myself, as I have in my
> religion, with the faith in which I was brought up, regulating my own
> conduct by its precepts, but leaving to abler heads the task of making
> converts.

So far as Irving was concerned this was not strictly true, for
his whole religious life was conditioned by his early rebellion
against home influences. Yet, for so determined a rebel he was
a curiously moderate one. The Irving children used to play at
preaching and taking the sacrament, and the boy Washington's
supreme act of defiance against his father's religion involved
neither irreligion nor immorality: he simply sneaked off to the
Episcopal church and surrepetitiously smuggled himself in
among the confirmation candidates. We have already seen that
his anti-evangelicalism may have helped to turn Emily Foster
against him; in any case, she was the only person to whom he
ever tried to explain himself in this aspect:

I feel deeply affected by your appeal to me on the subject of religion; but if this is a subject about which I am averse to enter into discussion it is not that I feel indifferent to it, or am disposed to thrust it from my thoughts. It is one about which I am disposed to *think* rather than talk. I must manage myself with respect to it, and must be left a little to my own management. I have some things to contend with as to the outward forms and ceremonies of religion that have nothing to do with the reason, but which are potent to the feelings. When I was a child religion was forced upon me before I could understand or appreciate it. I was made to swallow it whether I would or not, and that too in its most ungracious forms. I was tasked with it; thwarted with it; wearied with it in a thousand harsh and disagreeable ways; until I was disgusted with all its forms and observances. It was not until I had been my own master for several years that I voluntarily returned to what I had disliked so much in childhood. It required much effort of my reason to divest the outward ceremonies of religion of the dismal associations with which my young imagination had clothed them, and to behold religion itself in its real amiableness and beauty. I have all my life seen so much hypocrisy, cant and worldliness imposed upon mankind under the external forms of religion, that I remain to this day sensitive on the subject. If at any time it is pressed upon me I involuntarily shrink back. I am like a child that has once been thrust under the water and is afterwards shy of approaching the stream even to drink. I must be left to approach of my own accord. But you must not conclude from this that I am heedless and insensible, nor, because I am disinclined to discuss religion as a topic that I neither feel nor appreciate it. I have opinions and principles instilled into me by my early religious education, harsh and ill judged as it was, which still remain with me and influence my conduct. I have high feelings of reverence and veneration, which I believe to be, as far as they go, the religion of the soul, and, although doubtless far short of absolute devotion, are the sparks that in time may kindle up into it; but I know my own weak and imperfect nature and the treatment it requires. I feel that these sparks must be managed and in some measure left to themselves. A little eagerness to heap on fuel might smother them and in seeking too eagerly to blow them into a flame they might be blown out.

You are not to judge of my feelings in respect to religion for what might have been my deportment at Buckhill.[1] I felt out of tune there where you were all wound up to so high a key. I was a little jarred too by the well meant but unskilful and unseasonable handling of some of the professional persons I met there. If I held myself aloof in any degree, it was not from want of proper feeling for religion itself, but from an anxiety to avoid any chance of distaste to the form and manner in which it was administered.

Irving's later attitude toward his brother Ebenezer's piety was quite different from what he had felt toward his father:

I think him one of the most perfect exemplifications of the Christian character that I have ever known [he wrote his sister Mrs. Van Wart]. He has all father's devotion and zeal, without his strictness. Indeed, his piety is of the most genial and cheerful kind, interfering with no natural pleasure or elegant taste, and obtruding itself upon no one's habits, opinions, or pursuits. I wish to God I could feel like him. I envy him that indwelling source of consolation and enjoyment, which appears to have a happier effect than all the maxims of philosophy or the lessons of worldly wisdom.

Though Irving did not become a regular communicant in the Episcopal Church until late in life, he seems always to have thought of himself as belonging to the household of faith. It is "our faith" in his English Christmas papers and "our Saviour" that he finds on Spanish crosses. Clearly he tries to write of Mahomet from a humanist rather than a sectarian point of view, but though he achieves a reasonably sympathetic formulation of the Islamic faith, he views the problem from a Christian vantage-point and attributes the best in Mahomet himself to his having "drunk deep of the living waters of Christianity." In youth he was "solemnly convinced that there is a wise and good Providence that over-rules our destinies and directs everything for the best," and in his age he thanks God for preserving him. It is true that Henry Ellsworth was impressed by the liberality of his religious "sentiments." "He seldom speaks on this subject unless to condemn the strictness of puritanical folks." Finding a French Bible in the camp, "he commenced it and read many pages but made a great merriment about the curious things that took place in those ancient days— and made many strange remarks about courtships and marriages . . . during those old times." I have found no parallel to this, and in any case Ellsworth is not specific enough to make it clear that Irving was really irreverent. In *The Sketch Book* he feels a better man on Sunday in an English country church than anywhere else or at any other time, and in Spain the angelus had exactly the same effect on him: "There is always something pleasingly solemn in this custom, by which, at a melodious signal, every human being throughout the land unites at the same moment in a tribute of thanks to God for the mercies of the day."

On the other hand, Irving says little or nothing about specific Christian doctrines.[2] "If we can in another world meet and recognize the illustrious men who have gone before us," he once declared, "I think I should most wish to see and speak with him whom Halleck happily calls

The world-seeking Genoese,

and 'the myriad-minded Shakespeare.' " This seems rather conjectural and hypothetical, and though there are other passages which show that Irving took immortality pretty much for granted, I doubt that the hope of a life to come meant to him what it meant to Hawthorne, for example.

In Europe he found aids to devotion in the great cathedrals. In 1829 he wrote Madame D'Oubril from Seville:

I have seen the ceremonies and processions of holy week, which are still going on with great spirit, notwithstanding the bad weather. I have seen the ceremonies of Holy Week at Rome, yet find much of novelty and peculiar character in those of Seville. The cathedral of this city is a noble edifice, and, with its Gothic gloom and mystery rivals, in some measure, the classic splendor of St. Peters. The melancholy grandeur of these Gothic temples seems more analogous to the solemn and majestic nature of our faith; and accord wonderfully with the ceremonies of this festival, which celebrates the awful and affecting story of the sufferings and death of our Saviour.

And even though Irving was quite capable of recording, "As I have often leisure time on hand I now and then stroll into the churches to see the faces of the ladies and to see the church ceremonials performed," there is no sense in denying him, in this connection, a decent religious feeling.

The cathedrals of course belonged to what Irving thought of as an alien faith, and, like most American travelers of the nineteenth century, he found mingled attraction and repulsion in it:

There is certainly something very solemn and imposing in the ceremonies of the Roman church. Unwilling as we may be to acknowledge it, it must be confessed that forms and ceremonies and situations and places, have a powerful effect on our feelings in matters of religion. To enter a superb and solemnly constructed edifice

Whose ancient pillars rear their marble heads
To bear aloft its arched and ponderous roof—

gives us a dignified idea of the being to whom it is erected. Its long and lofty aisles and dimly lighted chapels adorned with paintings and statues pointing out some action or attribute of the Deity have an impressive appearance and the gloomy grandeur of the whole inspires us with reverence and respect.

Looking tranquility it strikes an awe!

Then the service itself has such an air of pomp and sublimity that I always feel more filled with an exalted idea of the deity than at any other time. The superb altars magnificently decorated and illuminated, the solemn movements of the priests and the humble prostration of the congregation the full chant of the choir, and the pealing sound of the organ swelling thro the arched aisles and dying away in soft gradations— the incense arising in fragrant columns before the grand altar as if ascending to the "heaven of heavens" a grateful offering of homage has altogether an effect on my feeling irresistibly solemn.

But the overwhelming spiritual suggestiveness of the Catholic service was combined with other things which he could not accept. To his way of thinking, priestcraft and superstition had combined with political despotism to produce a degenerate population in modern Europe, and he shuddered at the thought of young women entering "the living tomb" of the nunnery.

Perhaps I am prejudiced against the Romish religion from having been a witness to the gross ignorance superstition and misery it has intailed upon the inhabitants of these countries—but their grand ceremonies are to me the most pompous farces imaginable—To describe them would but be fatiguing you with descriptions of ostentatious humility and the grossest absurdities. The chief parts of the business that pleased me was the *Miserere* a fine piece of sad, melancholy music representing the passion of our Saviour.

With Napoleon smiling upon the Church in 1804, Irving expected it to regain its ancient hold upon France: "I expect the festivals of that religion will be again reestablished, and such is the fluctuating and capricious character of the French, that it is a chance if they will not be celebrated with more enthusiasm than ever." During the same year he was shocked by a Mass performed in the presence of the soldiers of a French garrison: "The music of the regiment played at different times during the service. At a certain signal of the divine all the soldiery presented arms, knelt down *and prayed*, at another signal. . . . It is something of a novelty to me to see soldiers pray by the word of command."

Anti-Catholic feeling in Irving was not wholly the fruit of his European observations, for his most anti-Catholic book was *A History of New York*. The same feeling appears as late as the *Spanish Papers*, where we find a reference to the Goths, who at one time had been "stout adherents of the Arian doctrines; but after a time they embraced the Catholic faith, which was maintained by the native Spaniards free from many of the gross superstitions of the Church at Rome." And of course it was in the Spanish books that Irving was primarily called upon as a writer to pass judgments on Catholic subjects. Columbus is progress, science, and the future, but the Church and the Council of Salamanca are bigotry and obscurantism. To be sure, even Columbus must be viewed in the frame of his time. His visions and his sense of mission Irving is able to take more or less in his

stride, and even his zeal for a crusade is not "preposterous, considering the period and circumstances in which it was made,
though it strongly illustrates his own enthusiastic and visionary
character." But even the great hero must be condemned when
he sins against nineteenth-century enlightenment: "in recommending the enslaving of the Caribs, Columbus thought he was
obeying the dictates of his conscience, when he was in reality
listening to the incitements of his interest." Ferdinand's sequestration of Jewish property in Spain was "disgraceful," nor are
Irving's sympathies always on the Christian side in the conflict
with the Moors. Even Isabella, much as he admired her, was
"almost bigoted in her piety, and perhaps too much under the
influence of ghostly advisers." Though she did well, she would
have done better without the priests, and insofar as she
wrought ill, it was because she followed their lead.

Catholicism was not the only faith foreign to his own with
which Irving came into contact. Early in life he attended
a Negro camp meeting; he always remembered the impression
it made upon him. Many years later he visited an establishment
of the Herrnhuters, to which he reacted as violently as Dickens
did to the Shakers; "surely we were not gifted with the delightful powers of the imagination thus to combat with them
and quench them." In *Salmagundi* my Aunt Charity had "a
considerable lean toward Methodism, was frequent in her attendance at love feasts, read Whitefield and Wesley, and even
went so far as once to travel the distance of five-and-twenty
miles to be present at a camp-meeting." But my Aunt Charity
is not treated roughly: "She was, indeed, as good a soul as the
Cockloft family ever boasted; a lady of unbounded loving-
kindness, which extended to man, woman, and child; many
of whom she almost killed with good-nature."

With the organized spiritualistic movement of his time Irving did not get far. In 1853 he participated in table-tipping at

Washington, but remained "among the unconverted—quite behind the age." Fulfilling a pact with John Nalder Hall, he tried to establish a contact with him after his death, with no results: "the ghosts," he once said, "have never been kind to me."

It was quite otherwise with popular superstitions. Intellectually Irving is "enlightened" here also, but when it comes to what James Russell Lowell calls "the harmless Jacobitism of sentiment," he is quite ready to indulge himself. "There is something . . . about these rural superstitions," he exclaims in *Bracebridge Hall,* "extremely pleasing to the imagination." "I feel convinced that the true interests and solid happiness of man are promoted by the advancement of truth; yet I cannot but mourn over the pleasant errors which it has trampled down in its progress." Even the gypsies are treated kindly because "they seek to deceive us into bright hopes and expectations. I have always been something of a castle-builder, and have found my liveliest pleasure to arise from the illusions which fancy has cast over commonplace realities."

> With what fondness [he exclaims in another connection], does the strongest mind dwell on the superstitions of the nursery—how do we often endeavor for a moment to conjure up past scenes and deceive ourselves for a moment in the pleasing fallacy of superstition we once felt— I recollect when a child the delicious horror I felt in hearing the stories of fairies ghosts and goblins—what then must have been the feelings of those in ancient times who trusted in them.

The young German who had that shocking adventure in Revolutionary Paris in *Tales of a Traveller* was a student of Swedenborg, and Irving himself refers longingly to

> rosicrucian mysteries, the ideas of sylphs hovering around—How delicious the idea that the souls of those whom we ever loved but who have been severed from us forever, have been suffered to revisit us—to watch over us, to protect us—such an idea calculated to make us more pure in our most secret actions.

Even in his published work Irving could write:

Are there, indeed, such beings? Is this space between us and the Deity filled up by innumerable orders of spiritual beings forming the same gradations between the human soul and divine perfection, that we see prevailing from humanity downwards to the meanest insect? . . .

Even the doctrine of departed spirits returning to visit the scenes and beings which were dear to them during the body's existence, though it has been debased by the absurd superstitions of the vulgar, in itself is awfully solemn and sublime. . . .

. . . Who yet has been able to comprehend and describe the nature of the soul, its connection with the body, or in what part of the frame it is situated? We know merely that it does exist. . . .

It would take away . . . from that loneliness and destitution which we are apt to feel more and more as we get on in our pilgrimage through the wilderness of this world, and find that those who set forward with us, lovingly and cheerily, on the journey, have one by one dropped away from our side. Place the superstition in this light, and I confess I should like to be a believer in it. . . .

There is also a very charming letter to a little girl, Nathalie Richter, written from Seville, April 22, 1829:

You have no idea what strange stories they tell about that neighborhood [a castle and fountain not far from Seville]. Not very far from the fountain there are the ruins of an old Spanish country seat, that was very grand and gay in former times; and used to be a great resort of all the fine people of the country round: but now the walls are all broken, the chambers roofless, and nothing inhabits it but bats and owls and lizards. But sometimes it will appear all lighted up at night, and there will be such a rattling of carriages as if all the gay people of Seville had come forth and were drawing up to its gates. Some of the country people say they have seen great old fashioned carriages drawn by six mules, with coachmen and footmen with cocked hats and old fashioned liveries; and gentlemen and ladies seated outside in ancient Spanish court dresses: but if they venture to speak to these gay people of a sudden the whole vanishes. All night too there will be heard from the old country seat the strumming of guitars and the rattling of castanets, and singing and dancing, and talking and laughing, but in the morning all is again a ruin, with the owls and bats and lizards swarming about it. Not far from this old country seat there is a grove of trees where in former times stood a convent; about the grove there keeps a little grey headed monk not above three feet high; who is sometimes seen walking on the tops of the trees reading in a great big book; but if you attempt to speak to him—bang! he slaps the book shut, and vanishes in a mighty passion.

When it came to the writing of fiction, Irving was obviously free to indulge his fancies as freely as he liked. Some of his best-known stories of the supernatural, including both "The Legend of Sleepy Hollow" and "The Spectre Bridegroom," are pseudo-supernaturalism of the kind that modern *aficionados* much dislike, with all the hair-raising events explained naturally at the end *à la* Mrs. Radcliffe. But in the case of the "Legend" at any rate, Irving is merely following his source, and it is in any event a shallow error to suppose that a writer cannot burlesque a kind of literature which he still thoroughly enjoys. In Irving's work as a whole, he has treated the supernatural in every conceivable way. *Tales of a Traveller* has all kinds of supernaturalism—real, mock, and ambivalent—and the supernaturalism of *The Alhambra* must, one would think, be sufficiently uncompromising to satisfy anybody. He was interested in recording true ghost stories as they were told to him in his journals, though it is true that in some cases an explanation is forthcoming. There is even a good Indian ghost story in *The Crayon Miscellany*.[3]

For the last seven years of his life, Irving was a pillar of Christ Church (Episcopal) at Tarrytown; his name appears as warden, member of the finance committee, and delegate to national diocesan conventions. Grace was said before meat at Sunnyside, and the master attended services whenever his health permitted (including the last Sunday of his life), even when tormented by nerves and asthma. The Reverend James Selden Spencer recorded Irving's having told him "that when he first attended church he felt but little interest in the service, and waited rather impatiently until it was over, and then settled himself down to listen to the sermon. But one Sunday, he said, as he was entering the church, the solemn exhortation to confession was being read, and the thought struck him that he

too had sins to confess." From that time on, the service became
to him "an increasing comfort and delight."

I do not know where the tone of Irving's devotion during his last years is better illustrated than in his enthusiasm
over Dupont's engraving of Ary Scheffer's *Christus Conso-
lator*, which he wept over when he saw it in a Broadway shop
and again when he unwrapped it at Sunnyside, where it may
still be seen. "He thought he had never seen anything so affecting—'there was nothing superior to it in the world of art.'"
Scheffer's is a beautiful Christ, though probably too feminized
for the taste of the twentieth century.

III

THE WORK

No American writer has been more succesful than Irving in
creating a legend. Henry Seidel Canby may pedantically object
that "his Dutch are quite false, except as satire, his Yankees no
more true than Yankee Doodle, his New Amsterdam a land of
Cocaigne." But since it is Irving's version, not the historians',
that survives in the popular imagination, what difference does
this make?

The vitality of legend is ever greater than that of fact, but
it does not always make for the survival of its creator as a
personality. And "Rip Van Winkle" might well have been expected to survive as a fragment of universal human experience
—and of humanity's endless dream of being delivered from the
tyranny of time—without permitting the personality of its author to get in the way. With Irving it has not worked out
that way.

It may well be, however, that contemporary readers do not
quite realize how great Irving's fame was in his own time.
Hotels, steamboats, public squares, wagons, and cigars were
named after him, as well as a spring in Oklahoma and a cliff in
New Jersey. The town of Dearman near his home changed its
name to Irvington. James Grant Wilson found that Niagara
Falls and Washington Irving were the two American topics
that excited the most interest among Britons. H. G. Wells's
father learned about the life of the English landed gentry by

reading Irving. When he died, New York closed down to honor him as if he had been some leading politician; his funeral procession contained 150 carriages, some 500 "citizens and strangers" on foot, and enough clergy to bury a bishop; the floor of the church sank slightly from the unaccustomed weight of those who crowded into it, while nearly 1000 more waited outside.

This, it may be said, is the kind of fame reserved for movie stars and sports celebrities today—and worth nothing. Be that as it may. From one point of view, all fame is worth nothing, but there is no genuine fame that leaves this element out. Moreover, Irving's réclame was not confined to this sort of thing. There was the flood of formal honors with which he was overwhelmed: the academic degrees, the gold medal from the Royal Society of Literature, the memberships in the Real Academia de la Historia, the Smithsonian Institution, and elsewhere. More importantly there was the lofty position accorded him in the literary world. It would be absurd to pretend that no Americans knew in 1859 that their country had already produced greater writers than Irving. It was even widely felt that in some respects his kind of literature was now "old hat" and that leadership had passed on to another "school" of younger and more vital writers. For all that, his was the first name that came to mind in connection with American letters, and he was universally recognized as having exercised considerable influence not only in English-speaking countries but on the Continent as well. In Spain he became a legend. As Melville said, the lilac he planted was a little slip,

And yonder lilac is a tree!

Melville is not the only writer whose homage to Irving may somewhat surprise a less susceptible generation. Look at Dickens's homage. Look at the way Scott accepted him. And what are we to make of Byron, who wept over "The Broken Heart" and called Irving's praise of *Don Juan* "feather in my (fool's) cap"? Crotchety Carlyle's reaction to *Bracebridge Hall* was not very favorable, yet when the news came of Irving's death, he wrote, "It was a dream of mine that we two should be friends!"

But this is history. History too is the extrinsic importance Irving acquired through becoming the first American writer to achieve a lasting vogue both here and abroad, and who initiated the long task of disabusing European readers of their prejudice against American books, "the first Ambassador," as Hellman said, "whom the New World of Letters sent to the Old." But what remains today as living literature?

"Rip Van Winkle," "The Legend of Sleepy Hollow," "The Devil and Tom Walker," "The Stout Gentleman," and a few more tales, plus the best of the essays in *The Sketch Book*, outstandingly those which, like "Westminster Abbey," sound the note of mutability which he never failed to strike with practiced hand—this much all would grant. There would be general agreement, too, upon the beauty of his style; whether or not you are interested in what he is saying, you can hardly fail to be pleased by his way of saying it. Canby, to be sure, finds the style "a patina upon the metal of his thought rather than the flexible soul of the thought itself," but this does not cancel out either the finish or the charm. And, for all his elegance, he was not verbose. "Had I more time," he once wrote Storrow about a manuscript submitted to him, "I should have taken the liberty occasionally of shaking some superfluous words out of the sentences, which weaken them."

The sentence quoted is not a model of construction; it may, therefore, conveniently illustrate the point that Irving's stylistic accomplishments are not wholly, or perhaps even basically, a mechanical matter. His editors tried to take care of his rackety spelling, but they were not able to do anything with the incurable addiction to the dangling modifier which sometimes turned him into an unconscious humorist. "Alas!" he cries in *Columbus*, "while writing that letter, his noble benefactress was a corpse!" And in *Mahomet* faulty syntax even drives the Deity into evil ways: "Having fallen into blind idolatry, God sent a prophet of the name of Saleh, to restore them to the right way." In his journals he writes of Dante's "L'Inferno," and misspells the names of intimate friends.[1]

Jonathan Oldstyle and *Salmagundi* may by common consent be passed over; they presaged a rather extraordinary number of themes afterwards developed, but they are not in themselves extraordinary supporters of reputation. *Knickerbocker's History* is another matter. Probably not many of us today nearly kill ourselves laughing at it as Fanny Kemble said she did, or even make our sides sore as Scott did his. But as a sustained imaginative effort it is still Irving's greatest book:

> I wrote the History of New York [wrote Irving in 1843], with the slightest materials. A complete history had been in course of preparation by Mr.————[2] and only knowing some of the ludicrous points of our city's history I could not imagine what would be found interesting enough for a volume on the subject and thought therefore of getting up Knickerbocker's idea of it. I offended many good families by bringing their names into it in ludicrous points of view and several persons never forgave me for it. It was a youthful folly.

The histories of colonial America supplied him with materials for Books II-VII, but William Smith's *History of New-York from the First Discovery to the Year 1732* (London, 1757) was practically all he had for the founding of New Netherlands and the actual history of the colony, and the only contemporary work he employed was Ebenezer Hazard's *Historical Collections Consisting of State Papers, and Other Authentic Documents . . .* (Philadelphia, 1794). "In order to populate his town of New Amsterdam," writes Robert S.

Osborne, who gives an excellent account of all these matters, "Irving simply took a Dutch community of his own time back into the first decade of the seventeenth century."

The first section (which may be Peter Irving's) contains an amusing digest of all the absurd ideas concerning the origin of the world and of pre-history that were—or were not—ever entertained among men. The author gets good fun out of the elaborate prolegomena employed by historians and their naïve attempts to settle questions on which no decisive evidence exists one way or the other by assuming that the reasonable thing must have happened. There are burlesque etymologies, and while a surprisingly large amount of the documentation is accurate, some of it refers to books which never existed. Probably no other book in American literature has a longer list of sources; [3] of these, Cervantes, Fielding, Sterne, and Swift are the most important.

Part of the fun is Knickerbocker's pretense of complete accuracy:

> But the chief merit on which I value myself, and found my hopes for future regard, is that faithful veracity with which I have compiled this invaluable little work; carefully winnowing away the chaff of hypothesis, and discarding the tares of fable, which are too apt to spring up and choke the seeds of truth and wholesome knowledge. . . . I have scrupulously discarded many a pithy tale and marvelous adventure, whereby the drowsy ear of summer indolence might be enthralled; jealously maintaining that fidelity, gravity, and dignity, which should ever distinguish the historian.

He records the legend that Peter Stuyvesant once shot Beelzebub with a silver bullet, but he will not vouch for the truth of this. "Perish the man who would let fall a drop to discolor the pure stream of history!" There is even one editorial footnote in which D. K. is criticized because, "in his scrupulous search after truth," he is "sometimes too fastidious in regard to facts which border a little on the marvelous."

Yet it is also true that D. K. claims to be an artist-historian. He admits that he introduced a storm into one of his chapters "to give a little bustle and life to this tranquil part of my work, and to keep my drowsy readers from falling asleep—and partly to serve as an overture to the tempestuous times which are about to assail the pacific province of Nieuw-Nederlandts." And while he cannot save the life of a favorite hero, or absolutely contradict the event of a battle, as a romancer might do, he can occasionally permit one whom he admires to "bestow on his enemy a sturdy back stroke sufficient to fell a giant; though, in honest truth, he may never have done any thing of the kind."

Knickerbocker's History is not a completely accurate book; neither Irving nor anybody else could have made it that with the materials available—but it is much more accurate than we have a right to require of a burlesque history. He cuts the number of Dutch governors down to three, making Wouter Van Twiller the third instead of the fifth; then in Book V he carelessly speaks of him as having surpassed "all who preceded him." He ridicules the Dutch for their eating, drinking, and smoking; for their phlegmatic temperament and their passion for scrubbing. But he does not save all his shafts for them— their Swedish and Yankee neighbors are, on occasion, handled quite as roughly—and it would be an insensitive reader indeed who should fail to recognize that in his pages Peter Stuyvesant, though at times a figure of fun, is also an heroic figure and almost a tragic one.[4]

It is not required of the author of a burlesque that he should be altogether consistent. Irving makes fun of Peter Stuyvesant for his fire-eating tendencies, but he also ridicules the pacifism of the second governor William Kieft, whom he describes with one eye on Thomas Jefferson. Irving's knowledge of history was not great, but he was quite sophisticated enough in his attitude toward it. He knew that complete accuracy is not possible in historical writing, and that history and fiction cannot be completely separated from each other; a good many contemporary conflicts of opinion concerning the nature of history are reflected in his pages. Diedrich Knickerbocker "explores the nature of history as *Don Quixote* had explored the nature of fiction, revealing the complexity of the problem without finally solving it," and a good many of the jokes are on the reader.[5]

As we have already seen, the common view that Irving was neo-classical up to *The Sketch Book* and romantic thereafter is much too simple to be maintained; it is true, however, that, once having begun to do his writing in a foreign land, he was less encouraged to develop that side of his talent which inclined him toward social and political satire. Publishing as he did on both sides of the Atlantic, he must appeal to two reading publics. When he wrote down what he observed in English villages, for example, he was as realistic as he could have been in America; he "added greatly to . . . [his] stock of knowledge, by noting down . . . habits and customs." Had he been merely a lover of fine scenery, he tells us, there would have been no need to leave his own country. "But Europe held forth the charms of stories and poetical associations."

Realism and romanticism can be much more easily separated in theory than in practice; there cannot have been many works of literature that were wholly one or the other. It is quite natural that there should be differences of opinion about these matters in Irving. Thus McDermott finds him reducing even the people he knew on his Western journey to literary types— "Irving is not a traveler reporting what he sees; he is ever the self-conscious literary man, the feature-story writer who, by the ready use of his imagination, makes a little fact go a long way"—while Nathalia Wright is so much impressed by his tendency to tie himself down to actual localities, even in such highly romantic stories as the banditti yarns in *Tales of a Traveller*, that she is willing to credit him with beginning a tradition in the American novel about Italy, "the chief characteristic of which, in contrast to the Gothic tradition, was an essential realism of background." Nobody can doubt that *The Sketch Book* has its romantic elements, but we can think of it as all romantic only by concentrating wholly upon "Rip Van Winkle," "The Legend of Sleepy Hollow," and "The Spectre Bridegroom" and ignoring everything else.[6]

All three of these stories have been derived from German sources, but the first two—the great ones—have been ingeniously transplanted to the Hudson River country. "When I first wrote the Legend of Rip Van Winkle," so Irving remembered it in 1843, "my thoughts had been for some time turned towards giving a color of romance and tradition to interesting points of our national scenery which is so generally deficient in our country." He succeeded so well that translators have always had trouble with the story.[7]

Irving's "Rip Van Winkle" is four times the length of Otmar's "Peter Klaus." He changes Otmar's knights to the ghosts of Henrik Hudson and his crew; he localizes; he characterizes Rip in his own manner, builds up his domestic background, and tells what happened after his return. If this is not a legitimate way to create literature, then Chaucer and Shakespeare will have to be cast into the outer darkness. As Longfellow once remarked, a modern writer cannot strike a spade into Parnassus anywhere without disturbing the bones of a dead poet.[8]

The sleep-motive in "Rip Van Winkle" has roots which run very deep in world literature. There is the classical story about Epimenides, who retired into a cave to escape the heat of the day when he should have been watching his flock, and slept

there for fifty-seven years.[9] Otmar himself tells of Frederick
Barbarossa, who sleeps in the Kyffhäuser, from which he will
return to succor his people in their need. Once a pair of lovers
visited the Emperor to borrow crockery for their wedding
feast, but when they got home again they found they had been
away 200 years.

Scott told Irving the story of Thomas Rhymer, who was
carried off by the Fairy Queen, and at Inverness he may have
seen the Hill of the Fairies and heard the story of the two
fiddlers of Strathspey, who were lured into this hill and de-
tained for 100 years. They recognized nothing and were recognized by nobody upon their emergence, and they crumbled to
dust when the Scriptures were read in church.[10]

After the three stories, the part of *The Sketch Book* that
is most read today comprises the several papers describing
English Christmas celebrations. It should be remembered that
this is pre-*Christmas Carol* material, though of course Addison had already described Sir Roger de Coverley's Christmas
in *The Spectator*. But there are twenty-six papers altogether
in *The Sketch Book* which concern English themes, and all but
six of them have their scene outside of London. Irving catches
the atmosphere of English rural life and the English Sunday as
well as he catches the Christmas spirit. There is an essay about
King James I of Scotland, the author of *The King's Quair*, and
there are two papers about Shakespeare, one describing a visit
to Stratford, and the other on Falstaff and the Boar's Head
Tavern. There is also an essay on "The Mutability of Literature," which is developed fancifully and imaginatively. The
same melancholy which the thought of time's triumph over
everything that is mortal calls forth here appears again in the
famous paper on "Westminster Abbey": "The coffin of Edward the Confessor has been broken open, and his remains
despoiled of their funeral ornaments; the sceptre has been

stolen from the hand of the imperious Elizabeth, and the effigy of Henry the Fifth is headless." And I suppose no reader of *The Sketch Book* ever forgets the passage in which Irving muses over the neighboring tombs of "the haughty Elizabeth" and "her victim, the lovely and unfortunate Mary." Despite his penchant for the picturesque, Irving's English papers are not mere antiquarianism: he was also seeking to understand the British character, as the essay on "John Bull" shows. "The Wife," "The Widow and Her Son," and "The Pride of the Village" have too much eighteenth-century sentimentalism to interest modern readers very deeply, but they are all based on realistic, not legendary, materials, and the incidents on which "The Wife" rests involved two of Irving's friends.

Of *Bracebridge Hall* Osborne has remarked that as Irving "had built *A History of New York* out of parts of *Salmagundi*, so he built *Bracebridge Hall* out of parts of *The Sketch Book*." But Osborne knows better than anybody else, and has clearly demonstrated, that *Bracebridge Hall* itself also descends not only from *Salmagundi* but even from *Jonathan Oldstyle*. Except for the four stories included (Irving finds a place for them on the pretext that they were told at the Hall), the book is considerably more unified than its predecessor. It is an attractive picture of English rural life, viewed from the upper-class standpoint, but the author does not neglect rural superstitions and May Day customs; this side of the volume is further developed through the device of bringing in a band of gypsies. It is clear that the old folk beliefs appealed to Irving by reason of their picturesqueness, and that he would like to accept them, but his usual balance and common sense do not desert him; he knows, for example, that in their time the May Day games were considerably less innocent than those who cherish them merely because they are old would like to believe.

As for the stories: "The Stout Gentleman" contains one of

the most artful uses of anti-climax in literature. "Dolph Hey-liger," a story of old New York, involves a doctor's idle apprentice and a search for buried treasure, and is one of the best of Irving's longer tales. "The Student of Salamanca" is pleasant enough reading about love, alchemy, intrigue, and the Inquisition.[11] "Annette Delarbre," the least substantial of the four, is another nineteenth-century tale about the tender-hearted maiden who could not distinguish between fidelity and fixation. Among them all, only *Evangeline* survives.

Irving himself thought *Tales of a Traveller* his best book, and his judgment was not absurd, for this was the only volume he had devoted entirely to fiction, and he was developing a new theory of narrative form[12] which might have come to more than it did if further experiments had not been discouraged by the savage press which the book received. Poe, Long-fellow, and Stevenson all loved it; perhaps Irving might find comfort here against not only the insensitiveness of contemporary reviewers but even the deplorably unimaginative tendency of many modern writers to echo them. It is true of course that the book lacks unity—but then it is called *Tales of a Traveller*—being divided into four parts: "Strange Stories by a Nervous Gentleman," "Buckthorne and His Friends," "The Italian Banditti," and "The Money-Diggers."

I do not understand Williams's judgment that "both the ghost stories and the robber tales designed for a public in love with German romantics and Gothic prestidigitators, are obsolete, as dead as the fashions which begot them." Most of the literature of the past is, in that sense, as dead as the fashions which begot it, but surely it ought to be possible for a scholar to read it and judge it in the light of the standards which prevailed when it was written. Williams continues: "we yawn over the machinery of haunted châteaux, sinister storms, mysterious footsteps, and hidden panels. Spirits sigh in the darkness; portraits wink; furniture dances; and brooding, sensitive heroes woo melancholy maidens—in vain."

There is no law against yawning, but it can hardly take the place of literary evaluation, and if we cannot enjoy these things, the loss is ours, for it means that one whole large area of Romantic literature is closed to us. "The Adventure of My Uncle" and "The Adventure of My Aunt," though "primitives" among ghost stories, do not, I think, lack the supernatural thrill, and of course it is not fair to judge any such tale by the standards which have evolved through the intensive development to which this type of literature has been subjected since Irving's time. But I do not see how anybody can snap his fingers at "The Bold Dragoon," whose merit was recognized by Anne Carroll Moore, when she gave it the place of honor in her collection, *The Bold Dragoon and Other Ghostly Tales*, by Washington Irving, which was delightfully illustrated by James Daugherty, and published by Alfred A. Knopf, in "New Amsterdam," as the title-page has it, in 1930. And nobody has ever been able to find a source for the horrible French Revolutionary tale, "Adventure of the German Student," which very much resembles one of Marjorie Bowen's supernatural stories. Here we have a dream which anticipates experience, quite in the modern manner, and an ending in a madhouse, which suggests the great German film, *The Cabinet of Dr. Caligari*. And here at least Irving's refusal to commit himself has less in common with the silly, shallow rationalism of Mrs. Radcliffe than with Hawthorne's skillful, subtle, and deliberate ambiguity.

"Buckthorne and His Friends," Irving's longest and most varied narrative, has perhaps been sufficiently discussed elsewhere in this volume. "The Italian Banditti" is made up of conventional romantic materials of the kind one might expect to encounter under that title, not particularly distinctive perhaps but thoroughly enjoyable; the plots seem to be Irving's own. "The Money Diggers" is American material again, centered on the ideas of digging for pirate gold or gaining wealth through diabolical means. "The Devil and Tom Walker" is, of course, the finest narrative in this part of the book—and in the book in general—but "Wolfert Webber; or Golden Dreams" is still well worth reading.

The Alhambra, as has already been said, combines *Arabian Nights* material, in the stories told, with honest, straightforward description of the place as it was in Irving's time, and of the people he encountered there. As he himself says, "Every thing in the work relating to myself and the actual inhabitants of the Alhambra is unexaggerated fact; it was only in the legends that I indulged in *romancing*." As romancing it was very good.

The rest of Irving's work was repetition and addenda, or else it was factual and historical writing. Though not widely or intensively read today, it still commands considerable respect.

That Irving was not a great historian goes without saying. He read enormously, and great libraries thrilled him as a voluptuary might be thrilled by a houris' paradise; he was even capable of hard, grueling work when necessary, but basically he did not malign himself when he wrote:

I have wandered through different countries, and witnessed many of the shifting scenes of life. I cannot say that I have studied them with the eye of a philosopher; but rather with the sauntering gaze with which humble lovers of the picturesque stroll from the window of one printshop to another; caught sometimes by the delineations of beauty, sometimes by the distortions of caricature, and sometimes by the loveliness of landscape.

"That work . . . was written so rapidly," he writes cavalierly of his life of Goldsmith, "with the printer's devil at my heels that I should not be surprised if many errors were detected in it. I had no time to refer to authorities that were not immediately at hand." He refused to "join in the severe censures that have been passed upon Sparks for the verbal corrections and alterations he has permitted himself to make even in some of Washington's letters." He even told Ik Marvel that he had no system—"you must go to Bancroft for that: I have, it is true, my little budget of notes—some tied one way, some another, and which, when I need, I think I come upon in my pigeon-holes by a sort of instinct. That is all there is to it."

"He had no taste for research," writes one distinguished modern student of historiography, "and confronted with the graver tasks of the historian he fails. In the lighter sphere of anecdote and romance he is supreme." [13] Alexander H. Everett anticipated this view in Irving's own time when he credited him with "the merit of plain and elegant narrative," but added that he did not "aspire to the higher palm of just and deep thought in the investigation of causes and effects, that constitutes the distinction of the real historian." Irving's burlesque of scholarship and the scholarly method in "The Art of Book-Making" and "The Boar's Head Tavern, Eastcheap" is very interesting in view of his own mining and sapping for books yet to come. He well knew that even when he wrote history he functioned as a man of letters. In 1837 it was suggested to him that he write a biography of Robert Fulton. Irving admitted that the subject was a good one,

but, somehow or other, I do not feel in the vein to undertake it; and unless a thing "jumps with my humour" I can make nothing of it—I wish, however, you could suggest some task to fill up intervals between such moods—the editing of any standard author or authors, or any other of those tasks which require judgment, taste and literary research, rather than fancy or invention. I need at this moment all the pecuniary aid that my pen can command.

It is interesting to note that the plan he conceived for his work on the conquest of Mexico was wider than the one Prescott finally used.[14] And Prescott himself, in his enthusiastic article about *The Conquest of Granada*, though clearly understanding and stating everything that Irving could not or would not do, also realized and paid tribute to his special gifts. "But all these particulars, however pertinent to philosophical history, would have been entirely out of keeping in Mr. Irving's, and might have produced a disagreeable discordance in the general harmony of his plan."

After *Knickerbocker*, *Granada* was the work most imaginatively handled. There he had exempted himself from the demands of strict fidelity by creating a burlesque; here he attributed the work to a mythical Fray Antonio Agapida; if the good friar is bigoted or credulous, Washington Irving's withers are unwrung. He recognized the work as "something of an experiment, and all experiments in literature or in anything else are doubtful." And he tells Colonel Aspinwall, "I have made a work out of the old chronicles, embellished as much as I am able, by the imagination, and adapted to the romantic taste of the day. Something that was to be between a history and a romance." The interesting thing is that both here and in *Knickerbocker* he was much more modest in taking advantage of the opportunities he had made for himself than he might have been expected to be. Substantially he was quite just [15] when he wrote Prince Dolgorouki of the *Granada*:

> I have introduced nothing that is not founded on historical authority, but I have used a little freedom of pencil in the coloring, grouping, &c— and have brought out characters and incidents in stronger relief than they are to be met with in the old histories. . . . I really believe the work will contain a fuller and more characteristic amount of that remarkable war than is to be found elsewhere.

It is quite inadequate, then, to attempt to differentiate between Irving and more "serious" historians by decribing his work as "narrative history." As Hedges says, it is "in a literary class almost by itself—which means, practically, it is in no class." Yet it shows the effect of most of the thinking of its time in the world of literary and historical theory. Irving was not uninterested in ideas or in generalizations, and he certainly was not less inclined than other historians to discern pattern in history or to see his characters as types or embodiments of forces larger than themselves.

Technically most of Irving's works in this field were biography rather than history. Because it lay farthest out of his range the *Mahomet* is the thinnest of these; the richest, in a sense, is the Goldsmith, not because Irving did independent research on the subject but rather because his own temperamental affinity for Goldsmith enabled him to make literature out of what John Forster and others had discovered. But the real tests of his skill and his methods came with the prodigious works on Columbus and George Washington.

The *Washington* began when the President placed his hand in blessing upon a six-year-old's brow. *The Life and Voyages of Columbus* may be said to have begun when that same boy pored over the geographical narratives in *The World Displayed:* "The early volumes treated of the voyages of Columbus and the conquests of Mexico and Peru. They were more delightful to me than a fairy tale, and the plates by which they were illustrated are indelibly stamped on my recollections."

As we have seen, the work grew out of—or took the place of—his plan to translate Navarrete's collection of documents, and though Irving thought it unnecessary to check Navarrete's work—"wherever I found a document published by him, I was sure of its correctness, and did not trouble myself to examine the original"—he would have resented the implication that he had relied entirely upon the Spaniard. As he described his plan in prospect to T. W. Storrow in 1826:

I shall form my narrative from a careful comparison and collation of the works of Las Casas and Columbus' son Ferdinando, both founded on Columbus' Journal—and shall at the same time make use of Oviedo, who lived in Columbus' time and in fact all the old Spanish writers. I have various works relative to the subject in Italian, French, &c. I am in fact surrounded by works of the kind. I shall endeavor to make it the most complete and authentic account of Columbus and his voyages extant and, by diligent investigation of the materials around me, to settle various points in dispute. It will require great attention and study & hard work, but I feel stimulated to it, and encouraged by the singular facilities which are thrown in my way. I want to do something that I must "take off my coat to." . . . My brother will be of much assistance to me in my researches and in the examination and collation of facts and dates, about which I mean to be scrupulously attentive and accurate, as I know I shall be expected to be careless in such particulars and to be apt to indulge in the imagination. I mean to look into every thing myself, to make myself master of my subject and to endeavor to produce a work which shall bear examination as to candor and authenticity.

When he had finished, it seemed to him that he had been faithful to this ideal:

I have woven into my work many curious particulars not hitherto known concerning Columbus, and I think I have thrown light upon some parts of his character which have not been brought out by his former biographers. I have labored hard to make the work complete and accurate as to all the information extant relative to the subject, which I have sought to execute in such a manner as would render it agreeable to the general reader.

Impartial judges have sometimes spoken nearly as sympathetically. Thus Bancroft gave *Columbus* "all kinds of merit— research, critical judgment, interest in the narrative, picturesque description and golden style." Nor is the distinguished Menèndez y Pelayo the only Spanish authority who has praised it warmly. Henry Harisse called it "a history written with judgment and impartiality, which leaves far behind it all descriptions of the discovery of the New World published before or since." Edward G. Bourne thought well of it, and though John Fiske charged and proved that Irving was sometimes guilty of misplaced eulogy and of attributing modern knowledge to the men of the past, he still felt respect and a warm regard for the work. "We have learned a great deal more about Columbus than Irving knew," writes Edward H. O'Neill, "but Irving has seldom been found wrong."

Yet, Irving's *Columbus* was less an independent piece of investigation than he claimed—and probably believed. He simply did not have the time or the knowledge or the training to make such an investigation; he probably did not even have the knowledge he would have needed to state the problem fairly. In assuming that Navarrete did not need his attestation, he was quite correct, and he could have added nothing substantial to Navarrete's labors if he had tried. His final claim must rest upon his having turned the story of Columbus into a work of art.

McCarter finds Irving's Columbus "the romantic hero of the nineteenth-century adventure-novel"; he cannot, he thinks, have been very unfamiliar to readers of Scott. Hedges is substantially in accord when he declares that, in *Columbus* and its successors, Irving "was to give almost free rein to the impulse to view history aesthetically, to organize it into a series of re-enactments of archetypal mythic dramas."

Such statements may be read disparagingly, but it is not necessary to read them thus. As Theodore Roosevelt perceived and proclaimed, imagination does not tend to distortion in the writing of history unless it is a distorted imagination. All historians select materials and make assumptions, and though many of Irving's superiors as research workers have certainly viewed history less aesthetically than he did, this does not in itself prove that they viewed it more accurately. Irving's uncritical state of mind has been well indicated by Hedges, as well as the fundamental reasonableness of his bent. He accepts what he has been told except when he runs into conflicts; then he tries to mediate between conflicting evidences, striking a balance between them, and generally assuming that the truth lies somewhere near that middle of the road in which his feet felt most at home. But though he "sins against literal accuracy," he often needs only to insert a "probably" or two to satisfy most historians, and though his annotation is somewhat sloppy, most of it is probably substantially accurate. In the end, Hedges defends *Columbus* against most of Stanley Williams's criticisms. It "does exactly what it was supposed to—utilizes the materials Navarrete had published and the manuscript histories in Rich's library. Thus it was, when it appeared, new and original, at least in one sense." Irving dramatized and highlighted and interpreted his hero on his own terms, and communicated his essence to the reader in a style which was the unmistakable expression of the writer's own personality. He expressed his own sense of values through him. His work might be done again and done better, but until another Washington Irving should be born into the world, nobody else could do what he had done. He had taken one of the momentous events of human history into the cosmos of his own mind and spirit.

As early as 1825 Archibald Constable asked Irving to write a life of Washington. On August 19 Irving wrote Constable from Paris and declined: "After the various works . . . which have appeared on the subject it would be very difficult to treat it anew in a manner to challenge public attention or to satisfy public expectation if much excited." He also objected that "it would require a great deal of reading and research, and that too of a troublesome and irksome kind among public documents and state papers; for Washington's life was more important as a Statesman than as a General." And he concluded: "I feel myself incapable of executing my idea of the task. It is one that I dare not attempt lightly. I stand in too great awe of it."

Ultimately, it would seem, the awe was overcome, and in his Preface to his first volume he outlined his formula for success:

My work is founded on the correspondence of Washington, which, in fact, affords the amplest and surest groundwork for his biography. This I have consulted as it exists in manuscript in the archives of the Department of State, to which I have had full and frequent access. I have also made frequent use of "Washington's Writings," as published by Mr. Sparks; a careful collation of many of them with the originals having convinced me of the general correctness of the collection, and of the safety with which it may be relied upon for historical purposes; and I am happy to bear this testimony to the essential accuracy of one whom I consider among the greatest benefactors to our national literature; and to whose writings and researches I acknowledge myself largely indebted throughout my work.

He tells us specifically where he got his information about Major André, Nelly Custis, and that tragic bride of darkness, Jane McCrea. There is a letter to Benjamin Silliman accepting the latter's offer to let him see Jonathan Trumbull's diary and offering to "defray the expense of having a copy made of it." On the other hand, when F. C. Yarnell wrote, offering to lend him a narrative of André's capture, he replied (after more than three months' silence), that he "had already disposed of the subject" and "had diligently consulted every authority I could find relating to it. I have endeavored to treat the matter as candidly and dispassionately as possible; which is not a very easy task where there is so much to touch and interest the feelings."

Irving returned to his use of Washington's own writings in an explanatory note at the end of Volume IV—"for never did man leave a more truthful mirror of his heart and mind, and a more thorough exponent of his conduct, than he has left in his copious correspondence"—and he also apologized for his inclusion of even those Revolutionary War campaigns in which Washington did not participate—"for his spirit pervaded and directed the whole, and a general knowledge of the whole is

necessary to appreciate the sagacity, forecast, enduring forti-
tude, and comprehensive wisdom with which he conducted it."
In a private letter of 1856, he explained himself more fully to
Henry T. Tuckerman:

You have discerned what I aimed at, "the careful avoidance of rhetoric,
the calm, patient and faithful narrative of facts." My great labor has
been to arrange these facts in the most lucid order and place them in the
most favorable light; and without exaggeration or embellishment; trust-
ing to their own characteristic value for effect. Rhetoric does very well
under the saddle but is not to be trusted in harness; being apt to pull
facts out of place or upset them. My horse *Gentleman Dick* was very
rhetorical and sheered off finely, but he was apt to run away with me
and came near breaking my neck.

I have availed myself of the license of biography to step down occasionally from the elevated walk of history and relate familiar things in a
familiar way; seeking to show the prevalent patterns, and feelings and
humors of the day, and even to depict the heroes of Seventy Six as they
really were, men in cocked hats, regimental coats and breeches; and not
classic warriors in shining armor and flowing mantles with brows bound
with laurel and truncheons in their hands.

But he also told F. S. Cozzens that he

had a great deal of trouble to keep the different parts together, giving
a little touch here and a little touch there, so that one part should not
lag behind the other nor one part be more conspicuous than the other.
I felt like old Lablache when he was performing in a rehearsal of his
orchestra . . . bringing out a violin here, a clarinet there, now suppress-
ing a trombone, now calling upon the flutes, and every now and then
bringing out the big bass drum. So I have to keep my different instruments in play, not too low in one passage nor too loud in another, and
now and then bringing in the great bass drum.

The orchestral comparison is interesting, and it shows that
Irving was as much the artist-historian when he was Irving as
when he was Diedrich Knickerbocker. But he goes on to add
that he wanted a style simple enough for a child to read. "I
want the action to shine through the style. No style, indeed; no
encumbrance of ornament. . . ."

Irving also said that he had been collecting material for
Washington for twenty years before he wrote the work, and
that to write it seemed a kind of duty. "Yet his character suggested the idea of a statue; however you might admire it, you
could not embrace it. But as I became better acquainted with
the real life of the man, his constant untiring benevolence, I
loved him more and more." This was precisely what Prescott
praised his biography for: "You have done with Washington
just as I thought you would, and, instead of a cold, marble
statue of a demigod, you have made him a being of flesh and
blood, like ourselves—one with whom we can have sympathy."
Later he added generously that he himself had never understood Washington's character until Irving had written about
him. Bancroft, too, was generous: "The narrative is beautifully
told, in your own happy diction and style, felicitous always;
never redundant; graceful and elegant."

Modern detractors of Irving, like modern detractors of
Longfellow, have generally been distressed over the fact that
he was neither Herman Melville nor Ernest Hemingway. This
much is undeniable, but why it should occasion so much distress is not quite clear. That he was a "genteel" writer admits
of no doubt, but in his time "genteel" was not a dirty word.
When he was seventy-five years old, he wrote a letter to a
young relative not yet out of his teens, in which he described
the personal qualities he admired:

> I have always valued in you what I considered to be an honorable
> nature; a conscientiousness in regard to duties; an open truthfulness; an
> absence of all low propensities and sensual indulgences; a reverence for
> sacred things; a respect for others; a freedom from selfishness, and a
> prompt decision to oblige; and, with all these, a gayety of spirit, flowing,
> I believe, from an uncorrupted heart, that gladdens everything around
> you.

His own possession of all these qualities was far above the average. And he valued their manifestation of themselves in books as well as in men.

It was not his function either to scale the heights or sound the depths of life; neither did he ever pretend to be able to do so. Though he was never so indifferent to either ideas or social evils as his critics would have us believe, he consistently inhabited a middle region which he surveyed and described with a winning, companionable charm. If you must have death in the afternoon and an orgy at night, he has nothing for you. And if life is flat and meaningless to you except in moments of rare spiritual ecstasy, he has nothing for you either. Between the heights and the depths, however, there still lies a very wide and attractive area. The reading public which dwells there may be smug, and it may be dull, but it does not need to be kicked every few minutes to stay awake, and it is possible that the tides of life run higher and stronger here than in many other publics, and that it will survive longer. This is the area that Irving inhabits, and whatever other shortcomings it may have, there can be no question that it embraces a good deal of what we generally mean to indicate when we speak of civilization.

NOTES

The following abbreviations are employed in this section and in the following bibliography:

ABC	American Book Company
AL	*American Literature*
BB	Bibliophile Society, Boston
BNYPL	*Bulletin of the New York Public Library*
ColUP	Columbia University Press
D	Doubleday & Company, Inc. (and their predecessors)
GC	Grolier Club
H	Harper & Brothers
HaM	*Harper's Magazine*
HB	Harcourt, Brace and Company
HM	Houghton Mifflin Company
Ht	Henry Holt & Company
HUP	Harvard University Press
I	Irving
JEGP	*Journal of English and Germanic Philology*
M	The Macmillan Company
MLN	*Modern Language Notes*
MLQ	*Modern Language Quarterly*
MP	*Modern Philology*
NYPL	New York Public Library
Okla	University of Oklahoma Press
OUP	Oxford University Press
P	G. P. Putnam's Sons
PMLA	*Publications of the Modern Language Association*
S	Charles Scribner's Sons
SP	*Studies in Philology*
SR	*Sewanee Review*
STW	Stanley T. Williams
WI	Washington Irving
YR	*Yale Review*
YULG	*Yale University Library Gazette*
YUP	Yale University Press

1 For Irving's association with Cabell, see Richard Beale Davis, "Washington Irving and Joseph C. Cabell," *English Studies in Honor of James Southall Wilson*, published as *University of Virginia Studies*, V (1941), 7-22. The volume is mislabeled IV.

2 See Stanley T. Williams, "Washington Irving's First Stay in Paris," *AL*, II (1930), 15-20.

3 The most elaborate study of both the *Letters of Jonathan Oldstyle* and *Salmagundi* is in Robert Stevens Osborne's North Carolina dissertation, "A Study of Washington Irving's Development as a Man of Letters to 1825." In the Jeremy Cockloft series, Osborne found "the original suggestions for *A History of New York* and also Irving's first humorous writings concerning the early Dutch settlers." Cockloft Hall marks the beginning of Irving's description of rural scenery, and much of *The Sketch Book* and *Bracebridge Hall* grew out of the Cockloft family. More interesting still is the emergence in "The Little Man in Black" of essentially the same pattern Irving was to employ in later, more famous tales: "A man of peculiar character is introduced into a society in which superstition plays a prominent part. Supernatural forces, real or imagined, motivate the action to bring about the major incident." Osborne's pp. 120-27 comprise the fullest discussion we have of the authorship of the individual *Salmagundi* papers, incorporating earlier studies; see also Williams's notes, *The Life of Washington Irving*, II, 263-73.

4 *The Picture of New-York; or, The Traveller's Guide through the Commercial Metropolis of the United States, By a Gentleman Residing in this City* (1807). Writers on Irving go on parroting one another to the effect that Mitchill's was an intolerably pretentious work, but those who have had an opportunity to examine the very rare volume can find nothing in it that could possibly have been burlesqued. See H. M. Lydenberg, "Irving's Knickerbocker and Some of Its Sources," *BNYPL*, LVI (1952), 544-53, 596-619. For Irving's services to the development of the Santa Claus legend in *A History of New York* see also Charles W. Jones, "Knickerbocker's Santa Claus," *The New-York Historical Society Quarterly Bulletin*, XXXVIII (1954), 357-83.

5 Williams, *The Spanish Background of American Literature* (YUP, 1955), II, 38, 295. Part III, Chapter 1 of this work is devoted to Irving.

6 See F. A. Sampson, "Washington Irving Travels in Missouri and the South," *Missouri Historical Review*, V (1910), 15-33.

7 Irving; Charles Joseph Latrobe; and Albert-Alexandre Pourtalès, Comte de Pourtalès.

8 Henry Leavitt Ellsworth, of Hartford. His appointment had grown out of the difficulties which developed after the Indian Removal Bill of 1830, especially the conflicts between Cherokees and Creeks. For his account of the journey, see *Washington Irving on the Prairie, or A Narrative of a Tour of the Southwest in the Year 1832*, ed. S. T. Williams and Barbara D. Simison (ABC, 1938)

9 The official account of *Washington Irving and Sunnyside*, now one of John D. Rockefeller, Jr.'s restorations, is in a work of that title by its director, Harold Dean Cater, originally published in *New York History*, XXXVIII (1957), 123-66, now reprinted in pamphlet form, by Sleepy Hollow Restorations, 1957. See, further, S. T. Williams, "Sunnyside, The Home of Our First Man of Letters," *House and Garden*, LXXXIV, July, 1948, pp. 51-5, 106, and especially the abundant Sunnyside material in October 1947 number of *American Collector* (Vol. XIV), which has been reprinted as a special edition and is available at Sunnyside.

10 The fullest account of Irving's life in Spain is in Claude G. Bowers, *The Spanish Adventures of Washington Irving* (HM, 1940), a work somewhat oddly neglected by students of Irving.

II THE MAN

1 HOW THE TREE WAS INCLINED

1 The only serious attempt to diagnose the precise nature of this malady was made by Francis Prescott Smith ("Washington Irving and France," p. 40), who collected the data given in various letters and journals and placed them before "two well-informed physicians" who returned a verdict of erythema multiforme. Smith describes this disease as "an ailment of toxic and septic origin with both cutaneous and visceral symptoms of some severity,—a disease which has often been confused with arthritis or articular rheumatism." Though chronic, it is subject to remissions. Not a common affliction, "it is known to occur in people of nervous or neurotic character." As Smith rightly observes, "this fact bears further testimony to what is implicit in Irving's journals,—that in spite of an outwardly phlegmatic demeanor, his was essentially a nervous nature."

2 In the last volume of his biography, and in more detail in his unpublished journal, Feb. 28-Nov. 30, 1859, in the Berg Collection. See also the published letter of Dr. J. C. Peters, Dec. 2, 1859, of which a copy is preserved in the Berg Collection.

3 In a letter from Madrid, Dec. 20, 1843 (Yale), he describes the changes he has made in his living quarters and furnishes a diagram.

1   Irving's feeling for—and use of—nature is studied formally and with Germanic thoroughness by Rudolf Grosskunz, *Die Natur in den Werken und Briefen des amerikanischen Schriftstellers Washington Irving* (Pöschel und Trepte, 1902), under such headings as "Die Jahreszeiten," "Die Tageszeiten," "Die Nacht," "Das Gewitter," "Der Himmel, Sonne und Mond," etc.

2   "A detailed analysis of the influence of graphic art on literary art is impossible, but there can be no doubt that after 1818 Irving's powers of observation became more and more those of the graphic artist. *Alhambra* is in many places little more than set descriptions; his 'Western Journal' is filled with word pictures which show his interest in the visual scene." Osborne, p. 277.

3   Pochmann, "Irving's German Tour," etc., calls his list of plays and operas seen and heard "unequalled in the record of any other American man of letters."

4   H. Earle Johnson, "Young American Abroad," *Musical Quarterly*, XLIV (1958), 65-75.

5   In 1805, in Italy, Irving first heard those "poor devils," the *castrati*. In spite of his preconceived horror, he found himself "captivated by their singing."

6   Irving was no more systematic in collecting books than he was in anything else, and once, when he ran out of shelf space at Sunnyside, he allowed Putnam to weed out some of the lumber, though he did pass on the exclusions afterwards and put some of them back. Nevertheless he was a true lover of books, taking almost as much physical pleasure in their format as intellectual satisfaction in their contents. It was fitting that he should use his influence with John Jacob Astor toward the founding of the great Astor Library. Williams thought Irving read comparatively little in later life, but this seems very doubtful. He read in bed, as he had always done, and his diligence in reading and commenting upon the many works sent to him is attested by many letters. He himself writes at sixty that "the doctor would . . . if he could, put a stop to my almost incessant reading, as he thinks that any fixed attention for a length of time wearies the brain, and in some degree produces those effects on the system which originated my [herpetic] complaint; but I cannot give up reading, in my otherwise listless state."

7   See W. B. Gates, "Shakespearean Elements in Irving's *Sketch Book*," *AL*, XXX (1959), 450-58.

8   The eighteenth-century influence is studied in detail, from the point of view of the older scholarship, in Ferdinand Künzig, *Washington Irving und seine Beziehungen zur englischen Literatur des 18. Jahr-*

hunderts (Heidelberg: Buchdruckerei Carl Pfeiffer, 1911). Künzig found *The Spectator*, Goldsmith, and Smollett the most important influences. Reichart, *Washington Irving and Germany*, pp. 152-3, takes exception to Williams's minimizing Goldsmith's influence on Irving (see Williams, *Life*, II, 219-23). McCarter, p. 170, finds "Buckthorne and His Friends" indebted to "The Philosophic Vagabond" in *The Vicar of Wakefield* and also to Goldsmith's essay, "Adventures of a Strolling Player."

9   The authors named, here and elsewhere in the various categories in this chapter, are of course merely representative.

10   J. Chesley Mathews, "Washington Irving's Knowledge of Dante," *AL*, X (1939), 480-83.

11   Francis Prescott Smith's Appendix C ("Washington Irving and France") lists the French books in Irving's library at Sunnyside and the French works and authors mentioned by him. It may be added that the most recondite language he ever attempted to study was Arabic. His Arabic notebook is in the New York Public Library. I am no judge of its profundity, but it certainly testifies to his diligence.

12   New York: Fords, Howard, and Hulbert, 1886.

13   When the English edition was going through the press, objection was made to a passage in "Marion's Men":

> And the British soldier trembles
> When Marion's name is heard.

There being no time to consult Bryant in America, Irving took the responsibility for a prudent alteration:

> And the foeman trembles in his camp.

Busybodies later tried their best to represent Bryant as having been angered by the liberty; actually he was nothing of the kind.

3   HOW THE TREE BORE ITS FRUIT

1   *Notes While Preparing Sketch Book* contains many entries, thoughts, reflections, even turns of speech afterwards worked up in published material. Cf. this (p. 56):

"Sultry afternoon, children relieved from school hurrying to river & plunging in sporting about   children brought up on the margins of our rivers are almost amphibious—

"Pond in the country inhabited by huge Bullfrog—his bellowing on summer evenings—superstitious horror that the children had of it—as we came home from school at twilight—

"Water snakes—Anthony Mitows (?) story of one which he saw when threshing (?)"

As Williams has already pointed out, in "Mountjoy" this became:

"Our greatest trial was to pass a dark, lonely pool, covered with pond-lilies, peopled with bull-frogs and water-snakes, and haunted by two white cranes. Oh, the terrors of that pond! How our little hearts would beat, as we approached it; what fearful glances we would throw around! And if by chance a plash of a wild duck, or the guttural twang of a bull-frog, struck our ears, as we stole quietly by—away we sped, nor paused until completely out of the woods."

2 Fred Lewis Pattee, *The Development of the American Short Story* (H, 1923), finds Irving's influence in the prose of Longfellow, Dana, Bryant, Whittier, Ik Mitchel, and George William Curtis. Even Bret Harte, "the leader of the new school of short story writers after the war, began by writing legends modeled after the legends of the Hudson. Poe was powerless in the 'thirties and 'forties in his attempts to change the technique of the form." Pattee gives Irving a long first chapter in his book, enumerating nine contributions which he made to the short story, then, somewhat strangely, calls him, a "detriment" to its development. "So far as modern technique is concerned he retarded its growth for a generation. . . . To him as much as even to Scott may be traced the origin of that wave of sentimentalism and unrestrained romance that surged through the annuals and the popular magazines for three decades." But why was the Poe form of short story necessarily superior per se to the Irving form? If so, then the contemporary short story, which has moved away from Poe's standards, must again be inferior.

On the other hand, Leonard B. Beach, "American Literature Re-Examined: Washington Irving, The Artist in a Changing World," *Univ. of Kansas City Review*, XIV (1948), 259-66, sees Irving anticipating a good deal of later American literature:

"The first great myth-maker (who was also the first great expatriate) experimented nobly with realism and romanticism in new proportions, studied our folk history, exploited the sovereign effects of humor, laid before readers for generations to come a simple, friendly philosophy of life and art."

"In 'National Nomenclature' Irving makes a plea for the euphonious Indian names and for a distinctive and poetic national appellation. . . . In 'The Creole Village' he anticipated the local color of the southern Mississippi valley made famous by G. W. Cable forty years later. . . . In 'The Great Mississippi Bubble,' he pried into Mark Twain's barrel with his account of the international swindler, John Law. 'The Early Experiences of Ralph Ringwood' . . . might have been written by Mark Twain himself. . . .

" 'Polly Holman's Wedding' . . . is replete with realistic detail, from the account of the backwoods ceremony with Kentucky Mountain fiddler, imported Methodist parson, dancing and moonshine to the description of a feast that rivals the Van Tassel banquet.... Strange that Irving should have come so close to Longstreet's and Craddock's property. Strange too that he should not have known what to make of it."

3 He was criticized for having "reviewed" *The Conquest of Granada* for Murray's *Quarterly Review* and accepted money for it. It is true, as he argued in his defense, that the article was explanatory rather than evaluative, but it was a bad system which permitted it to appear unsigned, with the author of the work under consideration referred to as "Mr. Irving."

4 See Andrew Breen Myers's introduction to "Washington Irving's Madrid Journal 1827-1828 and Related Letters," *BNYPL*, LXII (1958), 219, for evidence that Irving did not let up after completing *Columbus*, as Williams believed. A letter to Alexander H. Everett, April 15, 1829, in the Massachusetts Historical Society, provides some interesting sidelights on Irving's habits of composition and revision in *Columbus*, and perhaps by implication in other historical works: "Though I sometimes labor carefully at parts, I often write very rapidly; and what I write with facility of spirit, I am not apt to retouch with any great solicitude. I labor more to bring up careless and feebler parts to a tone in keeping with the rest, than nicely to finish what appears to me to be already good. Columbus had more slovenliness of style, in one stage of its preparation, than any work I ever wrote; for I was so anxious about the unity of the narrative and had to patch it together from so many different materials, that I had no time to think of the language. It was not until I had completely finished it as to facts, that I went over the whole of it and endeavored to bring up the style."

5 Harry Bergholz, "Was Washington Irving Stendhal's First American Critic," *Revue de Littérature Comparée*, XXVII (1953), 328-39, suggests that Irving reviewed *Rome, Naples, and Florence*, in the *Analectic*, July 1818, and that the review shows more critical power than he has generally been credited with.

6 Modern travelers will be more inclined to envy Irving in his poverty than to sympathize with him when they read that in Dresden in 1822 he had "a very neat, comfortable and prettily furnished apartment on the first floor of a Hotel: it consists of a cabinet with a bed in it, and a cheerful sitting room that looks on the finest square," for which he paid thirty-six shillings a month. See his letter to C. R. Leslie, Dec. 2, 1882, Berg Collection.

7 See his letter to C. R. Leslie, Jan. 9, 1832, in the Berg Collection. It is true that Murray does not seem to have been moved, but the mere

fact that he left the letter unanswered may testify to his knowledge that Irving's argument was unanswerable.

8 Pierre M. Irving, *Life*, IV, 411. Irving's total earnings from literature during his lifetime is set at $205,383.34. See further George Haven Putnam, *George Palmer Putnam, A Memoir* (P, 1912), especially pp. 85-6, 245-6.

4   How The Tree Grew In The Forest

1 The italics would seem to indicate that the paraphrase of Sterne's "They order this matter better in France" was conscious and deliberate.

2 One expression of Irving's snobbery seems all the more shocking in view of his own passion for the theater. In his *Analectic* paper on Robert Treat Paine, he refuses to go along with Paine's biographer in blaming his father for breaking with him after he had married an actress: "It is idle to rail at society for its laws of rank and gradations of respect. These rise, of themselves, out of the nature of things, and the moral and political circumstances in which that society is placed; and the universal acquiescence in them by the soundest minds is a sufficient proof they are salutary and correct."

3 See Richard Beale Davis, "James Ogilvie and Washington Irving," *Americana*, XXXV (1941), 435-58.

4 Irving has been accused of having wronged at least one man in his writings. J. F. McDermott, *Western Journals*, p. 59, finds nothing in Ellsworth's narrative "to sustain the concept of Tonish as he appears in the *Tour*," and prints letters (pp. 60-62) of E. A. Duyckinck in which Tonish is reported as resenting what Irving wrote about him: "he was a bad man—told a great many things that were not so." But the description of Tonish in the letter here quoted does not cause the reader to feel that he was a very reliable witness in his own behalf. Neither does his threat: "*Let me meet Irving on one of the Prairies and one or other of us shall lose his scalp!*"

5 A curious error for Little Nell in *The Old Curiosity Shop*. Barbara is another character in the same novel, the girl who marries Kit.

6 Irving's letter of thanks to Dr. Elisha Bartlett, who sent him his *Simple Settings in Verse for Six Portraits and Pictures from Mr. Dickens's Gallery* (Ticknor and Fields, 1855), is noncommittal so far as his attitude toward Dickens is concerned: "I am sure Dickens will feel flattered to see the offspring of his imagination thus poetically portrayed." See John T. Winterich, *An American Friend of Dickens* (New York: Thomas F. Madigan, Inc., 1933).

7 There is no word to indicate that Irving had heard any gossip concerning the cause of Dickens's separation from his wife.

8 See William Glyde Wilkins, *Charles Dickens in America* (S, 1911); J. W. T. Ley, *The Dickens Circle* (Chapman and Hall, 1919); Edward Wagenknecht, *The Man Charles Dickens* (HM, 1929), and five articles: John C. Eckel, "Washington Irving and Mint Juleps," *Dickensian*, II (1906), 214-16; W. G. Wilkins, "Charles Dickens and Washington Irving," *Dickensian*, XII (1916), 216-21; Ernest Boll, "Charles Dickens and Washington Irving," *MLQ*, V (1944), 453-67; W. C. D. Pacey, "Washington Irving and Charles Dickens," *AL*, XVI (1945), 332-9; Christof Wegelin, "Dickens and Irving: The Problem of Influence," *MLQ*, VII (1946), 83-91.

9 Albert Keiser, *The Indian in American Literature* (OUP, 1933), Chapter VII.

10 Irving also favored restoring the Indian names to American places. "New York" and "New London" stamped us, in his view, as "a second-hand people." He preferred the State of "Ontario" and the City of "Manhattan" and the United States of "Alleghenia" or "Appalachia." We might then speak of ourselves as Alleghenians or Appalachians, which would be more precise and exact than Americans, which also belongs to the people of the southern hemisphere. See "National Nomenclature," in *Spanish Papers*.

11 *Washington Irving, Esquire,* Chapter XIV.

12 On September 5, 1842, Irving wrote John Bandrell at the British Embassy in Madrid, expressing his concern over the Oregon boundary dispute, and warning against basing insupportable claims on the survey made by "Mr. Featherstonaugh," whom he bitterly denounced as "an adventurer and a charlatan—full of pretension, destitute of solid merit." The letter is in the Berg Collection.

13 D.K.'s scorn for Jefferson's reliance upon "instruments of writing," proclaiming embargoes, etc. is much like Theodore Roosevelt's contempt for President Wilson's famous "notes" to Germany before the United States entered World War I. But the attack on Jefferson was already in full tilt in *Salmagundi,* where Jefferson was even credited with a Negro mistress, like Thaddeus Stevens after him, clear down to D. W. Griffith's *The Birth of a Nation.* It may be noted that Tremaine McDowell, "General James Wilkinson in The Knickerbocker *History of New York,*" *MLN*, XLI (1926), 353-9, saw in the Van Poffenburgh episode an elaborate attack upon a contemporaneously notorious military man. Osborne, p. 195, dissents from this interpretation: "From Van Curlet to General Bracebridge, Irving presented military leaders as fat, stupid, and pompous; that the United States had such a man for military leader was pure coincidence."

5   How The Tree Was Deprived

1   See Clarence M. Webster, "Irving's Expurgation of the 1809 *History of New York*," *AL*, IV (1932), 293-5.

2   *Journal* . . . *1823-1824*, p. 92.

3   K. A. Spaulding, "A Note on *Astoria:* Irving's Use of the Robert Stuart Manuscript," *AL*, XXII (1950), 150-57.

4   There are a number of sympathetic references to Marie Antoinette in Irving's writings, and *The Sketch Book* testifies to his sympathy for Mary Queen of Scots. There is an interesting, unfinished essay on Mary in the Berg Collection, from which I quote the following paragraph:

"There is a wonderful charm attending every thing relating to this frail but interesting woman. Nothing can more bespeak the power of beauty than the universal sympathy which her story excites and the general disposition to disbelieve her crimes, speak lightly of her follies and deplore her misfortunes. The cool [?] historian when he comes to narrate the story of Mary warms into romance, and the most phlegmatic reader, who has ———— [?] with indifferent eye on the records of human misery, melts at the tale of her distresses and bursts forth into indignation at her tragical and untimely end."

5   "Recollections of Washington Irving," *Continental Monthly*, I.

6   F. P. Smith has also called attention to the many references Irving made to Madame de Bergh, wife of the Danish Minister at Dresden, during the same year 1823 in which he was most interested in Emily Foster.

7   The eldest son Algernon died in Dresden in September 1821.

8   George S. Hellman was sure that he did: see his *Washington Irving, Esquire*. Upon Hellman's evidence, Stanley T. Williams returned a verdict of not proven. Hellman replied in a review of Williams's edition of *Journal* . . . *(1823-1824)*, in *MLN*, XLVII (1932), 326-8; Williams replied to Hellman in "Washington Irving, Matilda Hoffman, and Emily Foster," *MLN*, XLVIII (1933), 182-6. Actually the controversy was something of a tempest in a teapot, for though Williams was undoubtedly right in taking up the position that no definite proof of a proposal existed, he still granted freely that all the probabilities favored the assumption; see his discussions in *Life*, I, 238-54, and in the introduction to S. T. Williams and Leonard B. Beach, eds., *The Journal of Emily Foster* (OUP, 1938).

Hellman was motivated by a desire to break down the traditional picture of Irving as having carried a broken heart through life from Matilda Hoffman's deathbed (which he regarded Pierre M. Irving as having established), and this introduced a certain emotional or propaganda element into his writings on the subject. In some of his references, he confused the Fosters with another English family; see Walter A. Reichart, "Washington Irving, the Fosters, and the Forsters," *MLN*, L (1935), 35-9.

The idea that Washington Irving loved Emily Foster did not originate with Hellman, however. We have positive evidence that Emily's sister, afterwards Flora Dawson, believed that Irving had made an offer (see *Life*, II, 240), and when Pierre's biography of his uncle was going through the press, Flora furnished the English publisher Richard Bentley with material drawn from the Fosters' Dresden diaries, which, without consulting Pierre, Bentley inserted at the close of Volume III.

Pierre has been blamed for the anger he displayed over this; actually he behaved with amazing restraint. Flora's lack of taste was shocking— and Emily's too if she was privy to the act. Pierre thought she was, but he may have been mistaken; she had been extremely reticent when he appealed to her for information concerning Irving's Dresden days, and it seems odd that she should have been willing to have her name brought in in such a sensational and controversial way. The greatest sinner, of course, was Bentley, who handled Pierre's work in an unbelievably highhanded way.

9 See Walter A. Reichart, "Baron von Gumppenberg, Emily Foster, and Washington Irving," *MLN*, LX (1945), 333-5.

10 Like Antoinette Bolviller, Leocadia Zamora never married but ended her life as founder and Mother Superior of a Carmelite convent. Claude G. Bowers discovered Leocadia's lost portrait and described her personality in *The Spanish Years of Washington Irving;* she had been little more than a name before.

11 There is a biography of Rebecca by Rollin G. Osterweis, *Rebecca Gratz: A Study in Charm* (P, 1935); see also her *Letters*, edited by David Philipson (Jewish Publication Society of America, 1929). It seems odd that Irving's friendship with the most distinguished early American Jewess did not give him more sympathy for her people, to whom he several times refers in stereotype terms.

To these documented cases of Irving's relationships with women there may be added a passing mention of what I may call the legendary connections in his life. The silliest—and the most spectacular—was the report printed in *Blackwood's Magazine*, XX (1826), 325, that he was engaged to marry the Empress Mary Louisa. The most interesting relates to Mary Shelley, widow of the poet, who was certainly enough interested in Irving to seek an introduction to him through John Howard Payne, who was interested in her, but there was not the slightest answering spark from Irving. For a full account of this matter, see H. H. Harper, *The Romance of Mary W. Shelley, John Howard Payne, and*

Washington Irving (BB, 1907); there are briefer accounts in the biographies by Williams and Hellman. The legend that Irving was once in love wtih Theodosia Burr was given currency by Charles Felton Pidgin, *Theodosia Burr: The First Gentlewoman of Her Time* (Boston, The C. M. Clark Publishing Co., 1907). Pidgin presented no evidence; neither did he state the connection as known fact. McCarter, "The Literary, Political, and Social Theories of WI," pp. 274-5, n. 9, has summed up the evidence against it with apparently conclusive finality.

6   How The Tree Praised Its Maker

1 Emily Foster's sister has recorded how, when he visited the Fosters in England, Irving was trapped into joining an ardent visiting Low Church divine in prayer upon his knees. She thought he was annoyed at the outset but later touched. See Flora Dawson, "The Author and the Divine; or, Washington Irving and the Rev. Charles Simeon," in her *Princes, Public Men, and Pretty Women: Episodes in Real Life,* 2 vols. (Bentley, 1864).

2 Jefferson's deism, roughly equated with atheism, is one of the reasons for the attack against him in *Salmagundi,* and Diedrich Knickerbocker thinks Moses' account of the beginnings of things quite as reasonable as those of any of the learned philosophers who followed him. But these are satirical passages, and not too much can be built upon them. Two of Irving's brothers were ardent Freemasons—Irving himself attended a Masonic dinner in England—and Freemasonry is not without its deistic aspects. Irving's *Tour in Scotland* notebook has some *memento mori* reflections, but this is not a characteristic note.

3 If he had been able to write it, Irving's supernatural masterpiece would have been the play "El Embozado." He was fascinated by the idea of writing about a man who should be baffled by his other self, and searched long and vainly for a play by Calderon in which he believed the theme had been treated. The best outline of Irving's attempts to write this play and of its literary associations is in M. M. Raymond's dissertation, "Washington Irving and the Theater," pp. 134-40, where see p. 140, n. 2 for evidence that Poe was indebted to it for "William Wilson." See also F. P. Smith, "Washington Irving and France," pp. 136-51.

III   THE WORK

1 Irving's standards in all matters of usage were very conservative, as see his letter to M. D. Phillips, Feb. 17, 1852, in the Berg Collection:

"I certainly do not make Webster's Dictionary my standard of orthography though I regret to say I often find myself inadvertently falling into some of the vitiations which the industrious circulation of his work has made so prevalent in our country. From the same cause also I find it almost impossible to have a work printed in this country free from some of his arbitrary modifications, which are pronounced provincialisms by all foreign scholars critical of the English language."

2   This passage is quoted from Irving's own memorandum in "Notes made in Madrid, Jan. 10-23, 1843," in the Sterling Library at Yale. The blank space is his.

3   These are well summed up by Williams and Tremaine McDowell in the introduction to their reprint of the first edition (ABC, 1927): "Passages reminiscent of Sterne jostle others from Cotton Mather. Sometimes a character speaks and acts in the idiom of Cervantes, or there is phrasing, perhaps half unconscious, which recalls . . . [Irving's] severe training in the Bible. Fielding is here, as are Swift and Rabelais, the New England historians, and the Jesuit fathers. It is not ostentatious learning, but a boyish pleasure of playing with words. Allusions tumble after one another throughout the book, occasionally badly assimilated or badly adapted, but all touched with the curiosity of the young writer's eager mind. . . . Interspersed are echoes from Shakespeare . . . the plays of Ben Jonson and John Dryden or the *Hudibras* of Samuel Butler. Irving can allude to Aesop . . . to Homer, Hobbes, Bacon, Sidney, Tom Paine, or Sheridan's Pizzaro. . . . He quotes from Hesiod, and he draws parallels from English, Greek, Roman, and Italian legend. . . . He was deep not merely in Cervantes, Rabelais, and Ariosto, but in Arthurian legend and in out-of-the-way tales of knighthood."

4   See C. G. Laird, "Tragedy and Irony in *Knickerbocker's History*," *AL*, XII (1940), 157-72.

5   See W. L. Hedges's Harvard dissertation, "The Fiction of History," for the most learned discussion of Irving as an historian that I have encountered. It is also the discussion which makes Irving himself appear, in this aspect, the most sophisticated.

6   And, of course, one would have to ignore the stylistic elements even in the works cited. Osborne has now shown that "five of the seven numbers of the *Sketch Book* were written to conform to a set and established pattern. Each issue was to contain one humorous writing, one pathetic writing, and one serious writing—usually concerned with relations between England and America. If the issue contained a fourth number, that added writing might be on any subject, but generally it took the form of nature description. . . . The humorous writings were generally in the tradition of the eighteenth century and remind one of Goldsmith's writing or even of the writings of Sterne, Fielding, and

Smollett. The pathetic writing was in the Romantic tradition, and 'The Widow and Her Son' and 'The Pride of the Village' remind one strikingly of such romantic writings as Wordsworth's *The Excursion*. . . . In some of the writings, as in 'The Legend of Sleepy Hollow,' there was a fortunate mingling of the Augustan style with romantic plot, and these works have proved extremely fortunate and have lasted well in the popular taste. Irving had had from his earliest writings a slight taste for what is generally considered romantic . . . and when this vein of Romanticism was introduced into his Augustan technique, his full powers were brought into his writing and the writings produced were those which have contributed most to his permanent fame."

7 See Williams, "The First Version of the Writings of Washington Irving in Spanish," *MP*, XXVIII (1930), 185-201. Daniel G. Hoffman, "Irving's Use of American Folklore in 'The Legend of Sleepy Hollow,'" *PMLA*, LXVIII (1953), 425-33, comments, "Although the original Peter Klaus was German, the themes of Rip Van Winkle are universal: the pathos of change, the barely-averted tragedy of loss of personal identity." I cannot, however, agree with Osborne (p. 287) that the "primary purpose" of "Rip Van Winkle" was "to illustrate the transformation wrought by democracy" in the community in which Rip lives. The machinery of the story is supernatural, but it derives its power from the theme of mutability plus the common human longing to escape problems by, in some form, throwing off the tyranny of time. Surely any sociological interest it may have is secondary. The changes which take place in Rip's village during his absence are important so far as the story is concerned merely because they help the reader to feel the lapse of time and contribute to Rip's isolation in his final phase.

8 See H. A. Pochmann, "Irving's German Sources in *The Sketch Book*," *SP*, XXVII (1930), 477-507; E. L. Brooks, "A Note on Irving's Sources," *AL*, XXV (1953), 229-30; and "A Note on the Source of 'Rip Van Winkle,'" *AL*, XXV (1954), 495-9; John T. Krumpelman, "Revealing the Source of Irving's 'Rip Van Winkle,'" *Monatshefte*, XLVII (1955), 361-2; Walter A. Reichart, "Concerning the Source of Irving's 'Rip Van Winkle,'" *Monatshefte*, XLVIII (1956), 94-5; see, also, the discussions in Reichart's *Washington Irving in Germany* (which plausibly explains why Irving apparently cited the wrong story as his source), and Williams, *Life*, I, 181-91.

9 Tieman de Vries, *Dutch History, Art, and Literature for Americans* (Grand Rapids, Michigan: Eerdmans-Sevensma Co., 1912) describes Erasmus's use of the story of Epimenides in his *Epistles* and absurdly accuses Irving of plagiarizing from Erasmus, with much hand wringing over his wickedness in maligning the Dutch.

10 William E. Griffes, *The Mikado's Empire* (H, 1896) summarizes

an ancient Chinese story in which Rip's part is played by "a pious wood-cutter," Lu-wen, who pursues a fox upon the holy mountain Tendai, and emerges into a clearing where two lovely ladies are playing checkers. He does not sleep but only stands watching them for a few minutes. When he turns to go, his limbs feel stiff, his ax-handle falls to pieces, and when he stoops to pick it up he finds his face covered with a long white beard. He returns to his village, where he finds everything as strange as Rip did. Finally an old woman identifies herself as "a descendant of the seventh generation of a man named Lu-wen. The old man groaned aloud, and, turning his back on all, retraced his weary steps to the mountain again. He was never heard of more, and it is believed he entered into the company of the immortal hermits and spirits of the mountain." For a "Rip Van Winkle" situation in a Spanish setting, see Irving's "The Adalantado of the Seven Cities," in *Wolfert's Roost*.

11   In the same memorandum cited above (n. 2), Irving says that he originally placed the scene of this story in Italy. The alchemist came partly from an old bookworm described by Isaac D'Israeli. His specula-tions on alchemy "were the result of an extensive course of reading in books on alchymy and the philosophers stone etc., in which I got very much interested and therefore handled the subject familiarly."

12   See McCarter, "The Literary, Political, and Social Theories of Washington Irving," p. 170.

13   G. P. Gooch, *History and Historians in the Nineteenth Century* (Longmans, Green, 1913).

14   See Pierre M. Irving, *Life*, Volume III, Chapter VI.

15   See Louise M. Hoffman, "Irving's Use of Spanish Sources in *The Conquest of Granada*," *Hispania*, XXVIII (1945), 493-8.

BIBLIOGRAPHY

For key to the abbreviations employed in this section, see p. 191. Additional bibliography will be found in the Notes.

There are two important bibliographies: William R. Langfeld and Philip C. Blackburn, *WI, A Bibliography* (NYPL, 1933) and STW and Mary Allen Edge, *A Bibliography of the Writings of WI: A Check List* (OUP, 1936). For writings about WI, see Robert E. Spiller et al., eds., *Literary History of the United States* (M, 1948), III, 578-83, and the *Bibliography Supplement*, ed. Richard M. Ludwig (M, 1959), pp. 143-4; Henry A. Pochmann, ed., *WI: Representative Selections* (ABC, 1934); Lewis Leary, *Articles on American Literature, 1900-1950* (Duke, 1954); also the quarterly bibliographies in *AL* and the annual bibliographies in *PMLA*.

G. P. Putnam's Sons have published a number of sets of I's works, including the "Author's Uniform Revised Edition" (1860-61), the "Spuyten Duyvil Edition" (1881), and the "Joseph Jefferson Edition" (n.d.). The first of these is regarded as standard, but the "Joseph Jefferson Edition" is the most lavish. See also *Spanish Papers and Other Miscellanies, Hitherto Unpublished and Uncollected*, ed. P. M. Irving, 2 vols. (P, 1886) and the reprint of the first edition of *Diedrich Knickerbocker's History of New York*, ed. STW and Tremaine McDowell (HB, 1927). *Letters of Jonathan Oldstyle* has been reproduced in facsimile from the edition of 1824, with an introduction by STW (ColUP, 1941). *The Wild Huntsman* and *Abu Hassan*, both ed. George S. Hellman, have been published by BB, 1924; for discussion see George R. Price, "WI's Librettos," *Music and Letters*, XXIX (1948), 348-55, and Percival R. Kirby, "WI, Barham Livius and Weber," same, XXXI (1950), 133-47. The play of *Charles the Second* is in Arthur Hobson Quinn, ed., *Representative American Plays* (Appleton, many editions); see also Thomas O. Mabbott, ed., "An Unwritten Drama of Lord Byron," *American Collector*, I (1925), 64-6. *Fragment of a Journal of a Sentimental Philosopher* . . . (New York, E. Sargent, 1809) may be a WI item. WI's verses have been collected by W. R. Langfeld, "The Poems of WI, Brought Together from Various Sources and for the First Time," *BNYPL*, XXXIV (1930), 763-79, to which should be added John Howard Birss, "New Verses by WI," *AL*, IV

(1932), 296, and Francis P. Smith, "WI, the Fosters, and Some Poetry," *AL*, IX (1937), 228-32. Minor items are I's review of Wheaton's *History of the Northmen, North American Review,* XXXV (1832), 342-71; Joseph F. Taylor, "WI's Mexico: A Lost Fragment," *Bookman,* XLI (1915), 665-9; S. T. Williams and Ernest E. Leisy, eds., "Polly Holman's Wedding," etc., *Southwest Review,* XIX (1934), 449-54; Howard C. Horsford, ed., "Illustration to the Legend of Prince Ahmed: An Unpublished Sketch by WI," *Princeton Univ. Library Chronicle,* XIV (1952), 30-36.

For WI's journals and note-books, see *The Journals of WI* (From July, 1815, to July, 1842), ed. William P. Trent and George S. Hellman (BB, 1919); *WI, Journal, 1803,* ed. STW (OUP, 1934); *WI: Notes and Journal of Travel in Europe, 1804-05,* ed. W. P. Trent, 3 vols. (New York, GC, 1921); Barbara D. Simison, ed., "WI's Notebook of 1810," *YULG,* XXIV (1949), 1-16, 74-94; *WI: Notes While Preparing Sketch Book &c 1817,* ed. STW (YUP, 1927); *Tour in Scotland, 1817, and Other Manuscript Notes,* ed. STW (YUP, 1927); *Journal of WI (1823-1824),* ed. STW (HUP, 1931); "WI's Madrid Journal 1827-1828 and Related Letters," ed. Andrew Breen Myers, *BNYPL,* LXII (1958), 217-27, 300-311, 407-19, 463-71; *Journal of WI, 1828, and Miscellaneous Notes on Moorish Legend and History* (ABC, 1937); *WI Diary, Spain 1828-1829,* ed. Clara Louisa Penney (New York, The Hispanic Society of America, 1926); *The Western Journals of WI,* ed. John Francis McDermott (Okla, 1944). See also "Peter Irving's Journals," *BNYPL,* XLIV (1940), 591-608, 649-70, 745-72, 814-42, 888-914.

Besides the biographies of WI by Pierre M. Irving and by STW, in both of which many letters are printed, generally only in part, letters of WI will be found in the following volumes: *Letters of WI to Henry Brevoort,* ed. G. S. Hellman (P, 2 vols., 1915; 1 vol., 1918); *Letters of Henry Brevoort to WI . . . ,* ed. G. S. Hellman, 2 vols. (P, 1916), with some letters from WI to Brevoort in Vol. II; *WI and the Storrows: Letters from England and the Continent, 1821-1828,* ed. STW (HUP, 1933); *WI: Letters from Sunnyside and Spain,* ed. STW (YUP, 1928); *Letters from WI to Mrs. William Renwick and to her Son, James Renwick, . . . written between September 10th, 1811 and April 5, 1816* (pamphlet, privately printed, n.d.); "Letters to Sarah Storrow from Spain by WI," ed. B. D. Simison, in *Papers in Honor of Andrew Keogh* (New Haven, Privately printed, 1938). More letters appear in the following articles: Thomas R. Adams, "WI; Another Letter from Spain," *AL,* XXV (1953), 354-8; W. B. Gates, "WI in Mississippi," *MLN,* LVIII (1943), 130-1; E. Herman Hespelt and STW, "Two Unpublished Anecdotes by Fernan Caballero, Preserved by WI," *MLN,* XLIX (1934), 25-31; Clara and Rudolf Kirk, "Seven Letters of WI," *Journal of the Rutgers Univ. Li-*

brary, IX (1945), 1-22, 36-58; X (1946), 20-27; "Letter from WI to George A. Ward, 1842," *Essex Institute Historical Collections*, LXXXIII (1947), 85; Thatcher T. P. Luquer, ed., "Correspondence of WI and John Howard Payne," *Scribner's Magazine*, XXIV (1910), 461-82, 597-616; V. H. Palsits, "WI and Frederick Saunders," *BNYPL*, XXXVI (1932), 218-9; Coleman O. Parsons, "WI Writes from Granada," *AL*, IV (1935), 439-43; Clara L. Penney, ed., "WI in Spain: Unpublished Letters, Chiefly to Mrs. Henry O'Shea, 1844-54," *BNYPL*, LXII (1958), 615-31; Milledge B. Siegler, "WI to William C. Preston: An Unpublished Letter," *AL*, XIX (1947), 256-9; STW, "WI and Andrew Jackson," *YULG*, XIX (1945), 67-9, "WI and Fernan Caballero," *JEGP*, XXIX (1930), 352-66, and "WI's Religion," *YR*, XV (1925), 414-6; STW and L. B. Beach, "WI's Letters to Mary Kennedy," *AL*, VI (1934), 44-65.

As stated in the Preface, the authorized biography of WI is Pierre M. Irving, *The Life and Letters of WI*, 4 vols. (P, 1863-4), and the fullest modern biography is STW, *The Life of WI*, 2 vols. (OUP, 1935). Other important modern books are G. S. Hellman, *WI, Esquire, Ambassador at Large from the New World to the Old* (Knopf, 1925); Henry Leavitt Ellsworth, *WI on the Prairie, or, A Narrative of a Tour of the Southwest in the Year 1832*, ed. STW and B. D. Simison (ABC, 1938); Claude G. Bowers, *The Spanish Adventures of WI* (HM, 1940); and Walter A. Reichart, *WI and Germany* (Univ. of Michigan Press, 1957). Harold Dean Cater, *WI and Sunnyside* (Sleepy Hollow Restorations, Inc., 1957) contains much useful information and many charming pictures. See also *WI and His Circle: A Loan Exhibition Observing the Restoration of "Sunnyside," October 8 through October 26, 1946*, with an Introduction by STW (New York, M. Knoedler & Company, 1946). Among the older studies, biographical and critical, the most useful is probably Charles Dudley Warner's graceful sketch, *WI*, in the "American Men of Letters" series (HM, 1890). Mention may also be made of Charles Adams, *Memoir of WI* (New York, Carlton & Lanahan, 1870); Egbert Benson, *Brief Remarks on The Wife of WI* (New York, Grattan and Banks, 1819), a worthless piece of cavilling which I list only because it is frequently referred to in WI literature; Henry W. Boynton, *WI* (HM, 1901); George William Curtis, *WI, A Sketch* (GC, 1891); David J. Hill, *WI* (New York, Sheldon and Company, 1879); Adolf Laun, *WI: Ein Lebens und Charakterbild*, 2 vols. (Berlin, Robert Oppenheim, 1870); C. D. Warner, *The Work of WI* (Harper, 1893); C. D. Warner, W. C. Bryant, and G. P. Putnam, *Studies of Irving* (P, 1880); *Irvingiana: A Memorial of WI* (New York, Charles B. Richardson, 1860); *WI: Commemoration of the One Hundredth Anniversary of His Birth by the WI Association* . . . (P, 1884).

Five important dissertations on WI are listed in the Preface. The appendix to M. M. Raymond, "WI and the Theater" includes a consideration of plays and musicals derived from Irving.

The following books have sections devoted to WI: Van Wyck Brooks, *The World of WI* (D, 1944); Henry Seidel Canby, *Classic Americans* (HB, 1931); George Carver, *Alms for Oblivion* (Bruce, 1946); John DeLancey Ferguson, *American Literature in Spain* (ColUP, 1916); Charles A. Ingraham, *WI and Other Essays* (The Author, Cambridge, N. Y., 1922); John Macy, *The Spirit of American Literature* (D, 1913); John Macy, ed., *American Writers on American Literature* (Liveright, 1931); R. B. Mowat, *Americans in England* (HM, 1935); Frederick Saunders, *Character Studies, with Some Recent Personal Recollections* (New York, Thomas Whittaker, 1894); William W. Waldron, *WI and Contemporaries, in Thirty Life Sketches* (New York, W. H. Kelley & Co., n.d.); STW, *The Spanish Background of American Literature*, Vol. II (YUP, 1955).

The following books, devoted primarily to other subjects, contain references to I: Homer F. Barnes, *Charles Fenno Hoffman* (ColUP, 1930); J. C. Derby, *Fifty Years Among Authors, Books, and Publishers* (New York, G. W. Carleton & Co., 1884); Waldo H. Dunn, *The Life of Donald G. Mitchell, Ik Marvel* (S, 1922); Amos L. Herold, *James Kirke Paulding, Versatile American* (ColUP, 1926); M. A. DeWolfe Howe, *The Life and Letters of George Bancroft*, 2 vols. (S, 1908); Joseph Jefferson, *"Rip Van Winkle": The Autobiography of Joseph Jefferson* (London, Reinhardt & Evans, Ltd., 1949); Frances Anne Kemble, *Records of a Girlhood*, (Ht, 1879); Charles Lanman, *Haphazard Personalities; Chiefly of Noted Americans* (Boston, Lee and Shepard, 1886); Charles R. Leslie, *Autobiographical Recollections*, 2 vols. (John Murray, 1860); Henry A. Pochmann et al., *German Culture in America . . .* (Univ. of Wisconsin Press, 1957); Robert E. Spiller, *The American in England during the First Half Century of Independence* (Ht, 1926); Bayard Tuckerman, ed., *The Diary of Philip Hone, 1828-1851*, 2 vols. (Dodd, Mead, 1889); Henry T. Tuckerman, *The Life of John Pendleton Kennedy* (P, 1871); N. P. Willis, *The Convalescent* (S, 1864); Minnie Clare Yarborough, ed., *The Reminiscences of William C. Preston* (Univ. of North Carolina Press, 1933).

Most of the following articles on I are of a scholarly nature. Some are critical; some are reminiscential.

Nelson F. Adkins, "An Uncollected Tale by WI," *AL*, V (1934), 264-7—cf. subsequent discussion by Ralph Thompson, VI (1935), 443-4, by Aubrey Starke, pp. 444-5, by P. K. McCarter, XI (1939), 294-5; Stockton Axson, "WI and the Knickerbocker Group," *Rice Institute Pamphlet*, XX (1933), 178-95; Adolph B. Benson, "Scandinavians in the Works of WI," *Scan. Studies and Notes*, IX (1927), 207-23; Jacob Blanck, "*Salma-*

gundi and its Publisher," *Papers of the Bibliographical Society of America*, XLI (1947), 1-32; G. L. Brooks, "A Note on I's Sources," *AL*, XXV (1953), 229-30, and "A Note on the Source of 'Rip Van Winkle,'" *AL*, XXV (1954), 495-9; Killis Campbell, "The Kennedy Papers," *SR*, XXV (1917), 2-19; Lewis Gaylord Clark, "Reminiscences of the Late WI," *Knickerbocker*, Jan. 1860, pp. 113-8, and "Recollections of WI," *Lippincott's Magazine*, III (1869), 552-60; John Esten Cooke, "A Morning at Sunnyside with WI," *Southern Mag.*, XII (1873), 710-6.

John C. Fiske, "The Soviet Controversy over Pushkin and WI," *Comparative Literature*, VII (1955), 25-31; Emilio Goggio, "WI and Italy," *Romanic Review*, XXI (1930), 26-33, and "WI's Works in Italy," XXII (1931), 301-03; Edwin Greenlaw, "WI's Comedy of Politics," *Texas Rev.*, I (1916), 291-306; William L. Hedges, "Irving's *Columbus*: The Problem of Romantic Biography," *The Americas*, XIII (1956), 127-40, and "Knickerbocker, Bolingbroke, and the Fiction of History," *Journal of the History of Ideas*, XX (1959), 317-28; G. S. Hellman, "I's *Washington* and an Episode in Courtesy," *Colophon*, Part I (1930); Thomas A. Kirby, "I and Moore: A Note on Anglo-American Literary Relations," *MLN*, LXII (1947), 251-5; John T. Krumpelman, "Revealing the Source of I's 'Rip Van Winkle,'" *Monatshefte*, XLVII (1955), 361-2; Charles Lanman, "A Day with WI," *Once a Week*, II (1859), 5-8; Louis Le Fevre, "Paul Bunyan and Rip Van Winkle," *YR*, XXXVI (1946), 66-76; Ernest E. Leisy, "I and the Genteel Tradition," *Southwest Rev.*, XXI (1936), 223-7; Terence Martin, "Rip, Ichabod, and the American Imagination," *AL*, XXXI (1959), 137-49; J. F. McDermott, "WI and the Journal of Captain Bonneville," *Miss. Valley Hist. Rev.*, XLIII (1956), 459-67; George D. Morris, "WI's Fiction in the Light of French Criticism," *Indiana Univ. Studies*, Vol. III, Study No. 30 (1916); Muriel Morris, "Mary Shelley and John Howard Payne," *London Mercury*, XXII (1930), 443-50.

James O. Noyes, "WI as an Invalid," *Knickerbocker*, Jan. 1860, pp. 118-22; Otto Plath, "WIs Einfluss auf Wilhelm Hauff," *Euphorion*, 1913; Henry A. Pochmann, "I's German Tour and its Influence on his Tales," *PMLA*, XLV (1930), 1150-87, and "I's German Sources in *The Sketch Book*," *SP*, XXVII (1930), 447-507; *Proceedings of the Mass. Hist. Society, 1858-1860*, pp. 393-424; G. H. Putnam, "WI," *Forum*, LXXV (1926), 397-409; G. P. Putnam, "Recollections of I," *Atlantic Mo.*, VI (1860), 601-12; Walter A. Reichart, "The Early Reception of WI's Works in Germany," *Anglia*, LXXIV (1956), 343-63, "Concerning the Source of I's 'Rip Van Winkle,'" *Monatshefte*, XLVIII (1956), 94-5, "WI's Influence on German Literature," *Mod. Lang. Rev.*, LII (1957), 537-54, and "WI's Friend and Collaborator: Barham John Livius, Esq.," *PMLA*, LVI (1941), 513-31; Irving T. Richards, "John Neal's Gleanings in Irvingiana," *AL*, VIII (1936), 170-9; Sara Puryear Rodes, "WI's Use of Traditional Folklore," *Southern Folklore Q.*, XIX (1956), 143-53; Jason A. Russell, "I: Recorder of Indian Life," *Jour. of Am. Hist.*, XXV (1931), 185-95.

Miriam R. Small, "A Possible Ancestor of Diedrich Knickerbocker," *AL*, II (1930), 21-4; F. P. Smith, "WI on French Romanticism," *Revue de Littérature comparée*, XVII (1937), 715-32; Joseph B. Thoburn, "Centennial of the Tour on the Prairies by WI (1832-1932)," *Chronicles of Oklahoma*, X (1932), 426-33; John B. Thompson, "The Origin of the Rip Van Winkle Legend," *HaM*, LXVII (1883), 617-22; Charles Watts II, "Poe, I, and *The Southern Literary Messenger*," *AL*, XXVII (1955), 249-51; STW, "WI and Matilda Hoffman," *American Speech*, I (1926), 463-9, "WI and Fernan Caballero," *JEGP*, XXIX (1930), 352-66, and "The First Version of the Writings of WI in Spanish," *MP*, XXVIII (1930), 185-201; James L. Wilson, "WI's Celebrated English Poet," *AL*, XVIII (1946), 247-9; Nathalia Wright, "I's Use of His Italian Experiences in *Tales of a Traveller:* The Beginning of an American Tradition," *AL*, XXXI (1959), 191-6; James Wynne, "WI," *HaM*, XXIV (1861), 349-56: Minnie C. Yarborough, "Rambles with WI: Quotations from an Unpublished Autobiography of William C. Preston," *South Atlantic Q.*, XXIX (1930), 423-39; Philip Young, "Fallen from Time: The Mythic Rip Van Winkle," *Kenyon Review*, XXII (1960), 547-73; Edwin H. Zeydel, "WI and Ludwig Tieck," *PMLA*, XLVI (1931), 946-7.

INDEX

C

Caballero, Fernan (Cecilia Böhl von Faber), 12, 62, 146
Cabell, Joseph Carrington, 7, 135
Cabinet of Dr. Caligari, The, 178
Campbell, Thomas, 12, 59, 77, 103-4
Canby, Henry Seidel, 167
Canova, Antonio, 45
Capital punishment, Washington Irving's attitude toward, 109
Carlyle, Thomas, 169
Cats, Washington Irving and, 43
Cervantes, 62
Chaucer, Geoffrey, 55-6, 154, 174
Chesterfield, Lord, 41
Childrearing, Washington Irving on, 120
Children, Washington Irving's love for, 119-20
Church, Frederick, 47
Classics, Washington Irving and the, 60
Clinton, DeWitt, 88-9
Cockburn, John, 38
Constable, Archibald, 185
Cooke, George Frederick, 48-9
Cooper, James Fenimore, Washington Irving and, 48, 64-5, 93, 121
Cooper, Thomas A., 144
Copyright, Washington Irving's views on, 108
Cozzens, F. S., 97, 187
✓ Criticism, Washington Irving's attitude toward, 77-80
Curtis, George William, 5, 26
Custis, Nelly, 186

D

Dana, Richard Henry, 81
Dante, 63
Daugherty, James, 178
Davidson, Margaret Miller, 74, 121-2
Decatur, Stephen, 38
Dickens, Charles, 39, 60, 74; Washington Irving's relations with, 94-9, 161, 168, 175
Dolgorouki, Prince, 14, 125, 181
Drinking, Washington Irving and, 137-9
Dryden, John, 78
Dueling, Washington Irving on, 108-9
Dunlap, William, 88
Duyckinck, E. A., 97-8

and theater, 47-53; reading and attitude toward literature, 53-5; readings in English literature, 55-60; in the classics, 60; in German, 60-61; in Spanish, 61-2; in Italian, 62-3; in French, 63; in American literature, 64-5. Section 3: literary theory, 65-70; ambition and attitude toward his own work, 71-4; methods of work, 74-7; attitude toward criticism, 77-80; toward the financial aspect of authorship, 80-83; relations with publishers, 83; investments, 83-4. Section 4: social proclivities and gifts, 85-93; friendships, 93-9; attitude toward Europe and America, 99-104; political and social views, 104-18. Section 5: family affections, 118-19; love for children, 119-20; attitude toward morality, 120-26; relations with women, 126-36; attitude toward smoking and drinking, 136-8; relations with Matilda Hoffman, 139-42; with Emily Foster, 142-6; friendships with various women in Spain, 146-9; with Rebecca Gratz, 149; attitude toward marriage, 150-54. Section 6: attitude toward religion, 154-65. Chapter III: success in creating a legend, 167; fame, 167-8; most durable work, 169; style, 169-70; creative writing, 170-79; as an historian, 179-88; position today, 188-9.

Writings:

Abu Hassan, 12
"Adventure of My Aunt, The," 178
"Adventure of My Uncle, The," 178
"Adventure of the German Student, The," 178
Adventures of Captain Bonneville, U.S.A., The, 20, 103, 113, 131
Alhambra, The, 16, 90, 164, 179
"Annette Delarbre," 133, 177
"Art of Bookmaking, The," 180
Astoria, 20, 41-2, 103, 113, 137
Biography and Poetical Remains of the Late Margaret Miller Davidson, 22, 74, 131-2
"Birds of Spring, The," 42
"Boar's Head Tavern, Eastcheap, The," 180
"Bold Dragoon, The," 57, 75, 178
Bracebridge Hall, 12, 17, 41-3, 54-5, 66-7, 70, 74-5, 99, 101, 105, 118, 122, 154-5, 162, 169, 176-7
"Broken Heart, The," 131-3
"Buckthorne and His Friends," 47, 70, 178
Charles II, 12
Conquest of Granada, The, 14-15, 79, 118, 122, 181
Crayon Miscellany, The, 16-17, 20, 164
"Desultory Thoughts on Criticism," 77
"Devil and Tom Walker, The," 109, 169, 179
"Dolph Heyliger," 43, 177

813.3 Wagenknecht, Edward
Irving   Washington Irving.

Wilmington Public Library
Wilmington, N. C.

RULES

1. Books marked 7 days may be kept one week. Books marked 14 days, two weeks. The latter may be renewed, if more than 6 months old.

2. A fine of two cents a day will be charged on each book which is not returned according to above rule. No book will be issued to any person having a fine of 25 cents or over.

3. A charge of ten cents will be made for mutilated plastic jackets. All injuries to books beyond reasonable wear and all losses shall be made good to the satisfaction of the Librarian.

4. Each borrower is held responsible for all books drawn on his card and for all fines accruing on the same.